Sonic Histories of Occupation

Sonic Histories of Occupation

*Experiencing Sound and Empire
in a Global Context*

Edited by
Russell P. Skelchy and Jeremy E. Taylor

BLOOMSBURY ACADEMIC
LONDON • NEW YORK • OXFORD • NEW DELHI • SYDNEY

BLOOMSBURY ACADEMIC
Bloomsbury Publishing Plc
50 Bedford Square, London, WC1B 3DP, UK
1385 Broadway, New York, NY 10018, USA
29 Earlsfort Terrace, Dublin 2, Ireland

BLOOMSBURY, BLOOMSBURY ACADEMIC and the Diana logo are trademarks of
Bloomsbury Publishing Plc

First published in Great Britain 2022
This paperback edition published 2023

Cover design: Terry Woodley
Cover image: Unattributed photograph of Chinese Boy Scouts in Japanese-occupied China,
circa 1942, © Imperial War Museum (HU 73372)

A catalogue record for this book is available from the British Library.

Library of Congress Cataloging-in-Publication Data
Names: Taylor, Jeremy E., 1973- editor. | Skelchy, Russell P., editor.
Title: Sonic histories of occupation : experiencing sound and empire in a global context /
edited by Russell P. Skelchy and Jeremy E. Taylor.
Description: [1.] | London ; New York : Bloomsbury Academic, 2022. | Includes bibliographical
references and index.
Identifiers: LCCN 2021028856 (print) | LCCN 2021028857 (ebook) | ISBN 9781350228085 (hardback) |
ISBN 9781350228092 (pdf) | ISBN 9781350228108 (ebook)
Subjects: LCSH: Music–Political aspects–History. | Sound–Political aspects–History. |
Military occupation–History.
Classification: LCC ML3916 .S6583 2022 (print) | LCC ML3916 (ebook) | DDC 306.4/84–dc23
LC record available at https://lccn.loc.gov/2021028856
LC ebook record available at https://lccn.loc.gov/2021028857

ISBN: HB: 978-1-3502-2808-5
PB: 978-1-3502-2811-5
ePDF: 978-1-3502-2809-2
eBook: 978-1-3502-2810-8

Typeset by Deanta Global Publishing Services, Chennai, India

Contents

Figures

Contributors

Tan Sooi Beng is Professor of Ethnomusicology at the School of Arts, Universiti Sains Malaysia (USM), Penang. She is the author of *Bangsawan: A Social and Stylistic History of Popular Malay Opera* (1993) and is co-author of *Music of Malaysia: Classical, Folk and Syncretic Traditions* (2017) and *Longing for the Past, the 78 RPM Era in Southeast Asia* (2013), which won the joint SEM Bruno Nettl Prize in 2014. She has also edited *Eclectic Cultures for All: The Development of the Peranakan Performing, Visual and Material Arts in Penang* (2019).

Iris Sandjette Blake is UC President's Postdoctoral Fellow in the Department of Musicology at the University of California, Los Angeles. She received her PhD in Ethnic Studies from the University of California, Riverside, and her MM in Ethnomusicology from the University of Texas at Austin. Her work has been published in the journal *Performance Matters*, and she is currently working on her first book project *Undisciplining the Voice*, which examines contemporary artworks and performances that attempt to de-link voice from its entanglements with the disciplinary apparatus of the colonial sensorium and the Western figure of the human.

Maya Cunningham is an Africanist/African Americanist ethnomusicologist, an Africana studies scholar and a cultural activist. She is completing her PhD at the University of Massachusetts, Amherst, in Afro-American studies with a concentration in ethnomusicology. Cunningham received an MA in ethnomusicology from the University of Maryland, College Park, an MA in jazz performance from the Aaron Copland School of Music at Queens College and a Bachelor of Music in jazz studies from Howard University. Her research focuses on intersections between African/African American identities and traditional Black music traditions.

Jim Donaghey is AHRC Research Fellow at Ulster University. He previously worked on the 'Sounding Conflict: From Resistance to Reconciliation' project at Queen's University Belfast, researching with the community music-making NGO Musicians Without Borders. The development of complementary, creative and innovative research methods was a core strand of that research relationship.

His wider research interests focus on the relationships between music and politics, primarily addressing punk counterculture and the anarchist movement in contemporary global contexts. He is Web Editor of www.AnarchistStudies. blog (associated with *Anarchist Studies* journal) and is a member of the editorial board of the journal *Punk and Post-Punk*.

Sophia Geng is Associate Professor at the College of Saint Benedict and Saint John's University. Her academic interests lie in Chinese studies, folklore and cultural heritage studies, as well as diaspora and gender studies. A recipient of the Robert Spaeth Professor of Distinction Award, Global-Local Leadership Award and Academic Advising Award, Dr Geng has been widely recognized for her dedication to teaching excellence. She is Vice Chair of ASIANetwork, a consortium of over 170 colleges striving to strengthen Asian studies in liberal arts education. She has published on topics such as the memory of the Second World War, diaspora and Chinese festivals.

DJ Hatfield is Associate Professor at the Graduate Institute of Music at National Taiwan University. A sociocultural anthropologist and sound installation artist, he is the author of *Taiwanese Pilgrimage to China* (2010) and numerous articles on Taiwanese popular religious practice, popular music and Indigenous cultural resurgence. His research interests include soundscapes, Indigenous media, gender and the ethics of locality. His sound artwork has appeared in the Taipei Biennial, the Mipaliw Arts Festival and the Taitung International Austronesian Arts Awards.

Fiona Magowan is Professor of Anthropology and Fellow of the Senator George J. Mitchell Institute for Global Peace, Security and Justice, Queen's University Belfast. She is author or editor of seven books and numerous articles on music, arts, emotion and conflict transformation. She is the author of *Melodies of Mourning: Music and Emotion in Northern Australia* (2007) and is co-editor of *Performing Gender, Place, and Emotion: Global Perspectives* (2013) and *Christianity, Conflict and Renewal in Australia and the Pacific* (2016). She is also PI on the PaCCS-funded project 'Sounding Conflict: From Resistance to Reconciliation' (2017–21) (http://soundingconflict.org/).

Annette McNelis is from Buncrana, County Donegal, close to the border with Derry/Londonderry. She has been involved in music for over forty years and has twenty years' experience working as a creative music educator. She is a keyboard tutor, songwriter, community music workshop leader and environmentalist.

Annette delivers CPD music training workshops for primary school teachers and develops environmentally themed music resources for primary schools. She has a passion for using music as a means for inspiring people to care more for the environment, and her Environment the Musical classroom resource was launched in 2014.

Russell P. Skelchy is Honorary Research Fellow with the ERC-funded Cultures of Occupation in Twentieth Century Asia (COTCA) project at the University of Nottingham. His research interests include decolonization, the music of Southeast Asia, sensory studies, imperialism and sound studies. Skelchy's publications have appeared in *Ethnomusicology, Sound Studies, South East Asia Research, Journal of Popular Music Studies* and *Action, Criticism and Theory for Music Education.*

Kevin Sliwoski is a writer and musician based in Oceanside, California, and is also the Family Readiness Command Team Advisor for Marine Corps Recruiting Station, San Diego. He holds a PhD in Music from the University of California, Riverside, as well as Master's degrees in US History and Musicology from the University of Oxford, and a Bachelor's degree in Music from the University of Hartford.

Dimitri Smirnov completed his PhD at the Centre for Cultural Studies at the University of Graz, Austria. His dissertation examines the political significance of literary sounds and how they convey violence in postcolonial prose fiction (Anglophone, Francophone and Russophone). He is currently a collaborator at 'Telling Sounds', a research project at the University of Music and Performing Arts in Vienna. His research interests and publishing activities lie at the intersection of comparative literature, sound studies and postcolonial studies.

Jeremy E. Taylor is Associate Professor of Modern Asian History at the University of Nottingham, UK. His research has been published in almost thirty different peer-reviewed journals including, most recently, the *European Journal of East Asian Studies* and the *Journal of Asian Studies*. His books include *Rethinking Transnational Chinese Cinemas: The Amoy-Dialect Film Industry in Cold War Asia* (2011), *Iconographies of Occupation: Visual Cultures in Wang Jingwei's China, 1939–1945* (2021), *Visual Histories of Occupation: A Transcultural Dialogue* (2021) and (with Lanjun Xu) *Chineseness and the Cold War: Contested Cultures and Diaspora in Southeast Asia and Hong Kong* (2021).

Acknowledgements

Earlier drafts of most of the chapters included in this collection were originally presented at the 'Resonating Occupation' Workshop, held in 2018 at the University of Nottingham (UK) under the Cultures of Occupation in Twentieth Century Asia (COTCA) project, or at the 'Sounding Imperialism in Twentieth-Century Asia' panel (also supported by COTCA), presented at the Association for Asian Studies Annual Conference in Denver in 2019. COTCA as well as this volume's Introduction and Chapter 8 were funded by the European Research Council (ERC) under the European Union's Horizon 2020 research and innovation programme (Grant Number 682081). This book would never have been started, let alone completed, were it not for the ERC's generous support.

It has been a privilege for the editors to work with the talented scholars who have contributed chapters to this volume. We would also like to acknowledge the numerous scholars who have attended or presented at COTCA events – as well as all members of the COTCA team (both past and present) – but whose work is not included in this collection. Their contributions via discussion, suggestions and mere enthusiasm have all helped to make this book a reality.

Special mention must be made of the team at Bloomsbury, particularly Maddie Holder and Abigail Lane, who have been extraordinarily supportive and enthusiastic editors. The anonymous peer reviewers offered valuable advice and suggestions, which helped to improve the book.

Introduction

Sonic histories of occupation

Russell P. Skelchy and Jeremy E. Taylor

Situating sound, occupation and history

Histories of occupation have been marked by the presence of iconic sounds. Second World War occupations of Europe, for instance, were famously known for the shattering explosions of rocket launchers and air-raid attack sirens, along with the low rumbling of armoured vehicles and the distinct hum of dive bombers (cf. Meilinger 2016). Sound, felt and heard in a wartime context, has also been weaponized to disorient, unnerve or disable opponents. During the 1942 German siege of Stalingrad, Soviet troops kept German forces awake late at night by playing Argentine tangos through loudspeakers. US forces employed similar tactics in the 1960s during the Vietnam War by blasting popular music, insults and the sounds of tanks and tigers through loudspeakers. During the 1989 US invasion of Panama, US forces did the same with loud heavy metal music, and more recently, following the 2003 US-led invasion of Iraq, military vehicles were mounted with loudspeakers that hurled insults in Arabic at enemy forces (Niiler 2018). Innovations in the field of sonic warfare have grown more sophisticated, especially through the development of acoustic weapons, both audible and inaudible, specifically ultrasonic (above 20 kilohertz) or infrasonic (below 20 hertz). Mysterious 'acoustic attacks' in Cuba (2016), China (2017), Austria (2021), and Vietnam (2021), causing abnormal sensations of sound, pressure and illness among US diplomats and leaders, have created suspicion about the use of ultrasonic weapons (McLoughlin 2018).[1] Furthermore, acoustic weapons classified as 'non-lethal', such as the Long-Range Acoustic Device (LRAD), which produces high-pitched piercing tones to disorient or disable, have been used by US and other military forces as well as law enforcement agencies to control large crowds and demonstrations (Huecho Pozo 2019).

Besides sonic warfare, the domestication or control of sound in occupied geographic spaces historically has been integral to imperial projects. In colonial Virginia of the early 1700s, European settlers were normally frightened by sounds emanating from surrounding forests, namely the howling of wolves at night and the whoops and cries of Native American hunters (McGill 2018). Efforts to smooth over the wild sounds of this setting included the use of 'instrumental sounds', or human-generated non-speech sounds such as bells, guns and musical instruments by Europeans to produce an auditory environment more familiar and secure. Large, heavy bells, for example, installed on plantations to summon children and others for meals and lessons, also made the colony sound more like England. The bells could be heard for several miles and, in some cases, became sonic beacons for lost travellers. These 'soundmarks' differentiated European settler spaces from the surrounding 'wilderness' inhabited by Indigenous people and animals. In this sense, the auditory environments created by European colonists in North America, similar to the sounds of sonic warfare, drastically reconfigured the contested soundscapes they had encroached upon.

Listening to the sonic histories of occupation in each of these instances involves the reception of multiple aural layers sensorially experienced through the body. Roland Barthes (1991: 245) differentiates *hearing* as a physiological phenomenon from *listening*, which is a psychological act, defined less by its object than its goal. In this context, listening to occupation does not entail an arbitrary hearing, but rather, as Nicole Huang (2013: 190) suggests, the close listening of a 'total soundscape', where politically charged sound bites saturate auditory space and social life. If we believe, as Peter Szendy (2007) does, that listening is an imperative (one must listen to be a 'conscious listener'), then intrinsically attached to the act of listening is a sense of responsibility and awareness. How does such awareness contribute to a listening of occupation? How do we listen to occupation? Or, more importantly, why *must* we listen to occupation? Such questions also suggest that the structures of occupation – and the sounds of it – require a built-in implicit (if not explicit) threat of physical violence and cultural destruction. How can a heightened attention to sound and auditory environments help to navigate the wider threat posed by occupation?

Sonic Histories of Occupation takes a transdisciplinary and comparative approach to addressing such questions. It brings together scholars from multiple disciplines, perspectives and geographic regions working at the nexus of sound, history and foreign occupation and/or colonialism. The book employs a comparative approach which places less emphasis on regional borders to explore unique cases of occupation in different geographic and temporal contexts.

Although the volume considers how these cases are unique, it also rethinks the existing nation-specific literature that shares the 'occupation' label. A significant number of fields, including legal studies, political science and history, have contributed definitions of the word 'occupation', namely in the context of (state) discourse on territory, legal frameworks and sovereignty (Gross 2017; Dinstein 2009; Stirk 2009; Hassan 2008; Gregory 2004). Although it is not necessarily the objective of this volume to add to this expanding list of definitions, it is worth noting that 'occupation' here is defined broadly to include words such as 'colonialism', 'imperialism', 'conflict' and 'war'. A wide definition is necessitated by the impossibility of establishing a catch-all definition of occupation that can provide a basis for a critical discussion about auditory expression under vastly different conditions bearing the label 'occupation'. As Jeremy E. Taylor (2021: 6–9) observes, debates about the meaning of 'occupation' should be encouraged without allowing such definitions to mark an end point of scholarly enquiry. This approach suspends the search for a single, all-encompassing definition while encouraging discussions around such definitions (a framework that is already used in cognate fields such as genocide studies).

It is also worth explicating how the words in this volume's title evoke themes and topics examined by its authors. Occupation has long been a locus of debate in scholarly and legal circles, generating a significant amount of academic literature. Much of this scholarship has addressed the ethical concerns of how occupation has been experienced by 'occupiers' and the 'occupied'. In popular culture, the circulation of sounds and images in mass media related to, for instance, the Israeli occupation of the West Bank and Gaza, Indigenous dispossession or the actions of the global Occupy movement has all created distinct associations with the word's meanings.[2] The US military invasions of Afghanistan (2001) and Iraq (2003) marked a trend towards what might be called 'occupation studies' (Taylor 2021). In sound studies, this same moment inspired an expanding subfield of literature describing and theorizing the sounds of war, some of which will be discussed later in this Introduction.

The term 'sonic histories' alludes to the ways that paying attention to sound and listening can inspire novel perspectives and 'storylines' of the past (Smith 2001). The word 'sonic' pertains to sound, or the physical vibrations that create audible waves of pressure that are transmitted through a medium and received and perceived by the body as sound. Sonic also alludes to movement and the perception of sound, namely in describing how fast sound moves through air. Think, for instance, of terms such as 'supersonic', 'subsonic' or 'ultrasonic' – all of which refer to the range of sound perceptible to the human ear.

Over the past thirty or more years, historians of sound have become increasingly interested in the types of knowledge produced by listening to the past. Mark M. Smith (2004: ix–x) has suggested that attempting to understand the aural dimensions of human experience is not necessarily a new endeavour, as scholars from classical antiquity through to the twentieth century considered aurality, listening and hearing. Historians of the *Annales* school, as well as other thinkers such as Marshall McLuhan and Walter Ong, have all contributed significantly to ideas on the history of the senses and the history of aurality (Erlmann 2004). In the 1970s, the emergence of social history amplified an interest in aural history, as did developments in intellectual history and the history of seeing. As Smith (2004) observes, interest in the field of aural history, while not qualitatively new, extends a deep genealogy that has flourished due to changes in historical research and a growing awareness of auditory technologies in contemporary life. For instance, Karin Bijsterveld's (2008) study of mechanical and industrial sound, building on the work of historians of sound such as Alain Corbin (1998) and Hillel Schwartz (1998), emphasizes a 'thoroughly historical' perspective by exploring a sequence of 'public problems of noise' over time. Attention to the audible has encouraged historians (and others) to listen with greater acuity not only to music and musicology but also to the materiality of sound (Hui 2013) and to a greater diversity of auditory environments and mediums (Rice 2016; Birdsall 2013). Studies of the history of sound and of hearing have been part of a wider trend towards a history of the senses, or a brand of social history that emphasizes intersensoriality (Rotter 2019; Classen 2018; Howes and Classen 2014; Morat 2014; Smith 2007a, 2004; Jay 2011). In fields such as deaf studies, an academic and activist field primarily associated with the teaching of sign language, clean divisions of hearing and seeing, and between hearing and deafness, have been called into question (Friedner and Helmrich 2012: 73). Deaf studies has urged a fresh response to the sonocentrism of sound studies that considers the visual (and other senses) as spaces of communicative and interactive possibility – for instance, reimagining how sound in the register of low-frequency vibration can challenge deaf–hearing dichotomies (Friedner and Helmrich 2012: 74–5; Gumperz 1962). By exploring the sonic histories of occupation, this volume interrogates how imperial power has created literal and metaphorical vibrations that have been interpreted, contested and perpetuated through the political, auditory and sensorial regimes of occupation and colonialism.

The relationship between sound and memory also correlates to how occupation has been experienced across the globe. As Jacques Rancière (2004) observes in the context of urban space, the historic dimensions of space have been constituted by a 'distribution of the sensible', where acoustic materializations, in the form of voices, acts of speech, sounds and music mark the collective imaginations of a space, comprised through a wider acoustic materiality he calls 'memoryscapes'. In this formulation, sound is not merely an object but the medium that structures remembrance. In some cases, the acoustic dimensions of a colonial or colonized past appear unmarked and may remain seemingly mute, even if these acoustic dimensions structure sonic memory and serve as the basis of remembrance (Kellerman 2019: 96). Conversely, actual physical silence may create a space of sonic memory by invoking, for instance, the repression and political silencing of a certain period (McCormack 2020: 12). As contributors to this volume suggest, sound and auditory environments are often weaved into memories of trauma, violence or liberation. Closely listening, in this sense, plays an integral role in reorienting how listeners choose to remember and tell stories about previous conflicts and negotiate their liberation in post-conflict sonic environments.

Although studies in sound (and music) have generally acknowledged the role of colonialism in shaping listening and performance practices, audition technologies and the science of audibility, few full-length studies have examined the role of sound in the imperial project globally. Although writers have discussed audibility and imperialism in diverse contexts and settings, such as war, jurisprudence, prison systems, noise reduction and urban spaces, a further examination of auditory environments beyond the scope of Europe and North America is needed. Part of the disconnect resides in orientation. Over the past decade, sound studies has emerged as a significant interdisciplinary field of inquiry in the humanities and social sciences, offering theoretical alternatives to visual studies of media and society that have innovatively 'unearthed repressed histories of sound and listening, while situating the ear as a major instrument in the production of social, cultural, and scientific knowledge' (Steingo and Sykes 2019).

In the early twenty-first century, the 'sonic turn' has produced useful ways to rethink the fundamental questions and assumptions of modernity, rationality, knowledge and experience. Important studies in technological modernity (Sterne 2003; Bijsterveld 2008), architectural acoustics (Thompson 2002), urban spaces (Bull 2000) and histories of aurality, listening, hearing and the body (Erlmann 2004, 2010; Szendy 2007; Schulze 2012) represent foundational works in the emerging field. Literature in the field of science and technology studies (STS) has also contributed to a focus on the materiality of sound as it is embedded not only in history and culture but also in technology and science, as well as its machines and ways of knowing and interacting (Groth and Schultz 2020: 420).

Some of these discussions are not entirely new to STS – for instance, historians of technology, such as Hans-Joachim Braun, have long advocated for the study of music and sound technology within the context of the history of technology (Pinch and Bijsterveld 2012: 10). The interweaving ideas and approaches of sound studies and STS have been particularly useful. As Pinch and Bijsterveld (2012: 103) suggest in the context of automobile technology, sound studies has been expedient in unravelling the early history of car sounds, their cultural meanings and the complexities of how these sounds are talked about, while STS has contributed robust theories on the testing and simulation of car sounds. These approaches together have clarified new sense-oriented ways of designing, testing and marketing cars. Although historians of science and technology and STS scholars have largely privileged the visual over the aural (and other senses), recent shifts in the STS field suggest further opportunities for interdisciplinary collaboration and exploration in the study of sound.

Nonetheless, an enduring critique of sound studies has been the lack of attention it has paid to research outside of North America and Western Europe. Writing in 2004, Veit Erlmann (2004: 4) observed, 'The number of accounts detailing how the West's sounds are cast back on it is still shockingly small. Even more striking is the absence from current debates of Third World scholars interested in auditory perception.' Although a shift appears to be taking place as sound as an object of study gains traction among researchers globally, and as sound studies as a disciplinary configuration remaps itself, Erlmann's comments remain pertinent. In this context, it is possible to surmise that one reason sound studies generally has not been attuned to the political conditions of occupation and imperialism is that few have conducted research in geographical regions where the experience of such oppressive conditions has been pervasive. Will simply shifting the focus of sound studies towards the so-called Global South change the fact the term itself has been formulated through colonialism and coloniality? (Chávez and Skelchy 2019). As Steingo and Sykes (2019) observe in *Remapping Sound Studies*, if the presumption that the South and sound lie at the heart of modernity, avoiding the reproduction of colonial logic may rest on approach and methodology rather than a simple remapping. A remapping implies more than reorienting the dominant ideas and narratives of a field focused on Europe and North America onto other world regions. Decentring Eurocentricism in the field requires that representations and knowledge of the world are situated both historically and geographically. In this regard, further efforts to decolonize the field of sound studies to address *who* produces knowledge on sound are as pertinent as how the field can be reoriented.

To a degree, these issues have been foregrounded in recent years as ethnomusicologists and anthropologists have become interested in sound studies, leading some to even question the privileging of 'music' as a cultural category based in relativism (Wong 2014). Since the 1950s, the field of ethnomusicology has maintained its commitment to a wide range of human musicality, especially of non-Western musical cultures, while attending somewhat to the traumas of colonialism. Although the discipline has been accused of appearing naïve at times to its own complicity in imperial projects, the work done by ethnomusicologists (and anthropologists) has resulted in shifts not only in geographic orientation but also in methodological approach to the study of sound. This is evident, for instance, in recent issues of journals (e.g. *Journal of Sonic Studies* and *Sound Studies*) and other publications where writers have examined auditory environments and practices in societies such as India, Turkey, Taiwan, Sri Lanka, Singapore, Thailand, Vietnam and the Caribbean (e.g. Basdurak 2020; Porath 2019; Lynch 2019; Hsieh 2019; Sykes 2018; Bronfman 2017; Cheung 2016; Östersjö and Nguyễn 2016). Researchers have focused primarily on the relationship of contested urban soundscapes to issues such as noise reduction, governmentality, spirituality and technology. Some of this literature consciously interrogates previously held theoretical ideas and approaches of sound studies by exploring how auditory environments outside of Europe and North America complicate (or disrupt) such ideas.[3]

Situating ideas on sound and occupation

Efforts to rethink and 'remap' sound studies are also evident in a growing body of literature exploring the relationship between sound and colonialism. In *Audible Empire: Music, Global Politics, Critique*, Ronald Radano and Tejumola Olaniyan (2016) present a selection of studies that encourage a rethinking of how music and sound are understood within the sensory realm of empire. Featuring a diversity of disciplinary perspectives, geographic and historical orientations, *Audible Empire* examines the power relations that underscore connections between the audible (in this case, music genres such as jazz, hip hop and Chinese musicals) and imperial institutions (schools, corporations, archives) and the listening practices they promoted (e.g. Western ideas of tonality as a universal and colonizing force). Although the volume focuses on music, it draws on a sound studies approach to address the concept of 'music' as it is articulated within a wider framework of sound and specifically how 'music' has been used to impose order on a sonically chaotic world. Furthermore, the volume reassesses how the celebration of modern technologies of sound established in earlier work in sound and popular music studies failed to account for capitalism's role in the emergence of internet social media platforms and technologies such as MP3. By re-emphasizing the importance of the local and cultural, Radano and Olaniyan move away from the 'excessive tendencies' in post-Cold-War cultural studies of sound towards emphasizing the historicity of empire's audible conditions that have resonated into the present (2016: 4).

Similar historical concerns regarding sonic practices in a colonial context, namely singing, listening, speaking and the writing of these practices, are explored in Ana Maria Ochoa-Gautier's *Aurality: Listening and Knowledge in Nineteenth-Century Colombia* (2014). As another instance of critically reorienting sound studies beyond the Euro-American world, Ochoa-Gautier foregrounds how distinctions between voice and ear, human and non-human, European and non-European, and nature and culture were created through networks that she calls 'acoustic assemblages' (Ochoa-Gautier 2014: 22–3). By simultaneously listening, theorizing about hearing and producing new political relationships, acoustic assemblages reference a colonial ontology of relationships that provides ways to think about the interactions between entities that produce or hear sounds. Through examining, for instance, the ways that the ear and voice 'imbued the technology of writing' with traces of the acoustic, Ochoa-Gautier describes how personhood and citizenship were denied (or granted) to certain groups or individuals in colonial Latin America. Often, these distinctions were made based on how Europeans interpreted sounds made by local people (e.g. as either animal-like or human) and how Europeans imagined or listened to the voices of the colonized.

Such interactions form the basis of volumes such as *Empire of the Senses: Sensory Practices of Colonialism in Early America* (2017), edited by Daniela Hacke and Paul Musselwhite. This book explores how European appropriations of the foreign were based on a sensory perception that shaped cultural encounters and European perceptions of distant environments. These perceptions, as Hacke and Musselwhite suggest, were observed, explained and reported via the senses. Focusing on sensory perception as a form of bodily practice (i.e. practices and modes as ways of understanding the world), the volume draws on the field of sensory history to explore how the historicity of the senses lies in the conceptualization and normative arrangement of the senses and their bodily affective experience.[4] Foregrounding the interdependency and interconnectedness of the senses in perceiving the world also demonstrates how Europeans, Indigenous peoples and enslaved Africans in the Americas constructed 'sensescapes' in the process of defining relationships with each other. By exploring how these sensescapes were consciously structured through the imperial project in the Americas, the collection explores how the creation and contestation of sensescapes as imperial devices were asserted through European institutions that defined intercultural sensory encounters between Europeans and non-Europeans (Hacke and Musselwhite 2017: 12).

As Carolyn Birdsall describes in the case of Nazi Germany, the struggle for public and social space involved not only the threat of physical violence but also multiple 'corporeal and acoustic strategies for achieving sensory appeal' (Birdsall 2012: 32). Creating 'resonance' within urban and rural acoustic settings suggests how the concept of 'resonance' spans from resonant systems of specific body parts (such as vibrations in the ear or vocal canal) and extends towards a wider notion of acoustic power (Augoyard and Torgue 2005: 108). The reverberance of sounds has historically been symbolic of sound as a source of potential power, used to mediate acoustic presence across distances. In the context of empire, the systematic weaponization of sound – for instance, the use of ammunition, heavy military vehicles, bells, loudspeakers and popular music – has made sound integral to the project of resonating imperial power.

The aftermath of the 11 September 2001 attacks in the United States and the subsequent US invasion of Iraq in 2003 marked a significant watershed in the study of the sound of conflict and occupation. These and other events provided a context for writers to interrogate the violent effects of auditory production in the global context of conflict and militarism. Earlier volumes to address the relationship between music and violence include Svanibor Pettan's *Music, Politics and War: Views from Croatia in the 1990s* (1999), which situates music in a wider field of sonic practices while documenting local perspectives on the crucial role of music in arduous periods of war. Another example is John O'Connell and Salwa El-Shawan Castelo-Branco's *Music and Conflict* (2010), which uses musicological and ethnographic analysis to focus on the role of music in social and political conflicts by examining how the practices and materials of music-making can promote and resolve conflict. Other examples include Jonathan Pieslak's *Sound Targets: American Soldiers and Music in the Iraq War* (2009), which describes the role of music in the everyday life of US military personnel, while key articles on the listening practices of US soldiers (Gilman 2010), the use of sound in interrogation and torture techniques (Cusick 2006, 2008), and the political economy of military experimentation with sonic booms as a form of state power in the Cold War (Suisman 2015) illustrate how the weaponization of sound has impacted people's bodies in the context of war.

Other notable publications explore the relationship between war and auditory experience as part of a historical setting – for instance, Carolyn Birdsall's *Nazi Soundscapes: Sound, Technology and Urban Space in Germany, 1933–1945* (2012) and David McDonald's *My Voice Is My Weapon: Music, Nationalism, and the Poetics of Palestinian Resistance* (2013). Birdsall's book examines how the Nazi regime used mediated sound and cultural phenomena (e.g. radio, voice, music) to transform acoustic environments, listening experience and urban space under wartime (and interwar) conditions. More specifically, Birdsall interrogates the role of sound, especially through radio, in constructing the 'people's community' (*Volksgemeinschaft*) as well as how the war decisively altered the city of Dusseldorf's auditory environment. By exploring public spaces and the implementation of surveillance and control through sirens, loudspeakers and special announcements, Birdsall studies how sound was used to encourage residents to self-monitor. McDonald uses popular song to explore the relationship between Palestinian nationalism, protest song and the ongoing 'Palestinian crisis' to provide an 'ethnohistorical' account of occupation and the significant events, musical styles and key artists active during his fieldwork. Employing a sociopolitical approach to examine the performativity of resistance, McDonald emphasizes how Palestinian cultural production has taken on dynamic approaches towards resistance, often utilizing and reshaping established discourses on national loss.

In sound studies, two landmark publications, namely Steve Goodman's *Sonic Warfare: Sound, Effect and the Ecology of War* (2010) and *Listening to War: Sound, Music, Trauma, and Survival in Wartime Iraq* (2015) by Martin Daughtry, explore the sonic dimensions of modern warfare, often overlooked in the experiences and representations presented through visual media. Both books share a transdisciplinary approach to theorizing the sonic experience of war and its affective dimensions of sound. As Daughtry (2015: 6) explains, *Listening to War* provides an ethnographic grounding to Goodman's broad ontological foundations by focusing on precise details and compelling stories. Furthermore, Daughtry describes how the 'belliphonic', a word he coins combining the Latin and Greek words for war and voice, respectively, represents the sonic dimension of the US military's 'Operation Iraqi Freedom' expressed through the layered sounds of weaponry, vehicles and voices. Importantly, Daughtry's rich and emotive accounts of war intertwine the perspectives of both Iraqi civilians and US soldiers in combat zones (and other spaces) to provide chilling immediacy to his theorization and sonic evidence. Goodman's focus is on how sound, specifically vibrational force within certain environments, contributes to an immersive atmosphere or ambience of fear and dread. Using the idea of the 'politics of frequency', *Sonic Warfare* foregrounds the relationship between vibration, power and war by analysing a diverse range of sounds including military sound bombs, the global clubbing industry and seemingly innocuous yet intrusive musical technologies such as Muzak.

The allusion to military occupations as not only noisy (in actual combat zones) but also musical has been studied in the context of 'musical militarism', a term associated with diverse implications including religious indoctrination, the introduction of instruments (e.g. brass), the reorientation of instrumental practices, musical pedagogy, the manipulation of aesthetics and musical style, European ideas of tonality and listening practices (Baker 2008; Irving 2010; Dolan 2013; Agawu 2016). Audible legacies of imperialism generally became absorbed aesthetically in taste preferences of the listening public and in the circulation of Euro-American popular music (and culture) across the globe (Radano and Olaniyan 2016: 5–6).

Without explicitly focusing on sound's relationship to war and colonialism, Jennifer Lynn Stoever's book *The Sonic Color Line: Race and the Cultural Politics of Listening* (2016) also examines how sensibilities, tastes and sensitivities are implicit in the control over a racialized soundscape. More specifically, Stoever explores how listening has operated as an organ of racial discernment, categorization and resistance in the United States. In the pre-Civil-War era, essentialist ideas about Black sounds and listening practices provided white elites with new methods to ground racial abjection in the body while cultivating white listening practices as critical, delicate and, more significantly, the standard of citizenship and personhood. Sound, in this formulation, functioned politically as a set of social relations and a medium for racial discourse. Through what Stoever (2016) calls the 'sonic colour line' – the process of racializing sound or how and why certain bodies in the United States are expected to produce, desire and live among particular types of sound – hierarchical divisions between 'blackness' and 'whiteness' are created. The codification of sound with racialized bodies, such as music and everyday ambient sounds, established 'noise' as sound's unruly 'Other'. Since the 1980s, for instance, the sound of hip-hop music pumped at a high volume through car speakers became a stand-in for the bodies of young Black men in US culture. As Stoever (2016: 12–13) argues, the labelling of such sounds as noise is not merely about measuring loudness in decibels but rather rendering as Other certain sounds (and the bodies that produce and consume them). Although Stoever's 'sonic colour line' does not reference occupation per se, it is not hard to situate it conceptually and historically within ideas of

US and European colonial hierarchies of ethnicity and sound. The 'sonic colour line', as a heuristic, encourages further questions about how dominant listening practices accrue and change over time while continuing to exert pressure to conform to the norms of the 'sonic colour line'. Through surveillance, discipline and interpretation, certain associations between sound and ethnicity become normalized and naturalized through dominant culture.

Situating *Sonic Histories of Occupation*

The issues raised in the critical literature on sound mentioned previously drive the methodologies and discussions explored in this volume. Besides adding to existing research in sound and music studies in a non-European/North American context, the case studies presented here examine how colonization and occupation have been experienced sensorially through specific 'auditory regimes' (Daughtry 2015; Morat 2014). The questions raised here urge readers to rethink ocularcentric histories of occupation or, as Radano and Olaniyan (2016: 2) suggest, how Western imperial orders and their political democracies have 'been matters of the ear'. This book contributes to an understanding of not only why sound is integral to the study of occupation and colonialism but also how sound has been deployed in efforts to control, negotiate and resist in disparate geographical, political and affective spaces.

The volume addresses a number of core questions, including:

(1) How is sound implicated in controlling and disciplining colonized or 'occupied' peoples and aural spaces?
(2) How do listeners under conditions of occupation form new types of auditory or vocal expression?
(3) How do sound and memory overlap in histories of occupation, conflict and trauma?
(4) How can the study of the sonic histories of occupation and colonialism contribute to the development of new research methodologies in sound studies and history?
(5) How does occupation give rise to distinctive auditory environments and music cultures?

In responding to these questions, the book is organized into three parts: 'Voice and occupation', 'Memory, sound and occupation' and 'Auditory responses to occupation and colonialism'. Each of these thematic parts represents compelling ways of examining the auditory experiences of those living through foreign occupation, imperialism or conflict, and each responds to at least one of the aforementioned core questions.

Part I, 'Voice and occupation', explores how the human voice has been discursively created and used to navigate conditions of occupation. For example, in Chapter 1 – 'The vocal apparatus' colonial contexts: France's *mission civilisatrice* and (settler) colonialism in Algeria and North America' – Iris Blake explains how the 'vocal apparatus', beginning in the late nineteenth century, was used discursively to describe how human bodily organs produced speech and sound. Blake suggests that the discursive formation of the vocal apparatus in medical, scientific and pedagogical literature was intended to not only consolidate its meaning but also align it with contemporary ideas about modernity, racial capitalism and colonialism. Indeed, she shows how scholarly advances in the study of the vocal apparatus were linked directly to the French colonial project in North Africa. Blake's chapter 'de-universalizes this Western conception of voicing [i.e., the vocal apparatus]', demonstrating how its 'historical and cultural construction' are 'inseparable from histories of colonial occupation'. She also introduces the notion of 'voice-as-territory', demonstrating not just how the vocal apparatus could be 'subjected to colonial spatial ideologies and disciplining projects' but also how it was linked directly to settler colonialism in the North American context. In doing so, Blake's chapter demonstrates how sound and the physical occupation of colonial territory are intertwined in discursive and physical ways.

In Chapter 2, 'The hush arbour as sanctuary: African American survival silence during British/American slavery', Maya Cunningham explains how 'in African American life during slavery, sound and silence . . . were closely related', with her chapter covering two seemingly opposite yet closely related 'sounds of occupation': 'coded speech by day, and secret meetings in hushed tones by night'. Drawing on accounts found in the Works Progress Administration (WPA) Slave Narratives, numerous published memoirs and anthropological work, Cunningham shows how enslaved African Americans on cash crop plantations in eighteenth- and nineteenth-century North America resisted enslavement through the performance of secret 'code songs', often within a religious context, that could be used to communicate clandestine messages to listeners while also representing a way in which to assert agency. At the same time, 'hush arbours' – spaces in which 'enslaved Blacks could speak, sing, pray and preach freely' but in hushed tones – represented a quite different form of sonic resistance. Be it in literal 'hush arbours' within wooded areas where trees muffled the sound of singing or worship, or in the use of objects (such as pots) that aided in muffling sounds of prayer or song, Cunningham shows not only that the deliberate practice of 'hushing' sonic expression enabled African Americans to create both physical and figurative spaces for sonic expression under slavery but also that such practices had legacies that stretched well beyond abolition.

In Chapter 3 – 'Music and sound in Weihsien Internment Camp in Japanese-occupied China' – Sophia Geng also touches on the use of 'coded songs', though in a very different context – internment camps for civilian Allied prisoners in Japanese-occupied China. Drawing from first-hand accounts of life in the largest of these camps, Geng describes how particular songs, especially those from a liturgical or Christian tradition, were used by internees to defy Japanese control. In addition, however, Geng argues that musical creativity in this wartime setting forged a sense of community among internees, and in some cases, helped them to survive a shared experience of trauma. Geng also details other examples of sonic transgression by inmates, from clandestine radio listening to more over acts of resistance – the ringing of bells by inmates to celebrate the surrender of Nazi Germany in 1945, for instance.

Part II of this volume, 'Memory, sound and occupation', considers the role of sound in reconciling communities to shared histories of conflict and/ or colonialism using methodologies that engage with Indigenous knowledge systems, ethnography and community-based research. Chapter 4, 'Occupying new sound worlds: Debordering sonic imaginaries in StoryMaps', demonstrates how new research methodologies in sound studies might be used to overcome the traumatic memories of sectarian violence and 'the Troubles' in Northern Ireland. In this chapter, Fiona Magowan, Jim Donaghey and Annette McNelis reflect on the ways in which sounds project and ameliorate community experiences, memories and narratives of conflict – but also reconciliation. The chapter focuses on the city of Derry/Londonderry in Northern Ireland as a case study to explore the different conflict/post-conflict settings of resistance and reconciliation, as well as the research potential of the StoryMap platform. In articulating the sonic memories and listening practices of Annette McNelis, a local musician, the chapter explores Annette's border crossing, analysed through her own StoryMap, to critically examine how the complexities emerging from border studies and human geography inform a theoretical shift from decolonization to 'debordering'.

In Chapter 5, 'Loud town, quiet base: Olongapo City, Subic Bay and the US Navy, 1950–70', Kevin Sliwoski recounts the sonic environments of the American naval base at Subic Bay in the Philippines and the adjacent Olongapo City, which grew to meet the needs of the base's 40,000 year-round residents in the period after the Second World War. Sliwoski explores how a wide range of sounds from war-fighting drills and air strips to nightclubs and cover bands became auditory signatures in that era of an ongoing US occupying presence that shaped the relationships between Filipinos and Americans in the immediate area. The chapter details the disparities between memories and records that depicted Olongapo City as dirty and noisy compared to the quiet and clean naval base at Subic Bay. Representations of sound, silence and volume, according to Sliwoski, were constructed along racial and gendered legacies of US colonialism in the Philippines later inherited by US service members and civilians alike. Referencing the literature on foreign occupation and US military bases – a growing body of research which explores military bases as a new form of occupation (e.g. Lutz 2009) – the chapter also explores how the US Navy exerted strict control over the sonic environment of the Subic Bay region through sound regulations and military life outside the confines of the base.

In Chapter 6, 'Registering sonic histories in a multiply occupied place: Sound and survivance in Mangota'ay Taiwan', DJ Hatfield explores how Indigenous Cepo' Pangcah communities in Taiwan register histories of occupation by various forces through the invocation of the sound of features of the natural environment, expressing and asserting their relationship to land (and sea) under settler occupation. As Hatfield observes, the intent of Pangcah sonic practices is revealed only through a close and informed listening of specific sounds that evoke massacres, oppression and other trauma. Cepo' Pangcah communities have survived the arrival of European merchants, navies and priests, Chinese settler colonists, the Japanese empire and, more recently, the government of the Republic of China (Taiwan). Through the registration of colonized histories expressed through sonic practice, the chapter shifts the question of 'what occupation sounds like' to explore how Indigenous people themselves record and inflect occupation in sound.

Part III, entitled 'Auditory responses to occupation and colonialism', articulates how the circulation of sounds through media, art, music and technology under colonialism and foreign occupation has created new identities and aural spaces. In Chapter 7, 'The sonic occupation of Central Asia: Sound culture and the railway in Chingiz Aitmatov's *The Day Lasts More Than a Hundred Years*', Dimitri Smirnov explores changes to the auditory environment of Central Asia brought about by the introduction of railway systems in the era of Russian colonialism as it is expressed in the literature of the Kyrgyz author Chingiz Aitmatov. As a way of consolidating its territorial possessions, the Russian Empire (and, later, the Soviet Union) pursued a practice of 'railway imperialism' – a development which meant changes not only to the landscape but also to the soundscapes of Central Asia. Smirnov's chapter recounts specific sounds and responses to sound in Chingiz Aitmatov's 1980 novel *The Day Lasts More Than a Hundred Years*, specifically referencing sounds from trains and railway stations to contextualize the novel's auditory dimension as part of a wider imperial heritage of the Soviet regime. As Smirnov observes, through the deafening roar of the trains and loud sounds emanating from the surrounding railway infrastructure (such as loudspeakers which were used for announcements and for playing music) the railway literally sounded the Russian occupation of Central Asia.

In Chapter 8, 'Auditory and spatial regimes of US colonial rule in Baguio, Philippines', Russell P. Skelchy explores how the creation of the hill station of Baguio was achieved both spatially and sonically through the work of US urban designers such as Daniel H. Burnham. In the early twentieth century, Burnham's plans for Baguio (and Manila) inspired a model of auditory and spatial planning that colonial administrators hoped to replicate across the archipelago. In this context, the chapter examines how the design and control of Baguio's auditory environment were part of a wider process to transforming the rural military outpost into a comfortable resort city for American expatriates, members of the Filipino elite and others to escape the noise, heat, disease and insurgency of Manila and the lowland areas. Furthermore, Skelchy explores Baguio as an 'auditory contact zone' where sound configured and framed the interactive dimensions of the imperial encounter between Filipinos and US expatriates. The re-engineering of urban spaces under the US colonial administration was integral in establishing sound as a material symbol of imperial power.

In Chapter 9, 'Soundscapes of diversity in the port cities of British Malaya: Cultural convergences and contestations in the early twentieth century', Tan Sooi Beng examines how the soundscapes of colonial port cities such as Penang and Singapore were articulated musically through Malay social dance and theatre forms such as *ronggeng* and *dondang sayang*. Tan argues that the diverse cultures of such port cities created new multiethnic identities that simultaneously engaged with global circulations of popular music genres and which featured texts promoting specific ideas of 'progress'. Listening beyond the cultural boundaries of the nation state, the chapter explores the permeability of borders in the colonial period and the ways that local musicians and communities defined a sense of place while interacting with structures of colonial power.

Sonic Histories of Occupation engages in a dialogue with other recent volumes published on sound and imperialism (e.g. Radano and Olaniyan 2016), engaging also with the recent literature foregrounding sound studies' Eurocentric epistemological and ontological history, however. This book seeks to widen such debates by addressing specific questions about the relationship between sound and occupation beyond Europe. This volume points to the ways that the study of occupation can contribute to a novel understanding of its legacies in different auditory environments across the world – from colonial North Africa to Soviet-controlled Central Asia and US bases in the Asia-Pacific region. Furthermore, the volume elicits greater nuance and perspective as to how listeners living under occupation (in various forms) have responded to auditory environments to create new forms of auditory expression. Finally, the volume reveals how comparative studies across geographical and temporal contexts can contribute to a better understanding of occupation and its multidirectional arrangements of power. Indeed, many of the chapters in this volume have sought to engage with the ways in which their own case studies respond to recent debates about the very definition of 'occupation'.

While the topics presented here are far from all-encompassing, the volume works towards a reorientation of sound studies through new ideas and geographic spaces. As the trend towards the 'remapping' or decolonizing of sound studies gains traction, *Sonic Histories of Occupation* features case studies from Asia, North Africa, North America and Europe by writers of diverse disciplinary, cultural and ethnic backgrounds. Undoubtedly, there are silences in this volume, especially related to sound in the context of well-known territorial occupations – Iraq, Afghanistan, the Occupied Palestinian Territories and various other well-documented cases of 'occupation' are not addressed in chapter form in this volume – or in addressing colonization in the context of gender, bodies and sexuality or constructions of civilization and migration/immigration. The editors nonetheless hope that the questions raised by this volume will help to widen the debate on both sound studies and the study of occupation. In this regard, *Sonic Histories of Occupation* encourages further collaborative explorations into the relationship between sound and occupation using a transdisciplinary and comparative approach.

Notes

1 'Kamala Harris trip delayed over possible "Havana syndrome" case,' BBC News, 25 August 2021. https://www.bbc.com/news/world-us-canada-58322593.

2 A shift in the use of the word 'occupation', which once belonged primarily to the military sphere, has now entered mainstream political discourse, especially since the Occupy movement started in 2011 (Rancière 2012). The words 'occupy' and 'occupied space' in this particular context referred to assembly (the material configuration of space or symbolic configuration of a community), horizontality (an anti-hierarchical subversion) and consensus decision-making in mass assemblies (Graeber 2011; Schneider 2013; Kinna 2020), anarchist ideas that defined the movement and its reconfiguration of public space. The word 'occupy' has taken on specific political meanings in settler-colonial societies where the word is associated with Indigenous sovereignty and dispossession (Kauanui 2016). For instance, during Occupy Wall Street, Indigenous activists and critics challenged the use of the term 'occupy' in relation to actual settler-colonial occupation. In this case, Indigenous dispossession was the precondition for the construction of Wall Street, a metonym for the US finance industry, where a wall was built to keep the Lenape people out of their homeland in an area now known as lower Manhattan (Barker 2011).

3 Sykes (2018) and Hsieh (2019), for instance, both argue against the idea of a 'singular, omnipresent' or 'holistic' understanding of the word 'soundscape'. Instead, both scholars argue for a soundscape that is moving, contested, relational and mutually constitutive. Although this shift does not necessarily derive from their case studies in Singapore and Taiwan respectively, it does suggest ways that research on non-Western auditory environments may inspire a rethinking of commonly understood terms in sound studies.

4 The field of sensory history also has contributed to the study of sound, occupation and imperialism, often in a European and North American context (e.g. Smith 2004, 2007b; Denney 2011; Morat 2014).

References

Agawu, K. (2016), 'Tonality as a Colonizing Force in Africa', in R. Radano and T. Olaniyan (eds), *Audible Empire: Music, Global Politics, Critique*, 334–56, Durham, NC: Duke University Press.

Alten, S. R. (2014), *Audio in Media*, 10th edn, Boston: Wadsworth Cengage Learning.

Augoyard, J. and H. Torgue, eds. (2005), *Sonic Experience: A Guide to Everyday Sounds*, trans. A. McCartney and D. Paquette, Montreal: McGill-Queen's University Press.

Baker, G. (2008), *Imposing Harmony: Music and Society in Colonial Cuzco*, Durham, NC: Duke University Press.

Barker, J. (2011), 'Manna-Hata', *Tequila Sovereign*, 10 October: Available online: https://tequilasovereign.wordpress.com/2011/10/10/manna-hata/ (accessed 12 October 2011).

Barthes, R. (1991), *The Responsibility of Forms: Critical Essays on Music, Art, and Representation*, Berkeley: University of California Press.

Basdurak, N. (2020), 'The Soundscape of Islamic Populism: Auditory Publics, Silences and the Myth of Democracy', *Sound Effects*, 9 (1): 133–48.

Birdsall, C. (2012), *Nazi Soundscapes: Sound, Technology and Urban Space in Germany, 1933-1945*, Amsterdam: Amsterdam University Press.

Birdsall, C. (2013), 'Sonic Artefacts: Reality Codes of Urbanity in Early German Radio Documentary', in K. Bijsterveld (ed), *Soundscapes of the Urban Past: Staged Sound as Mediated Cultural Heritage*, 129–68, New York: Columbia University Press.

Bijsterveld, K. (2008), *Mechanical Sound: Technology, Culture and Public Problems of Noise in the Twentieth Century*, Boston: MIT Press.

Bronfman, A. (2017), 'Sonic Colour Zones: Laura Boulton and the Hunt for Music', *Sound Studies*, 3 (1): 17–32.

Bull, M. (2000), *Sounding Out the City: Personal Stereos and the Management of Everyday Life*, Oxford: Berg.

Chávez, L. and R. Skelchy (2019), 'Decolonization for Ethnomusicology and Music Studies in Higher Education', *Action, Criticism, and Theory for Music Education*, 18 (3): 115–43.

Cheung, K. H. (2016), 'What do the Urban Soundscapes of a City Represent? Case Studies in Bangkok and Hong Kong', *Journal of Sonic Studies*, 12: Available online: https://www.researchcatalogue.net/view/251049/251050 (accessed 13 February 2020).

Classen, C., ed. (2018), *A Cultural History of the Senses in the Age of Empire*, London: Bloomsbury.

Corbin, A. (1998), *Village Bells: Sounds and Meanings in the Nineteenth-Century French Countryside*, trans. M. Thom, New York: Columbia University Press.

Cusick, S. G. (2006), 'Music as Torture/Music as Weapon', *Revista Transcultural de Música/Transcultural Music Review*, 10: 1–18.

Cusick, S. G. (2008), 'You Are in a Place That is Out of the World: Music in the Detention Camps of the Global War on Terror', *Journal of the Society of American Music*, 2 (1): 1–26.

Daughtry, J. M. (2015), *Listening to War: Sound, Music, Trauma, and Survival in Wartime Iraq*, Oxford: Oxford University Press.

Denney, P. (2011), 'Looking Back, Going Forward. Rethinking Sensory History', *Rethinking History*, 15 (4): 601–16.

Dinstein, Y. (2009), *The International Law of Belligerent Occupation*, Cambridge: Cambridge University Press.

Dolan, E. I. (2013), *The Orchestral Revolution: Haydn and the Technologies of Timbre*, Cambridge: Cambridge University Press.

Erlmann, V., ed. (2004), *Hearing Cultures: Essays on Sound, Listening and Modernity*, London: Bloomsbury.

Erlmann, V. (2010), *Reason and Resonance: A History of Modern Aurality*, New York: Zone Books.

Friedner, M. and S. Helmrich (2012), 'Sound Studies Meets Deaf Studies', *Senses annd Society*, 7 (1): 72–86.

Gilman, L. (2010), 'An American Soldier's iPod: Layers of Identity and Situated Listening in Iraq', *Music and Politics*, 4 (2): 1–17.

Graeber, D. (2011), 'Enacting the Impossible (On Consensus Decision Making)', *Occupy Wall Street* (29 October): Available online: http://occupywallst.org/article/enacting -the-impossible/ (accessed 2 December 2017).

Gross, A. (2017), *The Writing on the Wall: Rethinking the International Law of Occupation*, Cambridge: Cambridge University Press.

Groth, S. K. and H. Schulze (2020), *The Bloomsbury Handbook of Sound Art*, London: Bloomsbury.

Gregory, D. (2004), *The Colonial Present: Afghanistan, Palestine, Iraq*, Oxford: Blackwells.

Gumperz, J. (1962), 'Types of Linguistic Communities', *Anthropological Linguistics*, 4 (1): 28–40.

Hacke, D. and P. Musselwhite (2017), *Empire of the Senses: Sensory Practices of Colonialism in Early America*, Leiden: Brill.

Hassan, S. D. (2008), 'Never-ending Occupations', *The New Centennial Review*, 8 (1): 1–17.

Howes, D. and C. Classen (2014), *Ways of Sensing: Understanding the Senses in Society*, New York: Routledge.

Hsieh, J. C. (2019), 'Piano Transductions: Music, Sound and Noise in Urban Taiwan', *Sound Studies*, 5 (1): 4–21.

Huang, N. (2013), 'Listening to Films: Politics of the Auditory in 1970s China', *Journal of Chinese Cinemas*, 7 (3): 187–206.

Huecho Pozo, C. (2019), 'Ministry Plans Use of Acoustic Dissuasive Device', *Chile Today*, 9 December: Available online: https://chiletoday.cl/site/ministry-plans-use-of -acoustic-dissuasive-device/.

Hui, A. (2013), *The Psychophysical Ear: Music Experiments, Experimental Sounds, 1840–1910*, Cambridge, MA: MIT Press.

Irving, D. R. M. (2010), *Colonial Counterpoint: Music in Early Modern Manila*, Oxford: Oxford University Press.

Jay, M. (2011), 'In the Realm of the Senses: An Introduction', *The American Historical Review*, 116 (2): 307–15.

Kauanui, J. K. (2016), 'A Structure, Not an Event: Settler Colonialism and Enduring Indigeneity', *Lateral*, 5 (1): Available online: https://csalateral.org/issue/5-1/fo rum-alt-humanities-settler colonialism-enduring-indigeneity-kauanui/ (accessed 24 February 2020).

Kinna, R. (2020), *Government of No One: The Theory and Practice of Anarchism*, London: Penguin.

Kellermann, K. (2019), 'Silence, Motifs and Echoes: Acts of Listening in Postcolonial Hamburg', in P. Hildebrandt (ed), *Performing Citizenship: Bodies, Agencies, Limitations*, 93–110, New York: Palgrave Macmillan.

Lutz, C., ed. (2009), *The Bases of Empire: The Global Struggle Against U.S. Military Posts*, New York: New York University Press.

Lynch, J. A. (2019), 'Festival Noise and Soundscape Politics in Mumbai, India', *Sound Studies*, 5 (1): 37–51.

McCormack, R. (2020), *The Sculpted Ear: Aurality and Statuary in the West*, University Park: Pennsylvania State University Press.

McDonald, D. A. (2013), *My Voice is My Weapon: Music, Nationalism, and the Poetics of Palestinian Resistance*, Durham, NC: Duke University Press.

McGill, K. O. (2018), 'Sound in Colonial Virginia', *Encyclopedia Virginia*: Available online:https://www.encyclopediavirginia.org/Sound_in_Colonial_Virginia#start_ent ry (accessed 22 August 2020).

McLoughlin, I. (2018), 'Weaponizing Sound: Are Countries Using Intrusive Audio Surveillance?', *The Independent*, 6 June: Available online: https://www.independent.c o.uk/news/world/politics/sonic-attacks-china-cuba-sound-weapon-surveillance-us -diplomats-a8384341.html.

Meilinger, P. S. (2016), 'Sound and War', *The RUSI Journal*, 161 (5): 78–83.

Morat, D. (2014), 'Introduction', in D. Morat (ed), *Sounds of Modern History: Auditory Cultures in 19th and 20th Century Europe*, 1–12, New York: Berghahn Books.

Niiler, E. (2018), 'Sonic Weapons Long, Noisy History', *Sky History*, 27 August: Available online: https://www.history.com/news/sonic-weapons-warfare-acoustic.

Ochoa Gautier, A. M. (2014), *Aurality: Listening and Knowledge in Nineteenth-Century Colombia*, Durham, NC: Duke University Press.

Östersjö, S. and T. T. Nguyễn (2016), 'The Sounds of Hanoi and the After-image of the Homeland', *Journal of Sonic Studies*, 12: Available online: https://www.researchcatal ogue.net/view/246523/246546 (accessed 26 February 2020).

Pinch, T. and K. Bijsterveld, eds. (2012), *Oxford Handbook of Sound Studies*, Oxford: Oxford University Press.

Porath, N., ed. (2019), *Hearing Southeast Asia: Sounds of Hierarchy and Power in Context*, Copenhagen: NIAS Press.

Radano, R. and T. Olaniyan, eds. (2016), *Audible Empire: Music, Global Politics, Critique*, Durham, NC: Duke University Press.

Rancière, J. (2004), *The Politics of Aesthetics: The Distribution of the Sensible*, London: Continuum.

Rancière, J. (2012), 'Occupation', *Political Concepts: A Critical Lexicon*: Available online: https://www.politicalconcepts.org/occupation-jacques-ranciere/ (accessed 7 March 2020).

Rice, T. (2016), 'Sounds Inside: Prison, Prisoners and Acoustical Agency', *Sound Studies*, 2 (1): 6–20.

Rotter, A. J. (2019), *Empires of the Senses: Bodily Encounters in Imperial India and the Philippines*, Oxford: Oxford University Press.

Schneider, N. (2013), *Thank You, Anarchy: Notes from the Occupy Apocalypse*, Berkeley: University of California Press.

Schulze, H. (2012), 'The Body of Sound: Sounding Out the History of Science', *Sound Effects*, 2 (1): 196–208.

Schwartz, H. (1998), 'Beyond Tone and Decibel: The History of Noise', *Chronicle of Higher Education*, 9 January: B8.

Smith, M. M. (2001), *Listening to Nineteenth-Century America*, Chapel Hill: University of North Carolina Press.

Smith, M. M., ed. (2004), *Hearing History: A Reader*, Athens: University of Georgia Press.

Smith, M. M. (2007a), *Sensing the Past: Seeing, Hearing, Smelling, Tasting, and Touching in History*, Berkeley: University of California Press.

Smith, M. M. (2007b), *Sensory History*, London: Bloomsbury.

Steingo, G. and J. Sykes (2019), *Remapping Sound Studies*, Durham, NC: Duke University Press.

Sterne, J. (2003), *The Audible Past: Cultural Origins of Sound Reproduction*, Durham, NC: Duke University Press.

Stirk, P. M. R. (2016), *A History of Military Occupation from 1792 to 1914*, Edinburgh: Edinburgh University Press.

Stoever, J. L. (2016), *The Sonic Color Line: Race and the Cultural Politics of Listening*, New York: New York University Press.

Suisman, D. (2015), 'The Oklahoma City Sonic Boom Experiment and the Politics of Supersonic Aviation', *Radical History Review*, 121: 169–95.

Sykes, J. (2018), 'Ontologies of Acoustic Endurance: Rethinking Wartime Sound and Listening', *Sound Studies*, 4 (1): 35–60.

Szendy, P. (2007), *Listen: A History of Our Ears*. New York: Fordham University Press.

Taylor, J. E. (2021), 'Introduction: Visual Histories of Occupation(s)', in J. E. Taylor (ed), *Visual Histories of Occupation: A Transcultural Dialogue*, 1–23, London: Bloomsbury.

The Guardian (2009), 'G20 Protestors Blasted by Sonic Cannon', 25 September: Available online: https://www.theguardian.com/world/blog/2009/sep/25/sonic-cannon-g20-pittsburgh (accessed 22 August 2020).

Thompson, E. (2002), *The Soundscape of Modernity: Architectural Acoustics and the Culture of Listening in America, 1900–1933*, Cambridge, MA: MIT Press.

Wong, D. A. (2014), 'Sound, Silence, Music: Power', *Ethnomusicology*, 58 (2): 347–53.

Part I

Voice and occupation

Introduction to Part I

Jeremy E. Taylor

Part I of *Sonic Histories of Occupation* is entitled 'Voice and occupation'. The three chapters in this part address the extent to which voice – in its figurative and literal sense – has been discursively created and used to respond to conditions of occupation. Each chapter covers quite different temporal and geographic contexts, from the plantations of antebellum America to colonial North Africa and Japanese-occupied China, as well as contrasting interpretations of 'occupation'. In each case, a different emphasis is also placed on notions of 'the voice'.

For Blake, the scientific study of the human voice in the nineteenth century was directly linked to, and reflective of, the 'territoriality of [colonial] conquest'. She develops this argument through her 'voice-as-territory framework', highlighting the extent to which study of the human vocal apparatus took place in sites of, but also in parallel with, European colonial expansion in North Africa. In both the North African and North American contexts, study of the voice developed in parallel with the control of colonial territory.

In contrast, Cunningham's interpretation of 'occupation' stresses the 'interdependent colonization of both Indigenous land/people, and of the Black bodies of enslaved Africans' in colonial America and the independent United States. Her study of 'voice' in such a context is twofold. On the one hand, she stresses the 'hushing' of Black voices under slavery and racism, so that song, prayer and speech could be voiced beyond the ears of oppressors in the physical (and figurative) space of the 'hush arbour'. On the other hand, she explains how enslaved people used forms of vocal expression such as code songs to voice clandestine messages and meanings.

This latter interpretation of voice in Cunningham's Chapter 2 overlaps with the approach adopted in Geng's Chapter 3, in which songs and other forms of sonic expression that were used by European and American inmates in civilian camps in Japanese-occupied China are detailed. As Geng demonstrates, music could be used in such spaces to undermine Japanese control. But voice could also be used to establish some level of agency for people living in a state of captivity.

All chapters respond to some of the core questions which are addressed in this volume as a whole, such as how sound is implicated in controlling and disciplining colonized or 'occupied' peoples and aural spaces, and how listeners, under conditions of occupation, form new types of auditory or vocal expression. Be it under colonialism, slavery or military rule, the control or stifling of the voices of others was a crucial means through which to establish dominance – if only because it is through the voice that many forms of self-expression are made. By the same measure, the ability to harness the voice as an instrument of resistance, or to establish a 'voice' for oneself by circumventing or undermining the controls that are imposed on individuals and communities under occupation, represents a direct challenge to occupation regimes – a point that is stressed in a number of the works that were referenced in the Introduction to this volume.

1

The vocal apparatus' colonial contexts

France's *mission civilisatrice* and (settler) colonialism in Algeria and North America

Iris Sandjette Blake

Introduction

Manuel García II (1805–1906), a widely influential voice teacher who ascribed to a physiological theory of vocal production, began his 1894 work *Hints on Singing* with a section entitled 'Description of the Vocal Apparatus' that included anatomical drawings of the so-called vocal organs. For García (1894: 1), this 'Apparatus Constituting the Human Voice' was comprised of the following:

> Four distinct apparatus which combine their action; but with special functions, each being entirely independent of the rest. These apparatus are:
> The BELLOWS *namely*, the *lungs*.
> The VIBRATOR " " *glottis*.
> The REFLECTOR " " *pharynx*, and (when words are added)
> The ARTICULATOR " *organs of the mouth*.

Extending J. L. Austin's (1962) work on the performative capacity of statements, I understand García's explanation of the vocal apparatus to not just describe 'the human voice', but rather to performatively set boundaries around what counts within its rubric. In particular, I read García's recourse to the discourses and iconography of anatomy and technology as an attempt to mould the practice of voicing into a form that not only would be intelligible to modernity but would allow the human voice to cohere into a technology of modernity.

In this chapter, I examine how mid-to-late-nineteenth-century vocal scientists and pedagogues mobilized both scientific discourse and sound technologies, such as the laryngoscope, to universalize a biomechanical model of voicing, which they termed the 'vocal apparatus', that understood voicing as a human and sonic activity. In line with this volume's goals to rethink, reorient and remap sound studies, this chapter de-universalizes this Western conception of voicing, demonstrating its historical and cultural construction as inseparable from histories of colonial occupation.

While García was not the first to bring science and anatomy to bear on studies of the voice – for instance, Zaccaria Tevo's *Il Musico Testore* (1706) combined anatomical drawings of the vocal tract with a discussion of the effect of the four humours – his work represented a significant turn towards modernity. García's *Traité complet de l'art du chant* (*Complete Treatise on the Art of Singing* (1840; 1847)) was the first nineteenth-century work in music to address in detail 'the structures of the vocal tract' (Carter 2017: 158), and his 1894 work *Hints on Singing* was the first treatise on singing since Tevo's to include anatomical drawings of the vocal apparatus (158). However, rather than merely a return to, or extension of, this earlier work, García's use of anatomy as a supposedly descriptive mechanism for understanding the human voice cannot be separated from its shifting nineteenth-century context and position as an organizing schema of scientific racism. For example, diagrams of skulls similar to those included in *Hints on Singing* were used to produce, affirm and circulate the belief in a biological basis to hierarchized understandings of racial difference constructed by what musicologist Nina Eidsheim (2008: 57) describes as 'medical research, enabled by colonial force and fueled by the need to justify colonial activities'.

The mid-to-late-nineteenth-century elaboration of the vocal apparatus in technological terms was accompanied by the use of technologies to probe, examine, record, transmit and reproduce the human voice. One such technology was the laryngoscope, a small mirrored instrument that García invented in 1854 to observe the glottis and the larynx and 'confirm' what García and others had hypothesized regarding the internal structure of the vocal apparatus. As literary scholar Steven Connor (2000: 40) posits, vocal technologies can be understood as 'actualizations of fantasies and desires concerning the voice which predate the actual technologies'. The realizations of these vocal technologies, I argue, were conditioned by colonial fantasies and desires for scientific mastery of the body and the senses, which relied on a delimited definition of both 'the human' and 'the human voice'. In particular, vocal scientists and pedagogues' belief that the human voice was knowable and replicable because it was essentially a technological apparatus itself led them to overvalue studies of vocal physiology, eclipsing the social contexts of both physiology and vocal practice. In so doing, their theories of the vocal apparatus centred a genre of the human that Sylvia Wynter (2003) identifies as Man2: the human as a natural organism, a paradigm of the human that pretends to be race-neutral but remains structured by race. In line with natural philosophy's practice of isolating and inspecting each of the senses (Schmidt 2000), literature on the vocal apparatus demonstrated an investment in understanding sound as a distinct sensory category that was associated with the ears – an orientation that I understand as part of the colonial sensorium.

Bringing together (i) a colonial epistemology that located voice and power only in the racialized, gendered and classed figure of Man2 as the human and (ii) a colonial sensory order that insisted on the discreteness of sensory experiences, mid-to-late-nineteenth-century vocal scientists and pedagogues' elaboration of the vocal apparatus enabled the voice to become a technology for asserting colonial difference. Aligned with this particular (human) sensory regime, voice was an apparatus of the intertwined projects of modernity, racial capitalism, heteropatriarchy and settler colonialism by effectively silencing – or attempting to silence – otherwise modes of voicing that exceeded the colonial sensorium and Western constructions of who counts as human. I propose this formulation as my own (re)definition of the vocal apparatus. In this formulation, the 'apparatus constituting the human voice' is understood not just as a physiological accounting of body parts and processes but as co-extensive with the social effects of this definitional project: the suppression of alternative understandings of voicing that were already in praxis and that challenged the colonial, heteropatriarchal power structure by positing decolonial and undisciplined modes of being and relating.

In the first section of this chapter, I examine how the laryngoscope's invention was based on García's surgical experiences in French military hospitals during France's colonial occupation of Algeria. Thus, the laryngoscope's invention reveals the patriarchal and colonial desires that linked the spatiality of the body with the territoriality of conquest. I propose the expression 'voice-as-territory framework' to account for how the internal components of what vocal scientists and pedagogues identified as the vocal apparatus were subjected to colonial spatial ideologies and disciplining projects. In the second section, I examine how mid-nineteenth-century scientific, medical and pedagogical discourse on the vocal apparatus, influenced by and anticipating García's use of the laryngoscope, cultivated and circulated assumptions about voicing as a fundamentally human, sonic and biomechanical process.

The laryngoscope and the voice-as-territory framework

Born in Spain in 1805, García was a member of what voice professor Teresa Radomski claims to be 'the most important family in the history of singing' (2005: 25). His father, Manuel Populo Vicente García, was a famous tenor and singing teacher who had trained in the Italian opera tradition and was known for being a cruel disciplinarian in his pedagogical approach, and his sisters Maria Felicia (known as 'La Malibran') and Pauline Viardot were some of the most famous opera stars of their times. In addition to inventing the laryngoscope, García taught vocal pedagogy first at the Paris Conservatory from 1835 to 1848 and then at London's Royal Academy of Music from 1848 to 1895. While I disagree with Radomski's claim that García's was 'the most important family in the history of singing', as such a claim positions Europe as the centre of the history of singing, the notoriety and reach of García's family are important to note, as the cultural capital they held was key to the wide impact of García's texts and teachings on the science of singing.

While contemporary work on García has primarily celebrated his contributions to vocal pedagogy, the larger colonial context that informed his interest in vocal physiology – including García's participation in France's 1830 invasion of Algeria and his subsequent surgical experiences in French military hospitals – has remained largely unaccounted for. As Eidsheim asks, 'what kinds of power are produced when knowledge regarding vocal pedagogy is based on research enabled by colonial force and the rationalization of colonial expansion?' (2008: 56–7). I read García's use of the laryngoscope, first on himself and then on others (see Figures 1.1 and 1.2), as enacting a particular form of disciplinary power over the body and particularly the voice that is inseparable from the larger nineteenth-century context of colonial expansion.

According to García's memoirist and former student Malcolm Sterling Mackinlay, '"During all the years of study and investigation of the problems of the voice-emission", he [García] said, "one wish was ever uppermost in my mind – 'if only I could see the glottis!'"' (1908: 203–4). This scopic desire to see the glottis (the opening between the vocal cords)[1] and bring the scientific gaze to bear on the internal workings of the body is bound up with colonialist logics that, to paraphrase Diana Taylor (2003), value the archive – here, the voice hypostatized via anatomy – over the repertoire – the body's capacity to move and voice in a multitude of ways. Understanding the voice through science and anatomy as the biomechanical vocal apparatus was a technique to detach the voice from the field of relationalities in which voicing occurs and to discipline the body into a

1ᵉʳ ESSAI D'AUTO-LARYNGOSCOPIE
PAR LE CÉLÈBRE CHANTEUR GARCIA

Figure 1.1 'First attempt at auto-laryngoscopy by the famous singer García.' From an article entitled 'Famous Larynxes by the Dr. Poyet' in the French journal *Musica* (January 1904).

singular practice of voicing. As García claimed in his 1855 presentation to the Royal Society of London, 'the voice is formed in one unique manner, – *by the compressions and expansions of the air, or the successive and regular explosions which it produces in passing through the glottis*' (1855: 404, italics in original).

In this section, I begin with a discussion of García's early participation in acts of conquest and colonial institutions such as the military hospital to argue that French colonialism marks the unacknowledged conditions of possibility for García's desire to produce a uniform theory of the human singing voice by applying the voice-as-territory framework. Definitive records or accounts of García's level of involvement in France's invasion of Algeria are sparse, and in fact it was only when García was effectively on his deathbed that his family released documents pertaining to his colonial pursuits. An April 1905 article entitled 'Manuel Garcia' in *The Musical Times* (1905) noted that 'allusion has not

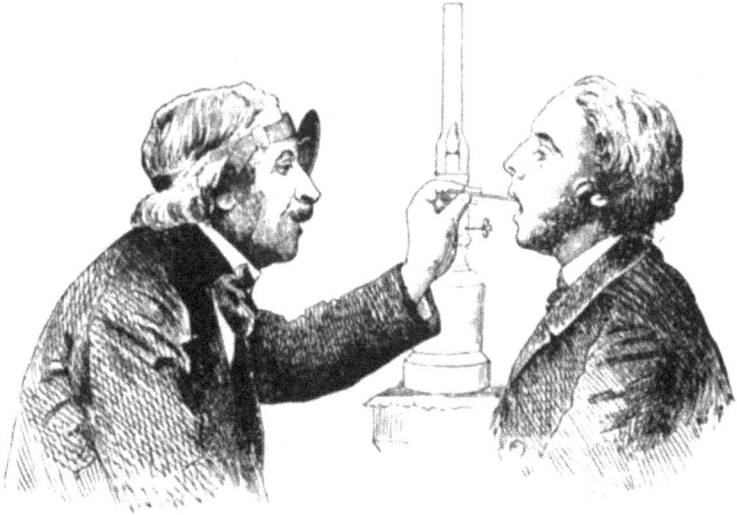

Laryngoscopic mirrors, half size :—

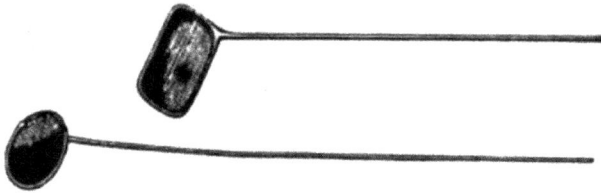

Figure 1.2 A sketch of García using the laryngoscope to observe someone else's glottis and of two laryngoscopic mirrors. From M. García (1894), *Hints on Singing*, London: E. Ascherberg and Co.

hitherto been made in any biographies of him' (226) to this period of García's life, apart from an article in *Le Guide Musical*. The March 1905 article referred to, 'Le Centenaire de Manuel Garcia' (The Centenary of Manuel García), was published in the week preceding García's 100-year birthday celebration with the intention of recounting García's life with the aid of unreleased documents. This article describes '*fait inconnu de la plupart de ses biographes*' (a fact unknown by most of García's biographers): relying on his sister and famed vocalist Maria Felicia Malibran's friendship with the French military's '*l'intendent en chef de l'armée*' (chief army officer, translated as 'commander-in-chief' in *The Musical Times*), García sought and secured an administrative position supporting the French Army's expeditionary forces, embarking at Toulon on 11 May 1830 as part of his 'second plan' following his exit from the opera stage due to vocal fatigue (Sand 1905: 205). García embarked with an army of approximately

37,000 under the command of Louis-Auguste-Victor, the Count de Ghaisnes de Bourmont – presumably Malibran's friend – and landed in Sidi Fredj, Algeria, on 14 June.

Though the accounts in these early-twentieth-century news articles do not give a detailed picture of García's involvement, these secondary sources do provide insight into the larger context and politics of France's invasion of Algeria. García's memoirist attributes France's invasion to a dispute over a debt the French government owed to the Algerian government incurred during 'the Egyptian expedition' (Mackinlay 1908: 97), culminating in the French consul's refusal of payment in 1827 which Hussein Dey, the dey of Algiers, responded to by hitting the French consul in the face with a fly swatter and 'fiercely abus[ing] the king' (98). Per Mackinlay, French soldiers were sent to Algeria to 'revenge the insult' (98), and García took this as an opportunity to escape from living with his father (97–8). However, this 'insult' was just a pretext for invasion, which was actually motivated by a desire for colonial expansion in competition with Britain (Halaçoğlu 2013). That a pretence was used as justification for invasion is not surprising, as according to philosopher and historian Abdallah Laroui:

> The history of Algeria from 1830 to 1870 is made up of pretenses: the colons who allegedly wished to transform the Algerians into men like themselves, when in reality their only desire was to transform the soil of Algeria into French soil; the military, who supposedly respected the local traditions and way of life, whereas in reality their only interest was to govern with the least possible effort; the claim of Napoleon III that he was building an Arab kingdom, whereas his central ideas were the 'Americanization' of the French economy and the French colonization of Algeria. (1977: 305)

As Laroui makes clear, the disciplining and acquisition of land was the driving force behind the invasion and occupation, and France modelled its settler-colonial practices in Algeria on those of the recently consolidated settler state of the United States. Another important pretext for France's invasion and conquest of Algeria was the *mission civilisatrice* (Duffy 2018). As Edward Said describes in *Orientalism*, '"la mission civilisatrice" began in the nineteenth century as a political second-best to Britain's presence' (1978: 169). Through this framework, the French imagined 'the Orient' as a feminized, exoticized and aestheticized place of 'memories, suggestive ruins, forgotten secrets' (170), whose Arab inhabitants required the French to teach them 'the meaning of liberty' (172) and as Laroui writes, 'to transform... into men like themselves' (1977: 305). The reproduction of a particular genre of the human, North American settler-colonial ideologies, and Orientalism were thus bound up together in the 1830 French invasion.

According to Mackinlay, García 'took part in the severe conflicts which ended in less than two months with the bombardment of Algiers and its surrender to the French armament under Bourmont and Duperre, the deposition of the Dey, and the total overthrow of the barbarian government' (1908: 98). Mackinlay's depiction frames the invasion as part of a civilizing mission that reproduces ideas of colonial difference between the supposedly civilized French government and what he comparatively frames as the 'barbarian government' of Algeria, demonstrating the Orientalist gaze of the West on the East.

I hear echoes of this so-called *mission civilisatrice* in the visual and narrative depictions of García's 1854 invention and use of the laryngoscope. In *Culture and Imperialism*, Edward Said connects the *mission civilisatrice* to metaphors of illumination, 'to benevolent as well as cruel schemes to bring light to the dark places and peoples of the world by acts of will and deployments of power' (1993: 30). According to French history of science scholar Patrick Petitjean, in nineteenth-century France the *mission civilisatrice* was revised, such that 'science replaced religion as the motive for colonization' (2005: 113). By continually making recourse to both the language of science and metaphors of illumination, the visual and narrative depictions of the laryngoscope's invention in nineteenth-century texts discussing the vocal apparatus aligned the laryngoscope with the *mission civilisatrice* and attempted to position the laryngoscope's invention at the crux of Enlightenment ideals, modernity, colonial scenes of discovery and white patriarchy.

For example, one of the earliest (self-)narrativizations of the laryngoscope's invention appears in 'Observations on the Human Voice', García's 1855 presentation of his 'discoveries' with the laryngoscope to the Royal Society of London, a British society of natural philosophers. García describes his method of observing the larynx:

> It consists in placing a little mirror, fixed on a long handle suitably bent, in the throat of the person experimented on against the soft palate and uvula. The party ought to turn himself towards the sun, so that the luminous rays falling on the mirror, may be reflected on the larynx. If the observer experiment on himself, he ought, by means of a second mirror, to receive the rays of the sun, and direct them on the mirror, which is placed against the uvula. (1855: 399)

Here, the use of the 'luminous rays' of the sun by the (masculine) 'observer' within the 'experiment' to observe the vocal apparatus performatively enacts a literal rendering of Enlightenment ideals of reason and scientific objectivity as a source of light, illuminating and making sense of the body's internal workings. Summarizing García's invention and citing this 1855 communication, Emil Behnke in *The Mechanism of the Human Voice* (1880) writes that after warming the mirror 'to prevent its becoming dimmed by the moisture of the breath. . . . The rays of the sun falling upon the mirror are reflected downwards into the voicebox, the image of which is clearly visible in the mirror' (1880: 73–4). Behnke uses similar language to García regarding the importance of the 'rays of the sun' and, extending the light imagery, cautions against the 'dimm[ing]' of the mirror. While the narrative depictions emphasize the sun as the light source, in the visual representations the light appears to be coming not from the sun but rather, in one image (see Figure 1.1), from a lantern that shines through the centre of the mirror García uses to observe himself and, in another (see Figure 1.2), from a candle which García himself reflects onto the laryngoscope with a mirror attached to his head. This incongruence demonstrates that the emphasis on sunlight performed metaphorical work even if it was not always used in practice.

Reading these narrative and visual depictions of the laryngoscope's invention in relation to the *mission civilisatrice*, the body's interior becomes akin to 'the dark places and peoples of the world' (Said 1993: 30), and the laryngoscope is the tool used to illuminate and 'discover' the glottis and define the vocal apparatus. However, in this voice-as-territory framework, opening the throat to 'receive' the light of Western science is presented as a voluntary act, even as the body's visceral resistance to being disciplined is alluded to as the breath's dimming of the mirror. The colonial underpinnings of the laryngoscope's reliance on illumination become explicit in Mackinlay's 1908 memoir celebrating García's life, *Garcia the centenarian and his times; being a memoir of Manuel Garcia's life and labours for the advancement of music and science*. Mackinlay writes, 'Before its [the laryngoscope's] invention threw light into places which had been dark since the birth of the human race, the larynx was an undiscovered country, and its diseases lay beyond the limits of medical art' (210–11). Here, Mackinlay directly compares García's observations of the larynx to an act of conquest. This memoirist further links the territoriality of conquest with the spatiality of the body, writing, 'While touching general medicine at many points, laryngology is also to a large extent an autonomous territory in the great federation of the human organism' (211), and he proceeds to refer to García as 'the discoverer of the hidden land' (212), presumably the larynx or the glottis.

Conveniently left out from these accounts is the way that placing a mirror in the throat against the soft palate and uvula often resulted in gagging and even vomiting. To sing and vocalize with the laryngoscope in one's throat required training one's body to accommodate a metal tool and moving one's head in such a way that light would be continuously directed onto the tool's small mirror. Rather than directly observing 'the vocal apparatus', García was observing the effects of using the laryngoscope, primarily on men,[2] which he then used to 'confirm' and universalize his ideas about the human voice. According to Mackinlay, 'By his examination of the glottis, he [García] had had the satisfaction of proving that all his theories with regard to the emission of the voice were absolutely correct' (1908: 205). Thus, this scene of technological observation and (self-)encounter – and the structures of power that inform its continued reproduction – become narrativized as foundational to the 'correct' definition of the vocal apparatus. In *Sounding Bodies Sounding Worlds: An Exploration of Embodiments in Sound*, Mickey Vallee proposes the term 'laryngealcentric voice' to refer to 'the voice brought through technics into the light of science', whereby 'the voice became a knowable object by virtue of its discovery through the technical tools that isolated the voice in the throat' (2019: 34). My use of the vocal apparatus and the voice-as-territory framework intends to extend this critique to account for the relationship of the 'laryngealcentric voice' to colonialism and modernity. For instance, a component of this usage of 'the light of science' was tied to the idea of awakening the people of 'the dark places' from their so-called deep slumber – an inherently colonialist framing that undergirded France's *mission civilisatrice*.

In addition to the laryngoscope's activation of the *mission civilisatrice* via the project of 'illumination', García's studies of anatomy undertaken in French military hospitals underscore how García's interests in observing and defining the vocal apparatus were linked to systems of colonial violence. Per Mackinlay, 'His [García's] predilections had always been scientific, and he was passionately fond of all such studies, but specially [*sic*] of anatomy and all that had to do with the human body' (1908: 96). In fact, after a failed operatic debut in Naples in 1829, García sent a letter to his father writing that the negative reviews meant he couldn't be an artist and that 'From now onward I am going to devote myself to the occupation which I love, and for which I believe I was born' (García in Mackinlay 1908: 91). Rather than joining his father as a voice teacher, García 'resolved to become an officer in the French mercantile marine . . . [and] began the study of astronomy and navigation' (Mackinlay 1908: 96) – suggesting that García's favoured 'occupation' was not vocal pedagogy but science in the service of militarism and colonialism, and demonstrating García's investment in an ideology of European planetary consciousness (Pratt 1992: 11).

While García's interest in science and militarism thus predated his military experiences in Algeria and anatomy studies in French military hospitals, it wasn't until his work in the military hospitals that he applied this towards the voice. The article in *Le Guide Musical* explains that García remained in Algeria until France had '*prise*' (taken) Algiers (Sand 1905: 205). García returned to France in late July of 1830, at the start of the July Revolution which overthrew King Charles X (Mackinlay 1908: 99). There, he sought out surgical experiences in metropolitan military hospitals in Paris, with the goal of finding out more about the science of the voice. According to *Le Guide Musical*, it was during his employment in these military hospitals that García attended medical courses and clinics and that he realized the importance of the study of physiology for '*l'éducation rationelle de la voix*' (the rational education of the voice) (Sand 1905: 205). Describing García's work in the military hospitals as 'crowned with success' – language that Mackinlay repeats verbatim – the article states that these experiences contributed to García's conviction to precisely determine the anatomy of the vocal cords (205).

While both the 1905 article and the 1908 memoir verify the linkage between García's medical experiences in French military hospitals and his work to define the vocal apparatus, the systems of colonial violence that these hospitals enabled are not acknowledged. They are treated instead as systems of education and medicine detached from colonial entanglements. An 1838 Paris guidebook describes how the civil hospitals of Paris were supervised by a general administration that was created in February 1801, consisting of an administrative committee and a general council comprised of 'some of the most notable functionaries of the state' including the Prefect of the Seine and the Prefect of Police (Galignani 1838: 93). The military hospitals, on the other hand, were governed by 'the état-major of the garrison of Paris' (93). Minimizing these direct linkages to state and military power, the guidebook lists all of these hospitals under the heading of 'charitable institutions'. In fact, one of the primary areas of research in the military hospitals was the treatment of venereal disease, a reminder of the way that militarism and sexual violence are inextricably linked. While this was still a major emphasis of the military hospitals in the 1830s, García's training in the military hospitals focused on 'medicine and some specialized studies which embraced the physiology of everything appertaining to the voice and the larynx' (Mackinlay 1908: 99).

Though they offer fairly brief accounts, the sources on García's 'specialized studies' in these metropolitan military hospitals confirm that anatomy classes were a central component of this course of study (Mackinlay 1908: 100; 'Manuel

Garcia' 1905: 226), and according to musicologist and voice instructor James Stark, it was in military hospitals that García 'had occasion to study the larynx in cases of neck wounds' (2003: 4). As Michel Foucault argues in *The Birth of the Clinic*, 'Nineteenth-century medicine was haunted by that absolute eye that cadaverizes life and rediscovers in the corpse the frail, broken nervure of life' (1963: 166). García's training in anatomy via dissections, I propose, trained García in this form of medical gaze that he would later apply to his invention and use of the laryngoscope. His sister Pauline Viardot, quoted by García's memoirist in 1908, recalls that García would bring back '[t]he throttles of all kinds of animals – chickens, sheep, and cows' (Mackinlay: 100) – from his anatomy classes, and they would conduct their own experiments on these vocal organs: 'He [García] would give me a pair of bellows, which I would insert in these windpipes one after another, and blow hard. Heavens! what extraordinary sounds they used to emit. The chickens' throttles would cluck, the sheep's would bleat, and the bulls' would roar, almost like life' (100). García's and Viardot's experiments in making the dissected vocal organs of animals sound 'almost like life' relied on a callous disregard for the body (here, of non-human animals; people's vocal organs were also used in this way), which was valued for the functionality of its discrete organs insofar as they might allow for the anatomists to hear 'in the corpse the frail, broken nervure of life'. In *The Philosophy of the Human Voice*, James Rush explains that such dissections were common practice:

> They [scientists] have removed the organs from men and other animals, and have produced something like their natural voices by blowing through them. They have inspected and named the curious structure of the cartilages and muscles of the larynx, with the absurd purpose to discover thereby the cause of intonation. . . . In short, they have tried to see sound, and to touch it with the dissecting knife. (1827: 4, cited in Vallee 2019: 37–8)

While Mickey Vallee in his work on sound technologies suggests that the laryngoscope represented a significant departure in scientific studies of the voice in that it 'allowed for non-surgical tracheal intubation and inspection' (2019: 38), I read García's 1881 re-narrativization of his invention of the laryngoscope for the International Congress of Medicine, which took place in London, as linking the laryngoscope to surgical practice. Describing himself as 'preoccupied with the ever-recurring wish so often repressed as unrealizable' – presumably, to see the glottis – García recounts:

> suddenly I saw the two mirrors of the laryngoscope in their respective positions, as if actually present before my eyes. I went straight to Charrière, the surgical

instrument maker, and asking if he happened to possess a small mirror with a long handle, was informed that he had a little dentist's mirror, which had been one of the failures of the London Exhibition of 1851. (1881: 197)

That García claims to have retrieved a mirror from the famed surgeon Joseph-Frédéric-Benoît Charrière to fashion the laryngoscope places the laryngoscope within a genealogy of 'surgical instruments'. Rather than a departure from surgical practice, the laryngoscope enabled the eye to function like the surgeon's knife. In his subchapter on the laryngoscope, philosopher Tim Scott writes that to use the laryngoscope 'one had to *learn to see* what could be disclosed by the instrument' (2010: 56), as exemplified by professor of physiology Eben Watson's clarification in his 1865 article 'Laryngoscopy and Its Revelations' that 'the part may be visible, and yet not seen by an unskilled observer; so that the beginner need not wonder if he cannot see all that even ought to be seen, in his first views of the larynx' (1865: 589, cited in Scott 2010: 56). Along with learning to see, the laryngoscope required its users to learn to hear a normative definition of the human voice; as Vallee describes, the laryngoscope's invention quickly inspired an entire industry to arise around the identification and treatment of so-called vocal defects (2019: 40).

García further positions himself and the laryngoscope in a genealogy of modernity and colonialism by pointing out that it was not just any mirror that he used but a dentist's mirror that had been created for the London Exhibition of 1851, the first World's Fair. García thus links his invention of the laryngoscope to the scientific-medical turn, inseparable from scientific racism and contemporaneous ideas about gender and sex. While also delivered to a professional society, this account marks a significant departure in tone and content from García's 1855 narration. Describing his use of the dentist's mirror as laryngoscope, he narrates,

I saw at once, to my great joy, the glottis wide open before me, and so fully exposed that I could perceive a portion of the trachea. When my excitement had somewhat subsided, I began to examine what was passing before my eyes. The manner in which the glottis silently opened and shut, and moved in the act of phonation, filled me with wonder. (1881: 197)

Alongside the usage of the first person 'I', which shifts the focus to García as innovator, García's use of more vivid temporal and affective language ('strolling', 'suddenly', 'impatient', 'joy', 'excitement', 'wonder') resonates with colonial travel narratives of encounter, discovery and sexual conquest ('wide open before me', 'fully exposed') that, as Said (1978) demonstrates, undergirded France's *mission civilisatrice* and the gendered and sexual tropes of Orientalism more broadly. In addition, I read García's comment that the instrument had been one of the London Exhibition's 'failures' as an attempt to heighten his own standing as a so-called genius – a category that historically has been used to consolidate power for white men and their ideas. In his own hands, García seems to suggest, the 'failure' of the famed Charrière was brought back into usefulness, modernity and progress through his observations of the vocal apparatus.

Mackinlay's narrativization of García's legacy similarly aims to position García as a father figure to the scientific-medical study of the voice – something that Stark reproduces in *Bel Canto: A History of Vocal Pedagogy* when he claims 'Garcia can be considered the father of modern voice science' (2003: xxii). Discussing García's centenary birthday celebration, Mackinlay writes, 'It must have brought the centenarian a great and justifiable pride when on that day he looked on the representatives of the Laryngological societies encircling the world, who united to call him Father' (1908: 213). This passage demonstrates the intertwining of colonialism and heteropaternalism (Arvin, Tuck and Morrill 2013: 13) in the legacy of the laryngoscope and the circumscribed understanding of the human voice it consolidated. While the imagery of the professional societies of laryngology 'encircling the world' evokes colonialism and empire, the positioning of García as a proud capital-F 'Father' to those 'united' representatives speaks to the heteropaternalism of this colonial order. That this heteropaternal colonial legacy was both apparent and embraced by García and his colleagues is further demonstrated by García's appellation, 'the Christopher Columbus of the larynx', given to him along with a floral arrangement by soprano and voice teacher Blanche Marchesi at this centenary celebration (Mackinlay 1908: 301).

The human, the senses and the management of hearing

While García popularized an investment in the 'science' of the voice and the voice-as-territory framework, he was by no means the sole adherent to this colonial ideology of the voice. An overvaluation of vocal physiology and the human also structured texts on the vocal apparatus that both preceded and followed García's use of the laryngoscope. Through their writings and teachings on the vocal apparatus, García's contemporaries in vocal science and pedagogy consolidated a set of assumptions about voicing: that voice was fundamentally human, that it was experienced through the sense of sound and that the voice could be understood and reproduced through the language of mechanics and technology. Centring Man2 as the human in their reliance on physiology, their work to universalize Western conceptions of the vocal apparatus laid the groundwork for the voice-as-territory framework to be taken up in disparate contexts of (settler) colonial occupation.

Descriptions of the human vocal apparatus by vocal pedagogues, scientists and physicians illustrate how voice was imagined to be fundamental to maintaining the hierarchization of forms of life, including the distinction between the human and the non-human, as is evidenced by García's attention to the vocal organs of non-human animals. However, the human vocal apparatus was consistently framed as comparatively more advanced than the vocal apparatus of non-human animals. For example, after describing the vocal organs of 'man' and birds in his lecture on the vocal apparatus and the voice, physicist and physiologist Carlo Matteucci affirms, 'We shall describe the vocal organ of man as being the most complicated and the most perfect' (1847: 370). Similarly, surgeon and anatomist John Bishop writes, 'It is in the human race that we find the most varied and perfect adaptation of vocal sounds to the communication of ideas, both of material and intellectual subjects' (1851: 10). Such descriptions of the human vocal apparatus as 'the most perfect', 'the most complicated' and 'the most varied' in comparison to the vocal apparatus of other species value the human and the human voice over that which is deemed non-human and reveal a world view that would map onto Darwinian theories of natural selection. While García typically relied on technical rather than philosophical language describing the functionality of the human voice, the laryngoscope was used by others as a means to scientifically verify the comparative complexity of the human vocal apparatus. For example, leading into his agreement with 'Mr. Bishop',[3] professor of physiology Eben Watson writes in 'Laryngoscopy and Its Revelations' that his own laryngoscopic observations of the movements of the vocal apparatus in the production of high notes demonstrate 'another among many instances of the complexity of the human mechanism which meet us at every step of the way' (1865: 591). This overvaluation of Man2 as the 'human' within mid-nineteenth-century studies of the vocal apparatus was subsumed into normative understandings of what constitutes voicing.

Moreover, such assertions of the superiority of the human voice over and above the non-human voice map onto what Mel Chen identifies as the animacy hierarchy – a hierarchized ontological scale that is racialized, queer and continuously produced and subject to power (2012: 2) – particularly in their comparative disavowals of the non-human. As these examples demonstrate, ideas about voicing and listening were fundamental to producing and reinforcing the animacy hierarchy. For example, physician James Copland claimed, 'Voice and speech are functions by means of which the human species claims and maintains an ascendency over all animated nature' (1858: 1491). Here, Copland points to the capacity to produce voice and speech as what distinguishes the human from the non-human, and aligns human voice and speech with power – in particular, power over 'all animated nature', or that which is non-human. However, Copland's insistence on voice as a method by which 'the human species' maintains its hierarchical position above 'all animated nature' can be read as responding to a categorical anxiety within this notion of 'the human' that recognizes the boundary between the human and the non-human is not already apparent but must be continuously produced and reasserted. As Chen argues:

> Recentering on animality (or the animals who face humans) tugs at the ontological cohesion of 'the human', stretching it out and revealing the contingent striations in its springy taffy: it is then that entities as variant as disability, womanhood, sexuality, emotion, the vegetal, and the inanimate become more salient, more palpable as having been rendered proximate to the human, though they have always subtended the human by propping it up. (2012: 98)

Thus, even as I argue that the voice-as-territory framework was invested in maintaining distinctions between the human and the non-human, these writings on the vocal apparatus simultaneously highlight the instability of the category of the human, which only coheres around categorical exclusions.

Along with such comparative disavowals of the non-human, the racialized regulation and management of the senses, and especially the sense of hearing, were central to the voice-as-territory framework. For instance, the surgical practices of dissecting the larynx to isolate and define the components of the vocal apparatus that García and others engaged in can be placed in relation to natural philosophers' partitioning of the senses into discrete and knowable categories. Focusing on the management of hearing during the Enlightenment, cultural historian Leigh Eric Schmidt notes that for natural philosophers, hearing in particular 'possessed an ambiguous, unstable power that made its careful management especially urgent. Marked as a spiritual, emotional, and superstitious sense, the ear posed a potential danger to the clearsightedness of reason' (2000: 7).

Nineteenth-century medical, scientific and pedagogical literature on the vocal apparatus contributed to the racialized management of hearing by focusing on the voice's connection to reason and rationality, and by distinguishing between sound versus noise and desirable versus undesirable types of vocal production. For example, in García's *New Treatise on the Art of Singing*, he asserts early on that 'The first essential for every singer is *mind* [italics original]' (1857: 8). In the treatise's second section, he emphasizes the centrality of expression to the human voice while insisting that 'Even while giving himself up to the strongest transports of passion, a pupil must nevertheless retain sufficient freedom of mind to examine those transports, one by one – to scrutinize the means by which they are pourtrayed, [*sic*] – and to classify them' (67). For García, then, while the voice acts as a vehicle for passion, the mind's ability to subject these passions to a classificatory schema ultimately takes priority – and in fact, his treatise includes an extensive classification of sentiments (martial enthusiasm, deep grief, tenderness, joy) and examples of how to produce the corresponding timbres that each 'requires' (69–71).

The valuation of reason similarly takes precedence in Copland's *A Dictionary of Practical Medicine*, where he claims, 'The sounds produced by the human organs of vocalization and articulation are the manifestations furnished to the species of the finest sentiments, of the deepest as well as the highest states of feeling, of the most profound and abstract results of thought, and the wisest and best revelations of mental reflection and of human reason' (1858: 1491). Along with his comparative valorization of the human, Copland mobilizes language that resonates with Wynter's description of how, with the Renaissance humanist institution of Man1, the Redeemed Spirit/Fallen Flesh master code was transumed into the racialized distinction between reason and rationality on the one hand and sensuality and irrationality on the other, with the humanists proposing that 'human reason had remained "lord over the senses similar to the way in which God is lord over his creatures"' (Wynter 2003: 287). In Copland's assertion, not only is voice directly associated with reason and the human but even the feelings attributed to the human species and which the voice can manifest suggest religio-rational overtones – 'the finest sentiments' the 'deepest ... [and] highest states of feeling' – perhaps to specify and distance these (human) feelings from the sensuous and the irrational. Moreover, the *sounds* produced by the vocal apparatus take centre stage as a method of manifesting a particular set of ethics, feeling and abstract thinking and as constituting 'the wisest and best revelations ... of human reason'.

Creating a distinction between sound and noise was another rhetorical technique used in literature on the vocal apparatus in an attempt to align the human voice with Man2. For instance, in a section on hearing following his description of the vocal apparatus, Matteucci clarifies:

By the word *sound*, we strictly understand a sensation which is preserved
uniform for a certain time, and which is susceptible of being measured and
compared. Sound differs, then, from a mere *noise*, inasmuch as the latter is the
effect of a single shock, or of a series of shocks which are repeated without any
regularity; whilst the sonorous sensation is that which we experience when the
acoustic nerve receives a certain number of successive shakings, separated from
each other by a certain and constant interval of time. (1847: 357–8)

Here, Matteucci posits sound in opposition to noise, and while the distinction
is proposed in scientific, acoustic and sensorial terms, as numerous scholars
have discussed, the discourse that separates sound from noise is a subjective
and often racialized and gendered discourse. Matteucci privileges uniformity of
sensorial experience over irregular repetitions or 'a single shock' and stresses the
importance of measurability, comparison and following a predictable temporal
schema – values that align with a belief in scientific objectivity and linear time.
However, even as Matteucci uses scientific-acoustic terminology, the distinction
he makes between them seems to follow a circular logic that ultimately breaks
down as he compares 'repeated shocks' to 'successive shakings', revealing the
social construction of the distinction.

García was relatively less concerned with the distinction between noise
and sound – in fact, he points to the usefulness of the 'noise' produced when
articulating the consonants *m*, *n*, *d*, *b* and *c* in prepping the singer for 'the
emission of sound' (1857: 47). When he does make a distinction between sound
and noise, it is typically to discuss 'the noise of the breath' (1857: 69). However, he
consistently emphasizes particular qualities of the voice as being more desirable
(especially 'freshness and steadiness') and cautions against the impairment of
the voice 'by too frequently using the high notes . . .; by exaggerating the timbres
. . . ; by loud and continued laughter; by animated discourse, &c', which García
claims can lead to irreparable damage resulting in a 'broken' voice (1857: 8).
As these examples demonstrate, and as Schmidt, Eidsheim and other scholars
have discussed, the sense of hearing – like other supposedly discrete senses –
and practices of listening do not exist *a priori* but are produced through the
workings of power. Scientific, medical and pedagogical literature on the vocal
apparatus was particularly invested in understanding the voice through the
sense of hearing as a discrete category because if voice could be understood
through sound alone – excising the messiness of multisensory perceptions of
voicing (Eidsheim 2015) and of the irruptive potential of the irrational/irregular
(noise) – it could be more easily disciplined to cohere around a particular genre
of the human and bolster the voice-as-territory framework.

In fact, despite the repeated discursive insistence on the superiority and perfection of the human vocal apparatus, and on the human-ness of voicing, the human voice was also frequently discussed in mechanical and technological terms, and writings on the vocal apparatus often compared its machinations to those of a musical instrument or acoustic technology. For example, influenced by the work of García, professor of elocution and vocal physiology Alexander Melville Bell fantasized about the potential mechanical inventions that an isolation and elaboration of scientific principles of speech might yield in his 1863 text *Principles of Speech and Dictionary of Sounds*:

> Scientific men . . . have elaborated theories of optics – and look at the result? Wonderful mechanical adaptations of optical principles, before undreamt of, and which, otherwise, would never have been discovered. Might not an analogous result attend the philosophical investigation of the faculty of speech; and acoustic and articulative principles be developed, which would lead to mechanical inventions no less wonderful and useful than those in optics? A subject so little explored, and so open to operations, is, at least, full *of promise* to science. (41, cited in Mills 2008: 1)

For Bell, understanding the acoustic and articulative mechanics of speech as distinct from and in distinction to optical principles was part of the promise the faculty of speech offered to science. Alongside Bell's colonial vocabulary/ imaginary of discovery and exploration in service of science, he imagines the faculty of speech (as well as that of sight) as a physiological process, the principles of which might be studied, delineated and harnessed into the production of mechanical inventions. In Alexander Graham Bell's revision of his father's colonial wish, the production of mechanical inventions related to the faculty of speech – such as the telephone, which he patented in 1876 in the United States and in 1877 in Canada – was not just full of promise to science but also full of promise for profit within the North American settler colonial context.

While Alexander Melville Bell was primarily concerned with speech as opposed to song or other manners of voicing, this quotation was preceded in his work by a section on voice that connects his so-called scientific principles of speech to the teachings of 'scientific singing-master' Manuel García (Bell [1863] 1916: 18). This section on voice also compares what Bell calls the vocal organ or apparatus to the mechanical operations of a musical instrument, one that 'combines the qualities of a wind and of a stringed instrument' (18). Bell suggests that the reader might create 'an experimental sonifier' (18) to verify these vocal principles using the reed of a bagpipe drone or a modified feather quill as a facsimile for the human glottis. For Bell, such an exercise is intended to demonstrate that the voice can be improved through scientific experimentation. He writes:

> It is important to all persons who labor under difficulties in the management of the voice, to be perfectly familiar with the process by which vocality is produced; to make themselves so by experiment; and to aim at the improvement of their vocal powers, by applying the same principles which they find to govern the mechanism of analogous sounds. . . . When the voice is otherwise commenced, much breath is wasted before vocality is obtained, and a clear resonant voice can hardly be produced by the loose expiration. (18)

Here, the vocal apparatus is mechanized, imagined to be an instrument that can be scientifically managed by humans towards the goal of improvement. Bell also links (and limits) the power of the voice to the sonic by suggesting a correspondence between 'vocal powers' and the mechanical production of 'analogous sounds'. However, despite Bell's claims that 'the more sonorous the voice, the more easy is its production' (18), he here admits that the management of the voice in the manners he advocates is not a natural principle but instead an act of labour that presented enough 'difficulties' and resistances to management that this passage would be addressed 'to all persons who labor under difficulties in the management of the voice'.

Bell's discussion of the need to 'manage' the voice reminds me of García's use of the laryngoscope, which also required the Western, masculine observer to respond to the 'difficulties' and resistances of the embodied voice-as-territory. In addition to 'managing' the breath's dimming of the mirror and the risk of the laryngoscope's expulsion by vomiting, returning to the 1865 article 'Laryngoscopy and Its Revelations', Watson discusses several techniques for overcoming 'frequent cause[s] of difficulty' such as the patient's fear and the presence and movement of the tongue. He recommends, for instance, 'gently taking hold' of the patient's tongue and pulling it out of their mouth, keeping the apparatus out of view of the patient and having the patient prep their own throat regularly with a solution of nitrate of silver 'to accustom the part to the presence of a foreign body in contact with it . . . [and to] gradually diminish its sensitivity' (589).

Bell's *Principles of Speech*, insisting on the centrality of the glottis, is likely referencing García's 1855 assertion cited earlier, that 'the voice is formed in one unique manner' (404) by the movement of air through the glottis – a universalizing gesture that localizes the source of the voice within a particular organ of the vocal apparatus. While Bell does at least allow for the possibility that the voice might be 'otherwise commenced', he still privileges García's model by aligning these 'otherwise commenced' voicings with wasted breath. For Bell and for García, the 'clarity' and 'resonance' of the voice – terms which rely on a listening practice that distinguishes between '"clear" (*clair*) or "dark" (*sombre*) sounds' and ringing (*voix eclatant*) versus 'veiled tones' (*voix sourde*) (García cited in Stark 2003: 36) – are valued over and above 'the noise of the breath', which Bell describes as a 'loose expiration'. In a similar vein, Boston-based vocal pedagogue Horace R. Streeter, in his work *A New and Correct Theory for the Mechanical Formation of the Human Voice*, argued against the use of certain vocal timbres, calling the chest register 'that obstructed, wrong, functional use of the parts' and insisting, 'We repeat it, that it is not at all the tone of the human voice' (1871: 37).

Whereas the voice-as-territory framework positions the commencement of the otherwise as breath that has been wasted, or in García's formulation, as noise, I understand 'otherwise commenced' voicings to be those that refuse the disciplinary procedures that would render the human vocal apparatus a technology of and for modernity. Recalling Emil Behnke's caution to work around the 'dimming' effects of the breath to observe the vocal apparatus using the laryngoscope, the framing of the voice in technological terms marks a disavowal of the flesh and messiness of bodies as well as a disavowal of the social context that gives rise to particular techniques of voicing and listening. The universalizing gesture that locates voice only within the (human, sonic) vocal apparatus model thus initiates a colonial disciplining of voice, and of the body through the voice, that attempts to silence the possibility that voicing can be – and is – otherwise commenced.

Conclusion

In this chapter, I have examined how aligning voice with the sonic and Man2 – through the nineteenth-century scientific, medical and pedagogical elaboration of the vocal apparatus model – has been a central component of the colonial project of modernity. In particular, García's use of the laryngoscope and the circulation of the vocal apparatus model more broadly linked voice and knowledge about voicing to science, modernity and heteropatriarchy through a set of assumptions: the human voice was knowable and replicable because it was essentially a technological apparatus itself; the voice was experienced through the sense of sound, so understanding voice required understanding mechanical and acoustic properties; and not only was the human voice, or the voice of Man, 'the most perfect' (Matteucci 1847: 370), but particular practices of voicing were superior to those that were 'otherwise commenced' (Bell [1863] 1916: 18). Because the laryngoscope influenced understandings of the voice and the vocal apparatus in the fields of science, medicine, elocution and vocal pedagogy, the emergence of technologies to record and transmit the voice in the latter half of the nineteenth century built on this framework.

While I propose that the laryngoscope's invention arose out of the specificities of French colonialism and in particular the nineteenth-century *mission civilisatrice*, interconnections between French colonialism in Algeria and settler colonialism in the North American context (Laroui 1977; Roberts 2015) facilitated settler capitalists' application of the voice-as-territory framework as they attempted to patent and monetize sound technologies in the settler-states of the United States and Canada. As demonstrated by Michael Taussig's (1993) work on the use of 'the talking machine' (victrolas) both in colonial expeditions and in films such as *Nanook of the North*, and via Roshanak Kheshti's (2015) analysis of white female comparative musicologists' recording and listening practices as effecting 'the phonographic subjectivation of the Native American as her necessary inferior' (8), technologies of voicing and listening, as '*instrument*[s] of modernity' (18; italics in original), came to play a central role in early-twentieth-century North American settler colonialism. While García's observations through the laryngoscope framed the vocal apparatus as an 'undiscovered country' among the 'dark places' of the body's interior, settler capitalists in North America extended colonial understandings of land as property to this voice-as-territory framework, such that the capacity to extract value from the biomechanical model of voicing took priority. The vocal apparatus model, with its attendant assumptions about the human and the human voice, impacted the invention and circulation of these technologies and produced the voice as an apparatus of modernity.

Notes

1   In García's *New Treatise on the Art of Singing*, he defines the glottis thus: 'the opening between them [the vocal ligaments] is termed the glottis (whence they are often called the *lips* of the glottis;) and to these ligaments, or lips, alone we are indebted for the vibrations of the voice' (1857: 5).

2 Musicologist Benjamin Steege explains that 'Garcia himself was primarily interested in the male voice' (2012: 186) and principally used the laryngoscope to examine the vocal apparatus of men.

3 Watson is referencing John Bishop's paper 'On the Physiology of the Human Voice', which he delivered to the Royal Society of London. Further demonstrating how studies of anatomy and dissection were central to defining the vocal apparatus, Bishop writes, 'The vocal cords are, as has been seen, rectangular-shaped membranes, and from experiments made on the larynx after death by Ferrien, Müller, and others (which the author has repeatedly verified), are found to vibrate like cylindrical cords' (1846: 555).

References

Arvin, M., E. Tuck and A. Morrill (2013), 'Decolonizing Feminism: Challenging Connections Between Settler Colonialism and Heteropatriarchy', *Feminist Formations*, 25 (1): 8–34.

Austin, J. L. (1962), *How to Do Things With Words*, Oxford: Clarendon Press.

Behnke, E. ([1880] 1890), *The Mechanism of the Human Voice*, London: J. Curwen and Sons.

Bell, A. M. ([1863] 1916), *Principles of Speech and Dictionary of Sounds, Including Directions and Exercises for the Cure of Stammering and Correction of All Faults of Articulation*, Washington, DC: Volta Bureau.

Bishop, J. (1846), 'On the Physiology of the Human Voice', *Philosophical Transactions of the Royal Society of London*, 136: 551–71.

Bishop, J. (1851), *On Articulate Sounds: And On the Causes and Cure of Impediments of Speech*, London: Samuel Highley.

Carter, S. (2017), 'From the Singer's Voice to the Listener's Ear: Zaccaria Tevo and the "Science" of Music', *Journal of Singing*, 74 (2): 155–61.

Chen, M. (2012), *Animacies: Biopolitics, Racial Mattering, and Queer Affect*, Durham, NC: Duke University Press.

Connor, S. (2000), *Dumbstruck: A Cultural History of Ventriloquism*, Oxford and New York: Oxford University Press.

Copland, J. (1858), *A Dictionary of Practical Medicine*, London: Longman, Brown, Green, Longmans, and Roberts.

Duffy, A. (2018), 'Civilizing Through Cork: Conservationism and la Mission Civilisatrice in French Colonial Algeria', *Environmental History*, 23 (2): 270–92.

Eidsheim, N. (2008), 'Voice as a Technology of Selfhood: Towards an Analysis of Racialized Timbre and Vocal Performance', PhD diss., University of California, San Diego.

Eidsheim, N. (2015), *Sensing Sound: Singing and Listening as Vibrational Practice*, Durham, NC: Duke University Press.

Foucault, M. (1963), *The Birth of the Clinic: An Archaeology of Medical Perception*, Paris: Presses Universitaires de France.

Galignani, W. (1838), *Galignani's New Paris Guide*, Paris: A. and W. Galignani and Co.

García, M. (1855), 'Observations on the Human Voice', *Proceedings of the Royal Society of London, 1854–1855*, 7: 399–410.

García, M. (1857), *New Treatise on the Art of Singing: A Compendius Method of Instruction with Exercises for the Cultivation of the Voice*, Boston, MA: Oliver Ditson Company.

García, M. (1881), 'On the Invention of the Laryngoscope', *Transactions of the Section of Laryngology of the VIIth International Congress of Medicine*, 3: 197.

García, M. (1894), *Hints on Singing*, London: E. Ascherberg and Co.

Halaçoğlu, C. (2013), 'Occupation and the Colonization of Algeria from 1830 to 1870: A Struggle for Dominance', MA diss., Middle East Technical University, Ankara.

Kheshti, R. (2015), *Modernity's Ear: Listening to Race and Gender in World Music*, New York and London: New York University Press.

Laroui, A. (1977), *The History of the Maghrib: An Interpretive Essay*, Princeton, NJ: Princeton University Press.

Mackinlay, M. S. (1908), *Garcia the Centenarian and His Times; Being a Memoir of Manuel Garcia's Life and Labours for the Advancement of Music and Science*, Edinburgh and London: W. Blackwood and Sons.

Matteucci, C. (1847), *Lectures on the Physical Phenomena of Living Beings*, London: Longman, Brown, Green and Longmans.

Mills, M. (2008), 'The Dead Room: Deafness and Communication Engineering', PhD diss., Harvard University, Cambridge, MA.

Petitjean, P. (2005), 'Science and the "Civilizing Mission": France and the Colonial Enterprise', in B. Stuchtey (ed.), *Science Across the European Empires, 1800–1950*, 107–28, Oxford: Oxford University Press.

Poyet, J. (1904), 'Les Larynx Celebres par le Dr. Poyet', *Musica* (January): 251.

Pratt, M. L. (1992), *Imperial Eyes: Travel Writing and Transculturation*, London and New York: Routledge.

Radomski, T. (2005), 'Manuel Garcia (1805–1906): A Bicentennial Reflection', *Australian Voice*, 11: 25–41.

Roberts, T. (2015), 'The Role of French Algeria in American Expansion During the Early Republic', *Journal of the Western Society for French History*, 43: 153–64.

Rush, J. (1827), *The Philosophy of the Human Voice: Embracing its Physiological History; Together with a System of Principles by which Criticism in the Art of Elocution May be Rendered Intelligible, and Instruction, Definite and Comprehensive, to which is Added a Brief Analysis of Song and Recitative*, Philadelphia, PA: J. Maxwell.

Said, E. (1978), *Orientalism*, New York: Random House.

Said, E. (1993), *Culture and Imperialism*, New York: Random House.

Sand, R. (1905), 'Le Centenaire de Manuel Garcia', *Le Guide Musical*, 51 (11): 203–6.

Schmidt, L. E. (2000), *Hearing Things: Religion, Illusion, and the American Enlightenment*, Cambridge, MA: Harvard University Press.

Scott, T. (2010), *Organization Philosophy: Gehlen, Foucault, Deleuze*, New York and London: Palgrave Macmillan.

Stark, J. (2003), *Bel Canto: A History of Vocal Pedagogy*, Toronto: University of Toronto Press.

Steege, B. (2012), *Helmholtz and the Modern Listener*, Cambridge: Cambridge University Press.

Streeter, H. R. (1871), *Voice Building: A New and Correct Theory for the Mechanical Formation of the Human Voice*, Boston, MA: White and Goullaud.

Taussig, M. (1993), *Mimesis and Alterity: A Particular History of the Senses*, New York and London: Routledge.

Taylor, D. (2003), *The Archive and the Repertoire: Performing Cultural Memory in the Americas*, Durham, NC: Duke University Press.

The Musical Times (1905), 'Manuel Garcia', 46 (746) (1 April): 225–32.

Vallee, M. (2019), *Sounding Bodies Sounding Worlds: An Exploration of Embodiments in Sound*, Singapore: Palgrave Macmillan.

Watson, E. (1865), 'Laryngoscopy and its Revelations', *The Lancet*, 1 (3 June): 588–91.

Wynter, S. (2003), 'Unsettling the Coloniality of Being/Power/Truth/Freedom: Towards the Human, After Man, Its Overrepresentation – An Argument', *CR: The New Centennial Review*, 3 (3): 257–337.

2

The hush arbour as sanctuary

African American survival silence during British/American slavery

Maya Cunningham

Introduction: African American slavery as occupation

African America was formed because of the British colonial project in North America. English colonists seized lands from Native Americans, and enslaved West and central Africans as colonial subjects, to form plantations that rendered 'cash crops'. This colonial project was only possible because of the transatlantic slave trade, the largest human-trafficking industry in world history. Europeans captured, enslaved and transported over ten million Africans to the Americas and Europe.[1] Between roughly 1500 and 1888, Blackburn (2013: 16) states that 'the plantation and mining slaves of the Americas toiled extraordinarily long hours to meet European consumers' craving for exotic luxuries'. These 'luxuries', which were previously only available to Europe through the silk routes, included sugar, cotton, coffee, spices, gold, silver and other items. Gomez (2005: 61) explains that in Europe, before the slave trade and colonial period, sugar had been a rare commodity, available only to the elite and often locked in 'spice cabinets'. He connects the early development of the transatlantic slave trade to the Spanish and Portuguese plantation cultivation of sugar in the late 1400s on Mediterranean islands and on Madeira and the Canary Islands, located off the coast of West Africa. 'The use of Black slaves to cultivate sugarcane therefore did not begin in the Americas, but in the Mediterranean and on West African coastal islands' (Gomez 2005: 62). Columbus's 1492 voyage to the Americas 'set in motion a process that . . . transferred a system of slavery from the Old World to the New' (Gomez 2005). Portugal and Spain began to transport enslaved Africans to the Americas to toil in mining and agricultural industries. Other nations, including Great Britain, the Netherlands, France and Denmark, quickly began to seize Indigenous lands in the Americas and established colonies to produce cash crops using the labour of enslaved Africans. Portuguese-held Brazil received the most Africans during the slave trade, with huge numbers going to British, French, Dutch and Spanish colonies as well. In the early 1600s, the establishment of tobacco as a cash crop in the Virginia colony triggered early British settlers to bring in large numbers of European indentured servants and enslaved Africans as free labour. The plantation economy in North America mushroomed to eventually include other cash crops, like rice, indigo, sugar and cotton. Scholars estimate that 305,326 Africans were trafficked into the pre- and post-revolution United States.[2] The brutality that enslaved Africans were subjected to cannot be understated. Yet, they resisted bondage in many ways, especially through escape, either to the northern United States and Canada (after slavery was abolished in these areas) or to Spanish-controlled Florida.

When escape was not possible for enslaved African Americans, surviving slavery depended on knowing when to speak and when to be silent. It is well documented that songs performed by African Americans during slavery were used as methods of resistance. Velma Maia Thomas (2001) confirms that spirituals such as 'Steal Away' and 'Swing Low Sweet Chariot' were often publicly performed on plantations as code songs used to secretly signal escape plans to freedom.[3] Larson (2004) records that Harriet Tubman publicly sang 'Bound for the Promised Land' to communicate to her family an encoded message of her plans to escape:

I'm sorry I'm going to leave you,
Farewell, oh farewell;
But I'll meet you in the morning
Farewell, oh farewell;
I'll meet you in the morning.

The 'Promised Land' lyric meant going either to heaven or to freedom in the North. Tubman also used spirituals with coded messages to help others escape during her return journeys South. She would sing an appropriate spiritual to warn her party of danger or to guide them to the next safe place (Larson 2004). These spirituals not only communicated escape messages but also asserted slaves' humanity, contesting their chattel status and the declaration in the US Constitution that they were only 'three-fifths of a human being' (Constitution of the United States, art. I, §2, cl. 3).

While scholarship on code songs is plentiful, less discussed are the contexts of secrecy and silence in which they were often performed. African Americans created spaces of refuge called hush arbours,[4] which were secret night meetings that often involved singing and religious worship. The study of early African American hush arbour practices is imperative to understanding the sonic history of African America under occupation via settler colonialism.

Tuck and Yang (2012) provide a useful framework for understanding the way in which settler-colonialism operates in the United States. Their analysis serves as a prismatic lens through which to better understand how African Americans used survival silence, via the hush arbour, to resist it:

> *Settler Colonialism* operates through internal/external colonial modes simultaneously because there is no spatial separation between metropole and colony. . . . The horizons of the settler colonial nation-state are total and require a mode of total appropriation of Indigenous life and land, rather than the selective expropriation of profit-producing fragments. . . . Settler colonialism is different from other forms of colonialism in that settlers come with the intention of making a new home on the land, a homemaking that insists on settler sovereignty over all things in their new domain. . . . Within settler colonialism, the most important concern is land/water/air/ subterranean earth. . . . Land is what is most valuable, contested, required. This is both because the settlers make Indigenous land their new home and *source of capital*. (2002: 5, emphasis added)

The land alone that formed the early United States had little value to the settler-colonial enterprise other than to provide homesteads and subsistence farming. However, British colonists had come to North America looking for profitability. The land could only be used as capital when paired with the labour that was necessary to produce cash crops of value in European markets. For example, the Virginia colony, settled in 1607, was a failed enterprise until the English settlers there began to raise tobacco as a cash crop that could be sold in England. They began to use tobacco as a form of currency and in other kinds of financial exchanges (Morgan 1975: 90–1; Berlin 2003: 13). With this in mind, we can understand the United States as an occupied settler colony that was executed through the interdependent colonization of both Indigenous land/people and the Black bodies of enslaved Africans who could make the land produce wealth through a cash crop economy. Therefore, freedom for Africans literally meant self-determination of their bodies, which had to be liberated and relocated away from slave plantations. Resisting occupation meant defying 'slave owners' attempts to control Black movement – and indeed, most aspects of black bodily experience' – this 'created a terrain on which bondspeople would contest slaveholding power' (Camp 2002: 534).

The context of this form of occupation – the colonization of African bodies, which were legally owned by slave masters as chattel – led Africans and their African American descendants to create a culture that had both an internal and external modus operandi. It was a culture that was essentially closed to dominant others and led to distinctive, bifurcated auditory environments and music culture that operated symbiotically. Secret hush arbour meetings, and the sonic practices that were central to those meetings, reveal one of the major ways that Africans resisted the colonial occupation of their bodies. When temporarily relocating to secret 'freedom spaces', African Americans spoke and made music in these meetings using their bodies, their voices and with body percussion, such as handclaps. These sounds can be seen (or heard) as 'silence', not only because they were hushed to avoid discovery but also because they were concealed from, and unheard by, colonial powers. Even though they were legal chattel, enslaved Black people asserted their personhood by choosing what their bodies would and would not sound in front of, and away from, slaveholders/landholders, who were in this instance an occupying force.

Building on historical research in African American studies on hush arbours (e.g. Nunley 2011; Harding 2007), I argue that strategies of silencing and sounding employed by African Americans under colonial occupation were equally important as methods of resistance. In this chapter, I excavate the WPA Slave Narratives (held at the Library of Congress) and African American autobiography as primary sources of recorded oral history to historically establish hush arbour practices. I will also examine the hush arbour imagery that is featured in Toni Morrison's highly acclaimed novel *Beloved* and in the film adaptation of this novel. I also draw on the anthropological work of Zora Neale Hurston, as well as Maya Angelou's autobiographies, which document Black American southern life during the Jim Crow segregation period, to find examples of hush arbour iterations after slavery that manifested as survival silence in African American culture.

Hush arbour as sanctuary

Fo' de war when we'd have a meetin' at night, wuz mos' always 'way in de woods or de bushes some whar so de white folks couldn't hear, an when dey'd sins a spiritual an' de spirit 'gin to shout some de elders would go 'mongst de

folks an' put dey han' over dey mouf' an some times put a clof in dey mouf an'
say: 'Spirit don talk so loud or de patterol break us up.'

(Becky Elzy, age 87, born 1848, Avery Island, Louisiana,
in McIlhenny 1933: 31)

Mrs Becky Elzy documents with her oral testimony the hush arbour meetings that she participated in on the Louisiana sugarcane plantation where she lived. What stands out is the symbiotic relationship between sounds and strategies of quieting that she describes. Enslaved Blacks like Mrs Elzy gathered during these secret prayer and song meetings to make sound that was not intended for slave owners' ears. Yet, their sounds still had to be hushed with a hand or a cloth to avoid discovery and to keep the meetings secret. I start with this example to demonstrate how in African American life during slavery, sound and silence seem different but were closely related. They were two sides of the same coin. As R. Murray Schafer argues in *The Soundscape: Our Sonic Environment and the Tuning of Our World*, there is really no such thing as silence, only the temporary absence of certain sounds (1977: 256). In the African American vernacular, when an elder says to someone 'hush' or 'hush your mouth', especially to a youngster, the command indicates either a lack of propriety or even the danger of the spoken words. In this sense, African American survival silence really means sounds that are hushed, secret and withheld until the proper time.

Hush arbours were the genesis of survival silence in African American culture. In African American studies, and theories of power, survival sounds and silence are sometimes called coded language, double entendre or the 'hidden transcript' – a term coined by James C. Scott in *Domination and the Arts of Resistance* (1990). Scott defines the 'hidden transcript' as the non-hegemonic, subversive discourse generated by subordinate groups and concealed from certain dominant others (Scott 1990, cited in Nunley 2011: 11). Scott juxtaposes the hidden transcript with the 'public transcript' – information that is deemed safe to reveal to the dominant group.

During slavery, African Americans were a people under occupation by British colonists who became 'Americans' after the United States was declared an independent country in 1776. The British first imported twenty Africans into the Jamestown Colony in Virginia in 1619 (see Figure 2.1). Due to their participation in the triangular slave trade, the population of Africans, in what eventually became the thirteen colonies, rapidly increased (Gomez 1998: 19–20). It is important to note that these Africans were not citizens of the colonies or of the United States. They were considered to be property and non-citizens.

Figure 2.1 'Landing negroes at Jamestown from a Dutch man-of-war, 1619', *c.* 1901. Library of Congress, LC-USZ62-53345.

According to the 1857 Dred Scott Decision, they had 'no rights which the white man was bound to respect'.[5]

The colonial slave owners had intimate familial and financial ties to Britain. Indeed, George Washington's English family crest forms the basis of the current design of Washington, DC's flag. In another example, anthropologist Joseph Opala has revealed the relationship between Richard Oswald, principal partner of the London firm Grant, Sargent and Oswald, and Henry Laurens, an American slave trader, as a key example of the British-American colonial occupation that was tied to slavery (see Figures 2.2 and 2.3). Oswald's firm took over Bunce Island, located off the coast of what is today Sierra Leone, and turned it into a 'slave factory' (see Figure 2.4). Through their business dealings, they forcibly supplied South Carolina's plantation owners with huge numbers of enslaved African men and women to undertake the laborious job of rice

Figure 2.2 'Henry Laurens Esq'r, president of the American Congress 1778', *c.* 1782. Library of Congress, LC-DIG-pga-01421.

planting. The forced migration that came of this business has resulted in the Gullah culture of the Georgia and South Carolina Sea Islands (Opala 1987). The fortune that Henry Laurens made by slave trading financed his political career, making him a key player in the American Revolution. His ill-gotten wealth led to him becoming president of the Continental Congress in 1777.

George Washington, Henry Laurens, Thomas Jefferson and all other plantation owners were the occupying force, the 'dominant others', that kept Blacks under constant surveillance. White slave masters were assisted by overseers and men who were called 'patrollers'. Patrollers were usually poorer white men who appointed themselves as guardians of southern rural roads. They often stopped and questioned Blacks about their travelling passes, searched for runaways, kidnapped and sold Blacks, lynched people and imposed general harassment.

Figure 2.3 'Benjamin Franklin and Richard Oswald discussing the Treaty of Peace, Paris', c. 1898. Library of Congress, LC-USZ62-55181 (image depicts events of 1786).

The dichotomy of guarded and open speech among African Americans was literally the sound of their occupation: coded speech by day and secret meetings in hushed tones by night. Keeping hush arbour meetings hidden from this occupying force of patrollers, overseers and slave owners was of the utmost importance, because, after the Stono Rebellion in 1739, colonies/states instituted 'slave codes', which criminalized unsupervised gatherings of Blacks in order to prevent conspiracies of escape or rebellion. In many instances, religious gatherings of the enslaved were also against the law or not allowed by slave masters. One WPA interviewee shared that when a hush arbour meeting he attended was discovered by a patroller, the man, while beating the group with his whip, declared 'we brought you here to serve us, not God' (Levine 2007: 42).

The religious nature of hush arbour meetings is an especially significant point when considering the sound of colonial occupation, because historical evidence

TO BE SOLD, on board the Ship *Bance-Island*, on tuefday the 6th of *May* next, at *Afhley-Ferry*; a choice cargo of about 250 fine healthy

NEGROES,

juft arrived from the Windward & Rice Coaft. —The utmoft care has already been taken, and fhall be continued, to keep them free from the leaft danger of being infected with the SMALL-POX, no boat having been on board, and all other communication with people from *Charles-Town* prevented.

Auftin, Laurens, & Appleby.

N. B. Full one Half of the above Negroes have had the SMALL-POX in their own Country.

Figure 2.4 'To be sold, on board the ship *Bance Island*, . . . negroes, just arrived from the Windward & Rice Coast', *c.* 1940–60. Library of Congress, LC-USZ62-10293 (photograph of newspaper advertisement from the 1780s).

shows that British-American slave owners exerted particular surveillance when slave preachers spoke to Black congregants on their plantations. At this point, white plantation society had developed its own settler-colonial version of Christianity. Their religious beliefs rationalized occupation and their rule over Indigenous land, and included justification for slavery. They told enslaved Blacks that their only way for 'salvation' was to 'obey your masters' and to be so-called good slaves (Escott 1979: 113). Escott asserts that formerly enslaved Blacks 'rejected white religion' as propaganda, even while slave masters either forced Blacks to attend their churches, where such erroneous doctrines were preached, or made Black slave preachers parrot these messages. When this happened, slaves of course dismissed what slave preachers repeated under white surveillance as 'hogwash', but they did not dismiss the preachers. Knowing the constraints that affected them, 'slaves understood the preachers and appreciated services that they were able to perform in secret' (Escott 1979: 68).

It is the role of slave preachers that serves as a pivot point into the secret lives of enslaved Blacks. Slave preachers often led hush arbour gatherings (see Figure 2.5). The meetings were almost always for the purpose of practising Christianity away from the scrutiny of white masters or to plan escape to freedom. Oftentimes, the two were intertwined. According to *Slave Missions and the Black Church in the Antebellum South*, 'African American perceptions and practice of Christianity had always emphasized freedom, community and the judgment day to come' (Cornelius 1999: 202). As historian Erskine Clarke contends (2015), they saw in biblical Christianity 'Jesus the Liberator'.

My research in African American autobiographies on hush arbour oral history reveals two key testimonies. Maya Angelou wrote in *Singing, Swinging and Getting Merry Like Christmas* (1976) about the oral history passed down by her paternal great-grandmother: 'My great-grandmother (who had been a slave), told me of praying silently under old wash pots, and of secret meetings deep in the woods to praise God. . . . Her owner wouldn't allow his Negroes to worship God (it might give them ideas) and they did so on pain of being lashed' (1976: 28). William Ford III, a Texas-based African American minister, has a hush arbour 'prayer pot' or 'prayer kettle' as a family heirloom (see Figure 2.6). In his writings, Ford (2007, 2015) shares the hush arbour legacy in his family:

Figure 2.5 'A negro camp meeting in the South', *c.* 1872. Library of Congress, LC-USZ62-63867.

Figure 2.6 Ford family prayer kettle, *c.* 2017. Copyrighted to William Ford III and used with permission.

> It begins with a 200-year-old black kettle pot, used by my Christian slave forbearers in Lake Providence, Louisiana. While used for cooking and washing clothes during the day, this kettle was secretly used for prayer. Forbidden to pray by their slave master, my ancestors were beaten unmercifully if found doing so. However, in spite of their master's cruelty, and because of their love for Jesus, they prayed anyway. At night, sneaking into a barn, they carried this cast iron cooking pot into their secret prayer meeting. As others looked out, those inside prayed. Turning this pot upside-down on the barn floor, they propped it up with rocks – suspending the pot a few inches above the ground. Then, while lying prostrate or kneeling on the ground, they prayed in whispers underneath the kettle to muffle their voices. The story passed down with the kettle is that they were risking their lives to pray for freedom for ensuing generations. One day, freedom did come. (Ford 2015)

As Angelou and Ford described, hush arbours often took place deep in woods that abutted southern plantations or in cabins, and were always at night (Cornelius 1999: 9). In these sanctuaries, enslaved Blacks could speak, sing, pray and preach freely, without using coded language, but they had to do so softly. Loud sounds had to be mediated into silence to avoid discovery by white patrollers. Participation in hush arbours was thus a form of resistance. Resistance in this context meant staying alive, being non-compliant with slave codes that forbade Black gatherings and holding onto the desire and determination to be free. Escott argued that 'the slaves' religion helped them to see themselves in a context removed from the slave owners' crippling perspective, thus sustaining mental resistance when physical opposition was not always possible' (1979: 115).

I have examined the WPA Federal Writer's Project Slave Narrative Collection, which are transcriptions of interviews conducted from 1936 to 1938 in twenty-six states, with over 2,000 members of the last living generation of Blacks who were formerly enslaved. My excavation yielded numerous accounts that confirmed that hush arbours were a common part of daily life. Raboteau (1978) and Ford (2018) also confirm that hush arbour meetings among enslaved African Americans were frequent and that they often used kettles to conceal their prayer meetings. 'The most common device for preserving secrecy was an iron pot usually placed in the middle of the cabin floor or at the doorstep, then slightly propped up to hold the sound of the praying and singing from escaping' (Raboteau, 1978, as cited in Ford 2018: 97). In an article in *The Atlantic*, historian William R. Black problematizes the WPA Narratives that were 'often filtered through the racism of white interviewers and their supervisors'. However, I use the narratives simply to confirm that Blacks engaged in these night meetings all over the South and to understand what usually happened during such gatherings.

One interviewee observed during slavery times that someone singing 'Steal Away to Jesus' signified that there would be a religious meeting that night 'in the woods, way down in the swamps' (Escott 1979: 111) (see Figure 2.7). The meetings usually took place in a four-part format: 'After the first hymn or spiritual came prayer, a major focus of the hush arbour service . . . (prayer) was an essential community action . . . prayer had overtones of liberation' (Cornelius 1999:11). Many narratives revealed that 'any member of the congregation could lead prayers, but the lesson and sermon were conducted by a preacher, chosen by the community for ability to interpret the sacred word' (1999: 11). 'After the sermon came the ring shout' – ring-shout lyrics performed in hush arbours, like 'Lay Down Body', often dramatized death and ascension to heaven, judgement for slave masters and escape to freedom. Silvia King was interviewed when she was 100 years old for the WPA Slave Narratives. During her interview, she described the ring shout: 'Dey gits in de ring dance . . . (it was) jes' a kind of shuffle, den it git faster and faster and dey gits warmed up and moans and shouts and claps and dances . . . sometimes dey sings and shout all night' (*Born in Slavery: Slave Narratives from the Federal Writers' Project, 1936–1938. Volume 16. Texas Narratives: Part 1 and Part 2* 1972: Part 2, 294).

Figure 2.7 'The sunny South – A negro revival meeting – a seeker "getting religion"', *c.* 1873. Library of Congress, LC-USZ62-117140.

The WPA Slave Narratives bring to life the real people who participated in these meetings and who witnessed the silencing or 'hushing' that was necessary to continue with them. Amanda McCray testified that on her Florida plantation there were praying grounds where 'the grass never had a chance ter grow fer the troubled knees that kept it crushed down' (*Born in Slavery: Slave Narratives from the Federal Writers' Project, 1936–1938. Volume 3 Florida Narratives* 1972: 212). Andrew Moss remembered that on the plantation where he grew up all of the slaves had their private prayer grounds: 'My Mammy's was a ole twisterd thick-rooted muscadine bush. She'd go in dar and pray for deliverance of de slaves' (*Born in Slavery: Slave Narratives from the Federal Writers' Project, 1936–1938. Volume 15 Tennessee Narratives* 1972: 49). Patsy Larkin recalled that on her plantation the slaves would steal away into the cane thickets and pray in a prostrate position with their faces close to the ground so that no sound would escape (Levine 2007: 42). On a Louisiana plantation, enslaved Blacks would gather in the woods at night, form a circle on their knees and pray over a vessel of water to drown out the sound (2007: 42). Richard Carruthers remembered the following:

> Us (negros) used to have a prayin' ground down in the hollow and sometime we
> come out of the field, between 11 and 12 at night, scorchin' and burnin up with

nothin to eat, and we wants to ask the good Lawd to have mercy. We puts grease in a snuff pan or bottle and make a lamp. We takes a pine torch, too, and goes down in the hollow to pray. Some gits so joyous they starts to holler loud and we has to stop up they mouth. I see (negros) git so full of the lawd and so happy they draps unconscious. (*Born in Slavery: Slave Narratives from the Federal Writers' Project, 1936-1938. Volume 16 Texas Narratives: Part 1 and Part 2* 1972: Part 1, 199)

Kalvin Woods, a slave preacher, described how women would take old quilts and rags and soak them before hanging them up in the shape of a small room, 'and the slaves who were interested about it would huddle up behind these quilts to do their praying, preaching and singing. These wet rags were used to keep the sound of their voices from penetrating the air' (Cade 1935: 87).

Building on these eye-witness accounts found in the WPA Slave Narrative Collection, Toni Morrison vividly illustrates the function of resistance in these gatherings, as well as the sounding/silencing dichotomy, in her novel *Beloved* (1987), as well as in *Beloved*, the film (1998). The book is an epic and dark tale of the main characters' lives during and after slavery: Sethe, Paul D and Baby Suggs. The story is set in a free Black community just outside of Cincinnati, Ohio, between 1861 and 1865. It is told in flashback to heighten the mystery of a baby ghost, Sethe's dead daughter, who haunts her home. Morrison brings to life the gruesome realities that African Americans had to endure during slavery. In this case, these realities took place in the lives of the main characters on a slave plantation in Kentucky that is ironically named 'Sweet Home'.

It is sometimes hard for us to envision what it meant to be considered a chattel. Morrison was inspired to write *Beloved* by a woman named Margaret Garner who, in 1856, escaped from slavery with her family, but after being tracked down by the slave catchers, killed her own child rather than allow her to be captured. With *Beloved*, Morrison seeks to answer one simple question. What were the conditions of slavery that drove this recently escaped Black mother to kill one child, and attempt to kill three others, in order to avoid recapture? Through the stories of each of her characters, Morrison forces us to know the egregious extent of the warped mind of the slaver and the physical, psychological and emotional damage done to the enslaved. Yet, amid all of this very real brutality, Morrison uses the African American hush arbour tradition to show us hope and freedom through the character of Baby Suggs, who is Sethe's mother-in-law and a spiritual leader in the community. Baby Suggs, who died eight years before the story begins, only appears when Sethe visits her through memory. Sethe's musings on the elder woman precipitate the first hush arbour scene in the film:

because slave life had 'busted her legs, back, head, eyes, hands, kidneys, womb and tongue,' she had nothing left to make a living with but her heart – which she put to work at once. Accepting no title of honor before her name . . . she became an unchurched preacher, one who visited pulpits and opened her great heart to those who could use it. . . . Uncalled, unrobed, unanointed, she let her great heart beat in their presence. When warm weather came, Baby Suggs, holy, followed by every black man, woman and child who could make it through, took her great heart to the Clearing – a wide-open place cut deep in the woods. . . . In the heat of every Saturday afternoon, she sat in the clearing while the people waited among the trees. (Morrison 1987: 43)

In the film, Sethe takes her two daughters to the 'Clearing' where Baby Suggs led outdoor church services in the woods – hush arbour meetings. The book and film bring to life what the tenor of these meetings might have been like. The film literally enacts the African American sound under occupation. Portrayed by the powerful actress Beah Smith, Baby Suggs fulfils the preacher role of the hush arbour tradition. With 'her great heart' she encourages the free Black community to celebrate themselves.

After situating herself on a huge flat-sided rock, Baby Suggs bowed her head and prayed silently. The company watched her from the trees. They knew she was ready when she put her stick down. Then she shouted, 'Let the children come!' and they ran from the trees toward her. 'Let your mothers hear you laugh', she told them, and the woods rang. The adults looked on and could not help smiling. Then 'Let the grown men come', she shouted. They stepped out one by one from among the ringing trees. 'Let your wives and your children see you dance', she told them, and groundlife shuddered under their feet. Finally she called the women to her. 'Cry', she told them. 'For the living and the dead. Just cry'. And without covering their eyes the women let loose. It started that way: laughing children, dancing men, crying women and then it got mixed up. Women stopped crying and danced; men sat down and cried; children danced, women laughed, children cried until, exhausted and riven, all and each lay about the Clearing damp and gasping for breath. (Morrison 1987: 43)

This scene in the book and film brings a vision of antebellum hush arbour meetings into sharp focus. In this case the meeting takes place in a homogenously free Black community and is therefore held during the day. However, the kind of reclamation of their humanity that Baby Suggs facilitates with her preaching was only safe to happen outside of the surveillance of whites, who in the book and film are the main employers of the Black community. The book and film also rightly depict this meeting as an expressive and emotionally cathartic experience with dancing (in ring-shout formation) and weeping, just as they are described in the WPA Slave Narratives.

The final scene of the film depicts the second half of the hush arbour scene in the book:

> 'Here', she said, 'in this here place, we flesh; flesh that weeps, laughs; flesh that dances on bare feet in grass. Love it. Love it hard. Yonder they do not love your flesh. They despise it. . . . And O my people they do not love your hands. Those they only use, tie, bind, chop off and leave empty. Love your hands! Love them . . . hear me now, love your heart. For this is the prize'. Saying no more, she stood up then and danced with her twisted hip the rest of what her heart had to say while the others opened their mouths and gave her the music. Long notes held until the four-part harmony was perfect enough for their deeply loved flesh. (Morrison 1987: 44)

Two things stand out in this passage. Even though this is a private meeting in a closed Black community, the hidden transcript is also duplicitously a public transcript because her words are sounded in the open during the day. Baby Suggs's choice of words 'hushes', in a sense, her declaration of the atrocities perpetrated by whites upon her Black congregation – atrocities they must still endure as non-citizens with no legal protection. She never names them or openly accuses them of the lynching and labour exploitation that she alludes to in her preaching. She simply uses the ambiguous word 'they', who the gathering's cultural insiders know refers to exploitative whites. The scene in the film once again envisions the emotional and transformative function of African American hush arbours, intensified for the viewers by the vocals of the *African Children's Choir* who sing Morrison's description of the 'long notes held in four-part harmony'. Beah Richards employs the intense, heartfelt preaching style that is traditional with many African American pastors. The documentary *Beah: A Black Woman Speaks* (2003) reveals that she learned this delivery from her father who was a pastor. The passionate 'amens' and 'halleluiahs' exclaimed by Richards, as Baby Suggs, and the African American actors as congregants reveal the emotional fervour of the meetings described in the WPA Narratives that required muffling with pots, kettles, clothes, hands and quilts.

The hush arbour church services embody the interdependent relationship between African American survival silence and sound when they were under occupation during slavery. The public and hidden transcripts became mirror reflections, or an interchangeable double jeopardy, that occurred at the same time. During the day, open and hidden communication moved back and forth between seemingly innocuous acquiescence to encoded speech and song at normal volumes. At night, true feelings, plain speech and messages of liberation were shared openly but had to be quieted. This 'twoness', as termed by W. E. B. Du Bois (1997: 2), or continual code switching, reflected the constant state of precarity in which enslaved Blacks had to live. In reaction, they created sanctuaries. Through hush arbours, they gained temporary physical freedom from plantations by making geographically distant closed cultural spaces. The hush arbour allowed them to claim freedom in their lives by making personal choices with their time spent outside of forced work through participating in all-night meetings, if they wanted to. The hush arbour also allowed them temporary emotional and psychological freedom by giving full voice to their feelings and enabling the free practice of their religion. Their Christianity allowed them to see themselves as children of God and not the chattel property of slave masters.

African American survival silence under racial apartheid (Jim Crow)

Hush arbour survival silence set a precedent for the continued operation of African American hidden and public transcripts during the Reconstruction and Jim Crow eras, from 1865 to the early 1960s. Jim Crow draws a dark parallel to the South African apartheid system. Even though the thirteenth and fourteenth constitutional amendments abolished slavery and granted citizenship to all persons born in the United States, many Blacks, especially in the South, still lived with few civil rights and no legal protection. In many cases, their livelihoods still depended upon what was spoken, or more importantly, what remained hushed, when under white surveillance. During this time in history, 'white surveillance' meant the presence among Blacks of anyone who supported and upheld the segregation system, and the idea of white supremacy and Black inferiority. This especially meant those who held power over Black lives, including white employers, landowners, public officials, law enforcement officers and even ordinary citizens who often deputized themselves to police Black behaviour.

From the late 1800s to the mid-twentieth century, African American cultural survival sounds and survival silence are well documented in proverbs, folklore, poetry, African American autobiography and in the anthropological work of Zora Neale Hurston. In *Mules and Men* (1935), Hurston's ethnographic book on Black folklore, she documents the so-called Uncle Remus folktales that abounded in early to mid-twentieth-century Black life. These were coded stories about the clever wit of Brer Rabbit (or Brother Rabbit) who always tricked larger and more dominant animals as a symbol for Blacks who outsmarted dominant oppressors. In the same work, Hurston also describes the 'hidden transcript' that manifested in 1930s Black Eatonville, as a 'feather bed of resistance'. Hurston describes a cultural form of 'hedging' done by Blacks in her hometown, Eatonville, Florida, in response to direct questions posed by whites: 'the theory behind our tactics: "All right, I'll set something outside the door of my mind for him to play with and handle. He can read my writing, but he sho' can't read my mind. I'll put this play toy in his hand, and he will seize it and go away. Then I'll say my say and sing my song"' (Hurston 1935: 2). She goes on to say, 'we let the probe enter, but it never comes out. It gets smothered under a lot of laughter and pleasantries' (Hurston 1935: 3).

Maya Angelou also documents this survival silence, which can also be thought of as the unsaid. In her autobiography *I Know Why the Caged Bird Sings* (1977), she quotes an African American proverb to describe a mechanism that was employed by many Blacks in Stamps, Arkansas, the racially oppressed, segregated town in which she grew up. This proverb is: 'Ask me where I am coming from and I will tell you where I am going.' In other words, avoid sharing information with the untrusted that can be used against you. Angelou also witnessed as a child in the early 1930s survival silence strategies used by Blacks in Stamps who still made a living in the post-slavery agricultural economic system as sharecroppers and day labourers in cotton fields. Trucks used her grandmother's store as a pickup point to transport Black workers to the white-owned fields. Angelou witnessed in these community members two very different modes of conduct: one that was a self-depreciating acquiescent, smiling pretence in front of whites, and another that was relaxed, natural, sassy and even proud when only Blacks were around. The smiling show for whites confused and disturbed Angelou until she read a poem by Paul Laurence Dunbar, a turn-of-the-century African American poet, that she said helped her understand. During an interview with Bill Moyers (*Going Home with Maya Angelou* 2014), she quotes Dunbar's 1896 poem:

We wear the mask that grins and lies
It hides our cheeks and shades our eyes
This debt we pay to human guile;
With torn and bleeding hearts we smile,
And mouth with myriad subtleties.

Why should the world be over-wise,
In counting all our tears and sighs?
Nay, let them only see us, while
We wear the mask.

In Black life during the Jim Crow era, the hidden transcript of survival sounds and silence took form in coded stories, hedging, deflecting and masking. As Angelou so eloquently explains, masking was self-silencing. This cultural pattern stemmed from the subordinate–dominant relationship carved out between Blacks and whites during slavery times.

Conclusion: The hush arbour legacy

While slavery has been over for more than 150 years, the hidden transcript in African American culture remains. Nunley (2011) investigates the contemporary manifestations of the hush arbour as safe places for Black people to speak openly. He argues that many African Americans still tend to moderate what they say in front of whites. He contends that contemporary iterations of the hush arbour remain in African American culture in Black barbershops, front porches and other insider cultural spaces that facilitate uncensored Black speech, which he calls 'African American hush arbour rhetoric' (Nunley 2011: 1–2).

This study is important for considering 'sonic histories of occupation' because it examines auditory environments in circumstances, like African American slavery and racial apartheid, that are not often considered under common definitions of occupation. It speaks to the question of survival silence and sound under the conditions of British/American settler colonialism. With this in mind, this study opens the possibilities for similar work in sound studies concerning other Black populations, like those in South Africa, that have also been subjected to settler colonialism and/or occupation. If African Americans formed the hush arbour tradition, and an internal hidden transcript of survival silence in these circumstances, then it might be possible to use this as a basis of comparison with other communities or societies that may have formed similar auditory environments in resistance to occupation.

To conclude, however, I ask that we consider another legacy of the hush arbour. What I have found so far suggests that the impact of this practice continued into the twentieth century, and beyond, transforming silence into loud, amplified sound that openly contested the Jim Crow system and reverberated all over the United States during the 1950s and 1960s. After emancipation, hush arbour congregations became free Black churches. Many still met in outdoor 'brush arbours' on Sunday mornings, just after slavery ended (Cornelius 1999: 9). These hush arbour congregations, which scholars call 'the invisible institution', became the blueprint for the Black church, which became the highly visible foundation

Figure 2.8 Martin Luther King, Jr, at a freedom rally, Washington Temple Church, 1962. Photo by O. Fernandez. Library of Congress, LC-USZ62-111157.

of the African American Civil Rights Movement. Pastors of Black churches were the leaders of the movement. The Rev. Dr Martin Luther King, Jr, descended from a lineage of preachers that began during the hush arbour era. His maternal great-grandfather, Willis Williams, was a slave-era preacher (National Archives and Records Administration n.d.) (see Figure 2.8). Considering how profoundly the Civil Rights Movement changed the United States as a nation, and infused generations who came after with an ethos of justice and equality, further historical research might suggest that we all have been affected by the prayers for liberty uttered by hopeful enslaved Blacks in the hush arbours of old.

Notes

1   See www.slavevoyages.org, an online platform where scholars of the transatlantic slave trade contribute the most current research findings. This database details the

timeline of the slave trade, the nation states involved, specific voyages and other statistical information.

2   According to www.slavevoyages.org, the United States received lower numbers of enslaved Africans, an estimated 305,326, compared to other New World countries such as Brazil, which received the most at an estimated 5,848,266. However, these numbers must be understood in the context of the systems of slavery and the agricultural enterprise in operation in these countries. Sugarcane plantations dominated Brazil, which involved gruesome working conditions and back-breaking work, and importation numbers were higher there because it was less expensive for plantation owners to brutally work enslaved Africans to death, and then replace them with others because the distance between the east coast of Brazil and west central Africa was relatively short. The average lifespan for enslaved Africans in Brazil was seven years. During the time of the slave trade, tobacco was a dominant cash crop in North America (the cotton boom came after the legal end of the US slave trade in 1808). The cost was much higher to import Africans into the United States, because, among other things, the distance was longer from West and west central Africa. However, the lower importation numbers in the United States did not mean that the population of Africans was necessarily less than that of other New World countries, because the African population in the United States was the only one in the New World to reproduce itself (Berlin 2003).

3   See *Underground Railroad: The William Still Story* (2018), [Film] USA: PBS.

4   Hush arbours are also often referred to as 'hush harbours'. The term 'arbour' references a roof formed by a close grove of trees. These spots were chosen because tree branches effectively muffled sound.

5   Taney (1856).

References

Angelou, M. (1976), *Singin' And Swingin' And Gettin' Merry Like Christmas*, New York: Bantam.

Angelou, M. (1977), *I Know Why the Caged Bird Sings*, New York: Ballantine.

Battle, M. (2006), *The Black Church In America: African American Christian Spirituality*, Malden, MA: Blackwell.

Beah: A Black Women Speaks (2003), [Film] Dir. L. Hamilton, USA: HBO.

Beloved (1998), [Film] Dir. J. Demme, USA: Touchstone Pictures.

Berlin, I. (1998), *Many Thousands Gone: The First Two Centuries of Slavery in North America*, Cambridge, MA: Harvard University Press.

Berlin, I. (2003), *Generations of Captivity: A History of African-American Slaves*, Cambridge, MA: Harvard University Press.

Black, W. (2018), 'Abraham Lincoln's Secret Visit to Slaves', *The Atlantic*, 12 February: Available online: https://www.theatlantic.com/politics/archive/2018/02/former-slaves-stories-abraham-lincoln/552917/ (accessed 30 April 2018).

Blackburn, R. (2013), *The American Crucible: Slavery, Emancipation and Human Rights*, London: Verso.

Born in Slavery: Slave Narratives from the Federal Writers' Project, 1936–1938. Volume 3. Florida Narratives (1972), Washington, DC: Library of Congress.

Born in Slavery: Slave Narratives from the Federal Writers' Project, 1936–1938. Volume 15. Tennessee Narratives (1972), Washington, DC: Library of Congress.

Born in Slavery: Slave Narratives from the Federal Writers' Project, 1936–1938. Volume 16. Texas Narratives: Part 1 and Part 2 (1972), Washington, DC: Library of Congress.

Cade, J. (1935), 'Out of the Mouths of Ex-Slaves', *The Journal of Negro History*, 20 (3): 294–337.

Camp, S. (2002), 'The Pleasures of Resistance: Enslaved Women and Body Politics in the Plantation South, 1830–1861', *The Journal of Southern History*, 68 (3): 533–72.

Constitution of the United States: Available online: https://www.constituteproject.org/constitution/United_States_of_America_1992?lang=en (accessed 29 April 2018).

Cornelius, J. (1999), *Slave Missions and the Black Church In The Antebellum South*, Columbia: University of South Carolina Press.

Dubois, W. E. B. (1997), *The Souls of Black Folk*, Boston, MA: Bedford Books.

Erskine, C. (2015), 'Public Lecture: A Slave's World', Savannah, GA, 22 June.

Escott, P. (1979), *Slavery Remembered: A Record of Twentieth-Century Slave Narratives*, Chapel Hill: University of North Carolina Press.

Family Across the Sea (1991), [Film] Dir. D. Boulware, T. Carrier and A. Baker, USA: South Carolina Educational Television Network.

Ford, W. (2007), *Created for Influence*, Dallas, TX: Chosen Publishing.

Ford, W. (2015), 'The Prayers of My Forefathers (Former Slaves) Echo Today, 150 Years After the Civil War', *Will Ford Ministries.org*: Available online: https://willfordministries.com/2015/11/29/the-prayers-of-my-forefathers-former-slaves-echo-today-150-years-after-the-civil-war/ (accessed 1 December 2018).

Ford, W. and M. Lockett (2018), *The Dream King: How the Dream of Martin Luther King, Jr. Is Being Fulfilled to Heal Racism in America*, Redding, CA: NewType Publishing.

Going Home With Maya Angelou (2014), [TV programme], USA: Moyers and Company: Available online: https://billmoyers.com/episode/going-home-with-maya-angelou/ (accessed 30 April 2018).

Gomez, M. (1998), *Exchanging Our Country Marks: The Transformation of African Identities in the Colonial and Antebellum South*, Chapel Hill: University of North Carolina Press.

Gomez, M. (2005), *Reversing Sail: A History of the African Diaspora*, New York: Cambridge University Press.

Harding, R. (2007), 'You Got a Right to the Tree of Life', *Cross Currents*, 57 (2): 266–80.

Heilbut, A. (1971), *The Gospel Sound: Good News and Bad Times*, New York: Simon and Schuster.

Hurston, Z. N. (1978), *Mules and Men*, Bloomington: Indiana University Press.

Larson, K. (2004), *Bound for the Promised Land: Harriet Tubman, Portrait of an American Hero*, New York: Ballantine.

Levine, L. W. (2007), *Black Culture and Black Consciousness: Afro-American Folk Thought from Slavery to Freedom*, Oxford: Oxford University Press.

McIlhenny, E. A. (1933), *Befo' De War Spirituals: Words and Melodies*, Boston, MA: Christopher Publishing House.

Morgan, E. (1975), *American Slavery, American Freedom*, London: Norton.

Morrison, T. (1987), *Beloved*, New York: Knopf.

National Archives and Records Administration (n.d.), 'From the Roots of a Tree: The Genealogy of Martin Luther King, Jr.': Available online: https://www.archives.gov/files/atlanta/education/resources-by-state/images/mlk-supplemental.pdf (accessed 17 February 2018).

Nunley, V. (2011), *Keepin' It Hushed: The Barbershop and African American Hush Arbor Rhetoric*, Detroit, MI: Wayne State University Press.

Opala, J. A. (1987), 'The Gullah: Rice, Slavery, and the Sierra Leone-American Connection': Available online: https://glc.yale.edu/gullah-rice-slavery-and-sierra-leone-american-connection (accessed 30 April 2018).

Prahlad, A., ed. (2006), *The Greenwood Encyclopedia of African American Folklore*, Westport, CT: Greenwood Press.

Raboteau, A. (1978), *Slave Religion: The Invisible Institution in the Antebellum South*, New York: Oxford University Press

Schafer, M. R. (1977), *The Soundscape: Our Sonic Environment and the Tuning of the World*, Rochester, VT: Destiny Books.

Scott, J. (1990), *Domination and the Arts of Resistance: Hidden Transcripts*, New Haven, CT: Yale University Press.

Smithsonian Folkways, Wade in the Water Volume II: African American Congregational Singing: Nineteenth Century Roots (1996), Washington, DC: Smithsonian Folkways Recordings.

Taney, Roger Brooke and Supreme Court Of The United States (1856), *U.S. Reports: Dred Scott v. Sandford, 60 U.S. 19 How. 393*.

Thomas, V. (2001), *No Man Can Hinder Me: The Journey from Slavery to Emancipation Through Song*, New York: Crown.

Tuck, E. and W. Yang (2012), 'Decolonization is not a Metaphor', *Decolonization: Indigeneity, Education and Society*, 1 (1): 1–40.

United States Department of State (n.d.), 'Introduction to The Court Opinion On The Dredd Scott Case': Available online: https://usa.usembassy.de/etexts/democrac/21.htm (accessed 30 April 2018).

Walker, W. T. (1979), '*Somebody's Calling My Name*', *Black Sacred Music and Social Change*, Valley Forge, PA: Judson Press.

3

Music and sound in Weihsien Internment Camp in Japanese-occupied China

Sophia Geng

Introduction

On 7 July 1937, Japanese forces based in Manchuria charged southward towards Beijing, invading north China and hence starting the Second Sino-Japanese War (1937–45). On 7 December 1941, Japan attacked Pearl Harbor, transforming the Second Sino-Japanese War into the Pacific War. As a result of Pearl Harbor, the status of Allied citizens living in China at the time changed from neutral to 'enemy aliens'. These Allied citizens included individuals and their families who worked in China as government officials, executives, engineers and Christian missionaries. They were forced into internment camps under the watchful eyes of the Japanese. At the end of 1942, the Japanese authorities decided to concentrate all 'enemy aliens' into larger camps. The chosen site for one such camp in north China was a Presbyterian mission compound called Ledao yuan (Courtyard of the Happy Way) in Weihsien (now Weixian) in Shandong Province. The Japanese referred to this site as the Weihsien Civilian Assembly Centre. From March 1943 to October 1945, anywhere between 1,500 and 2,000 foreign nationals were imprisoned in the camp. After the war, dozens of internees shared their experiences of imprisonment at Weihsien in memoirs, (auto) biographies and oral histories. Over thirty such accounts have been published, and there are many more unpublished accounts. This chapter taps into the large number of resources collected by internees and published through a digital memorial.[1]

This chapter examines the distinctive auditory environments and music cultures that arose within the Weihsien Internment Camp and argues that the Weihsien internees forged a sense of belonging and community through their creative engagement with music and sound. A large variety of musical activities occurred during the camp's two and a half years of existence. This included institutionalized activities such as the formation of a choir, an orchestra, a theatre and a band organized or sponsored by the camp's Entertainment Committee. In addition, a wide range of informal and spontaneous music-making took place within the camp. The music that the internees performed ranged from popular pre-Second World War songs, folk music and dance melodies to classical repertoire. The internees also created new songs or creatively revised old songs to express their views of their involuntary confinement in the camp. The wide range of music-making and creativity displayed at Weihsien Internment Camp was similar to that which emerged in Nazi-controlled ghettos and labour camps across wartime Europe which have been examined by scholars in the field of Holocaust studies (e.g. Gilbert 2005).

The music analysed in this chapter includes three types: missionary music of faith, secular music of resilience and internees' music of resistance. At Weihsien Camp, about half of the internees were missionaries from America and Europe. These missionaries were allowed to practise religious services, in which prayers, chants, hymns and Mass were an integral part of their daily lives. Life within Weihsien was harsh, and hunger haunted the camp. The Japanese guards strictly controlled the camp's provisions. As a result, by October 1945, internees were so emaciated that they looked like skeletons of their former selves. However, throughout the existence of the camp, the Japanese did permit secular musical performances, either organized or spontaneous, as a form of entertainment. As a result, an array of musical productions that showcased the internees' resilience and creativity were developed in Weihsien Camp, despite the difficult situation that internees faced.

Sound and music were also used to discipline and manage internees. As McGinnis (2020: 226–30) points out, it was not uncommon to employ music as a tool to control or regulate prisoners' behaviour in camps operated by various governments during the Second World War. In the eyes of the captors, the captives' engagement with music was a harmless diversion providing that it was undertaken with the consent of camp administrators and under official supervision. Moreover, music offered the potential for captors to realign internees' views. The Japanese guards closely monitored music performed and produced by internees at Weihsien. Music had to be practised and performed in designated spaces. In addition, they forbade musical activities that proclaimed the internees' allegiance to their kings, queens or Allied governments. Thus, national anthems and patriotic songs were outlawed. Furthermore, musical productions that portrayed the Japanese government or army negatively (or even insinuated such sentiments) were not tolerated. Defiance of such regulations would result in harsh punishment, which included verbal reprimands, solitary confinement, severe beatings or transfers to prisons that were notorious for their cruelty. The Japanese also threatened the withdrawal of privileges such as holding performances or gatherings to regulate the behaviour of internees.

Despite such hardships, internees created new forms of auditory expression through their ingenuity, and these forms of expression enabled them to defy, protest against or resist Japanese control. Japanese guards' limited understanding of the English language and Western musical traditions meant that defiance and resistance could be expressed through music in the camps in a clandestine fashion. The internees used music to warn their fellow internees of the approach of patrolling guards, for example. They improvised lyrics to transmit secret messages. They omitted lyrics of forbidden songs in order to practise them in secret. And on special occasions, they openly sang national anthems or taboo songs and braced for the wrath of their captors.

The production as well as the appreciation of musical performances offered comfort and a sense of connection with pre-occupation normalcy. Music could uplift people's spirits and offer emotional support to those who had to confront unbearable circumstances. Moreover, music could consolidate the communal bonds that were formed within the camp. Subsequently, music became a survival mechanism for the imprisoned and a way in which to respond to occupation and persecution. As Mary Taylor Previte (2019), who spent her formative years at the camp, put it: 'In a world of guard dogs, roll calls, and prisoner numbers; a world of hunger, guard towers, and barrier walls with electrified wire; men, women and children shaped their response to this world with music.'

Music matters in understanding the history of occupation. As Gilbert argues (2005: 4), music is 'a unique legacy of the time: fragments of shared ideas and interpretation, orally conveyed and preserved, from communities that otherwise left few traces'. Music provides a medium through which we can study occupation as it was taking place, rather than examining it retrospectively. Music also captures the makers, performers, listeners and non-participants in their diverse social roles as captors, prisoners, collaborators and bystanders.

In this chapter, literary analysis, archival and historical research and psychological interpretations are employed to understand the features and functions of music under the circumstances of internment in wartime China. By studying sonic histories of occupation, we can explore issues as broad as oppression, hegemony, hierarchy, disparity, resilience, resistance and memory. Sonic histories of occupation connect major forces shaping the modern world, such as imperialism and colonialism, and individualized experiences including capitulation, abandonment, appeasement, submission, acquiescence, endurance and resistance. In addition, the study of 'sonic occupation' offers us a venue in which to examine inequality and empowerment, including but not limited to race, gender, class, ability, sexuality, language and nationality. Music functioned in many ways under occupation. It was an expression of identity, as well as a common language that could both bridge and enlarge sociocultural, political and economic gaps.

Music of faith

Internees began to arrive at Weihsien Internment Camp in late March of 1943. Eventually, over 2,000 Allied prisoners would be squeezed into this space of 150 by 200 yards (approximately 137 metres by 182 metres). Internees found themselves in barren rooms behind barrier walls with electrified wires and guard towers. Among the interned were some 800 British citizens, 600 Americans, 250 Dutch citizens, 250 Belgians, some Greeks, some Russians (mainly spouses of British and American men) and one Norwegian. Among this group were about 1,000 missionaries, with approximately 600 Catholics and 400 Protestants. The remaining 1,000 were Allied citizens who had been working in China at the time of the attack on Pearl Harbor. In terms of age, there were about 400 internees over 60 years old and about 400 under 15 years of age (Langdon 1966: 20–1). The Japanese left it to internees themselves to do all the manual labour of the camp, such as pumping and boiling water, cooking, cleaning and laundry duties.

The Japanese authorities only supplied internees with two small meals a day. Breakfast was dry bread soaked in hot water with Chinese leeks and tea. Dinner was stew, bread and tea. As a result of the scanty portions and heavy manual labour, hunger began to spread (Wolf 1990: 175–6). Sister Wibora Muehlenbein, OSB, recollected in her memoirs that 'We were always hungry. People were dropping pounds without the worry of modern diets. Also, sanitary conditions – aside from the problem of contaminated water – were such that dysentery and other intestinal diseases were soon common. We needed more food – more nutritious food – and better sanitary conditions under which to prepare it' (Muehlenbein 1962: 163). Sister Ann Colette Wolf, SP, described the scarcity of food in her book *Against All Odds: Sisters of Providence Mission to the Chinese*: 'All those who had eggs saved the shells so that they could be washed, dried, and pounded into powder. This powder was mixed with food to supply the needed calcium in the body' (1990: 179).

Although the situation was harsh, the missionaries in the camp actively participated in musical performances and productions. Christians believe that a liturgical song has a pre-eminent place in the *ars celebrandi*, for not only is it a means of active participation but it is another source of power. In adversity, the religious at the camp turned to song and music with even more intensity, which in turn created an extraordinary auditory experience for singers as well as listeners. Herbert Hudson Taylor, a leader of the China Inland Mission, was 80 years old when Pearl Harbor was attacked. In his two-and-a-half-year internment at Weihsien, early each morning his fellow internees would hear him sing, 'Courage, brother, do not stumble; though the path be dark as night. There's a star to guide the humble, trust in God and do the right' (Taylor n.d.). His singing, which was a natural expression of his faith, carried a message of courage to his fellow internees and was mentioned in several memoirs.

The Japanese guards allowed music for several reasons. First of all, Weihsien was a civilian camp, and no captured military personnel or intelligence officers were held there. The purpose of the camp was not to exterminate such captives but to isolate them and potentially use them in exchange for the release of Japanese citizens. Second, the initial commandant of the camp was Lieutenant Colonel Jimbo Nobuhiko – a Catholic. Unlike some commandants in other Japanese internment camps, Jimbo showed more restraint at Weihsien. Before being assigned as head of the camp, he had been part of the Imperial Japanese Army occupying the Philippines. Due to his refusal to carry out an order to execute Manuel Roxas,[2] Jimbo had been threatened with court martial. He was later transferred to Weihsien as punishment (Ocampo 2018). Although Jimbo rejected the internees' request for more provisions at the camp canteens, he showed more restraint in using intimidation and punishment compared to his counterparts in similar camps (such as Stanley Camp in Hong Kong). Finally, the Japanese intended to use Weihsien as their 'model camp' for publicity purposes. The encouragement of certain sounds at the camp was therefore one way for them to create the image that they were competent operators of well-managed 'civilian assembly centres'. For instance, when there were external visitors to Weihsien, they would let interned children in the camp do the headcount in Japanese. The innocent voices of children counting in Japanese presented a seemingly harmonious scene to visitors (Previte 1985).

Missionaries in the camp kept their hopes and spirits alive by invoking the power of sound: singing hymns at Mass, chanting and praying. Sometimes they even added a sense of humour to their songs. Sister Francetta Vetter recalled how 'We had vegetables, the ever-present bean sprouts. The bean sprouts were so prevalent that one of the great missionaries composed a little song, and the refrain of this song was "All things do have an end; only bean sprouts are without end'" (Vetter *c.* 1955–8).

The primary location of liturgical music was the camp's assembly hall, which had a seating capacity of about 500 people. Every morning, priests offered a large number of Masses there: daily Masses began at about 5.00 am and continued until the 7.30 am roll-call. Fourteen altars were set up in the assembly hall, but they were insufficient in accommodating more than 300 priests and bishops. Many priests said Mass in their rooms. They placed a board on their beds, covering it with a small linen cloth to use as a makeshift altar. Each congregation of sisters also had 'altars' set up in their rooms, so that the priests were able to celebrate Mass daily (Wolf 1990: 179).

Some Masses were so galvanizing that they left a long-lasting impression on both singers and listeners. Years later, when missionaries took up the pen to recount their lives in the camp, many described in detail the uplifting effects of religious singing. Sister Francis de Sales, SP, recounted the High Mass on the first Sunday after the internees arrived at the camp:

> When the Mass began, one of the Belgian priests, director of the choir at Tatung Regional Seminary, mounted the sanctuary step and lifted his hand as the signal for the congregation to begin. It was a thrilling moment. Without any practice, missionaries from Europe and America here in Asia lifted up their voices and sang in beautiful tones, perfect rhythm and accent, the Mass of Angels. Here was the one, holy, Catholic and apostolic church in action. Non-Catholics spoke, even after months of seeing the weekly Catholic ceremonies, of the impression that first High Mass in camp made on them. (Wolf 1990: 179)

The power of ecumenism was also displayed in their Sunday Masses as Sister Muehlenbein (1980: 168) recounted in her memoir:

> Our Sunday Mass was always as solemn as possible. Usually one of the six bishops present in the camp officiated with the other five, in all their regalia, on the stage which served as sanctuary. The Scheut Fathers took charge of the singing. Their Christus Vincit was truly raising the roof right off the building. Every Sunday found the windows crowded with non-catholics [*sic*] who said only one word when we came out from the service, 'Beautiful'. Several conversions among the internees resulted.

Internment brought different styles of religious music together. This confluence enabled listeners to experience a variety of liturgical and religious musical traditions. Seeing non-Catholics gathered around the church windows, Sister

Muehlenbein was proud of the awe-inspiring music of her Catholic faith. In her opinion, the experience of listening was so impressive for the non-Catholic audience in the camp that it played a decisive role in the conversion of several of them. In this case, music was not only a way to sustain the faith of the Catholic religious in the camp but also a magnet to draw non-believers to their religion, thereby ultimately fulfilling their mission's call (i.e. conversion to Catholicism).

Music of faith was sung not only by the adult missionaries but also by children at Weihsien. Mary Taylor Previte's *Songs of Salvation at Weihsien Prison Camp* (1985) captures the important role music played in children's lives. As a daughter of inland missionaries, Previte had been studying at Chefoo School in Shandong Province. After Pearl Harbor, this school was taken over by the Japanese and turned into a military centre. Students were first put into a concentration camp on Temple Hill in Chefoo. In September 1943, the staff and students were relocated to Weihsien, where they remained until the end of the Second World War. The situation was grim: 'Separated from our parents, we found ourselves crammed into a world of gut-wrenching hunger, guard dogs, bayonet drills, prisoner numbers and badges, daily roll calls, bed bugs, flies, and unspeakable sanitation' (Previte 1985). However, thanks to the uplifting environment created by the adults around them, children's memories of their years in Weihsien were not purely about the cruelty of war; this was also 'a story of heroes, a story of hope, a story of triumph' (Previte 2005).

In a 2014 interview with *This American Life*, 82-year-old Mary Previte reflected on how the music of faith shaped her formative years:

> It was like you weren't going to be afraid if you could sing about it. We would sing, (SINGING) 'Day is done'. Gone the sun from the sea, from the hills, from the sky. All is well, safely rest. God is nigh. How could you be afraid when you're singing about all is well, safely rest, God is nigh? How could you be afraid of that? So we were constantly putting things into music. (*This American Life* n.d.)

Music of resilience

In tandem with religious music that called for faith and courage, there was a wide variety of secular music in the form of concerts, choirs, dramatic performances and operas at Weihsien. A large proportion of this music was organized by the Entertainment Committee, which was composed of missionaries as well as secular internees. The establishment of the Entertainment Committee (alongside committees that focused on the survival needs of the internees) testified to the importance of entertainment in the hearts of the internees. As Sears Eldredge explains, 'The most difficult time psychologically was their leisure hours between the evening meal and "Lights Out!" Some activity had to be found to fill these hours; something they could participate in, or look forward to, that would occupy their minds and prevent them from brooding on their future as POWs' (2012: 21). To Eldredge, music and theatre in these wartime camps were not entertainment but a strategy for survival.

Internees involved in the Entertainment Committee not only sent uplifting messages through music but also practised resilience and ingenuity themselves. Sister Francetta Vetter shared her recollections of the committee after the war: 'One of our sisters, Sister Ursuline, was on this committee to provide entertainment. There were a number of sisters and a number of lay people, men and women who composed a song and they also wrote music because they had very few copies' (Vetter *c*. 1955–8). Vetter recounted how the Entertainment Committee had to spend many hours copying songs and musical pieces so that all those who took part could have a copy. After many years, Sister Francetta still remembered the 'very beautiful choir' organized by the Entertainment Committee. To her, the music performances served an important purpose. As she concludes, 'In this way some of our sad moments were made very cheerful' (Vetter *c*. 1955–8).

Mary Taylor Previte (1985) also remembered the shield that musical activities created for them in the camp:

> Someone found a battered piano mouldering in the church basement and made it the centrepiece of a 22-piece symphonette. It was a glorious combination – brass by the Salvation Army band, woodwinds by the Tientsin Dance Band, and violins and cellos by assorted private citizens.... There was also a choral society that sang classical songs and madrigals – Handel's *The Messiah*, Mendelssohn's *Elijah* and Stainer's *The Crucifixion*. And yet another group of prisoners organized a sophisticated drama society, whose ultimate triumph was its production of George Bernard Shaw's *Androcles and the Lion*. To costume 10 Roman guards with armor and helmets, stage hands soldered together tin cans from the Red Cross food parcels. . . . The church was always jammed for these performances. It was our escape from the police dogs, barbed wire barriers, stinking latrines and gnawing hunger.

Mary Taylor Previte's account throws light on the ingenuity of the internees. Alongside the active choral society, a drama society creatively recycled tin cans from Red Cross food parcels to make Roman guard costumes to be used in performances. Greg Leck, in his *Captives of Empires*, quoted an internee called Marie Regier, who recounted:

Shaw's *Androcles and the Lion* was produced, a play which the amateur club of Tientsin would have discarded as requiring too expensive a setting. Not so at Weihsien. Every soldier was enveloped in a perfect suit of armor created out of Red Cross tins invisibly welded together while Red Cross cartons piled on top of each other gave the illusion of Roman pillars. (Leck 2006: 273)

A Weihsien Dramatic Club poster designed by Jacqueline De St. Hubert advertised 'Red, Hot, Blue: A Nonstop Vaudeville', which was held on 31 March and 1 April 1944. The programme for this performance was suitably colourful. It included an 'Introduction', a 'Page from History', 'Hula', 'Ignorance is Bliss', 'Waltz', 'Song', 'Pettin' in the Park in Paree', 'Shades of Hawaii', 'French Cancan', 'Duologue', 'Rhumba, Adapted from the French' and a 'Finale'. This vaudeville performance provided an escape from the harsh realities of camp life. It also shows the internees' desire for a peaceful world in which they could resume lives filled with colour and joviality.[3]

In addition to producing posters to advertise such performances, the internees composed lyrics depicting camp life. Resilience and hope shine through in the lyrics of all of these songs. For example, an internee whose name has been lost with the passing of time wrote a song titled 'The Weihsien Chorus' to the tune of Solomon Levi:

Oh the joys of Weihsien! Oh the Weihsien day!
Good old Weihsien, tra-la-la-la-la-la-la!
We rise in the dark, and light the fires with coal that's really rocks,
We carry the water, collect the porridge, and empty the garbage box.
They cry 'puhsing' at everything, we smile and shout 'hooray'.
We'll live to see another year, and another Christmas Day.
And now we've come to the end of the song, and we hope it won't be long
Until we leave this Weihsien Camp – in that we can't be wrong.
So let's decide before we go that we will always strive
To whistle and sing a merry song in nineteen forty five.[4]

This song, possibly written for Christmas 1944, captures the optimism in the camp. As Greg Leck eloquently surmises (2006: 282):

concerts and plays fostered a community spirit, and helped provide relaxation and fun. They provided diversions from the dreary, and sometimes suffocating, atmosphere of the camp. They could be uplifting [. . .] In addition to serving as a diversion and temporary escape from camp life, such entertainments also served as reminders that there was another world, one of refined living and conveniences, and enjoyment.

Other songs had a more humorous spin. 'Weihsien's Sure a Dandy Place' is a case in point:

> Weihsien's sure a hungry place,
> I like it awfully well,
> You wait in queue eternally,
> And only get a smell . . .
> Weihsien's sure a sumptuous place,
> With kitchens only three,
> And when you've gone in all of these,
> There's nil for you and me . . .
> Weihsien's sure a newsy place,
> I like it more and more,
> With rumours, whispers that you hear,
> You know less than before. (Leck 2006: 278)

This song depicts the harsh conditions at Weihsien: the scarcity of food, long queues, limited cooking facilities, rumours and gossip. Its clever use of contrasting phrases such as 'dandy' with 'awful', and 'sumptuous' with 'nil', creates a satirical effect. The internees, after a long day's work, could relate to the details in the song and felt validated and pleased by its satire.

The 'Weihsien Camp Song' (with lyrics by Nancy Cochran and music by Solomon Levi) is another good example of this humorous and light-hearted spirit. The song portrays the dramatically changed lives of the secular internees of the camp. Former high-ranking executives of international companies now had to engage in back-breaking manual labour:

> We used to be executives who labored with our brains,
> With secretaries neat and quick to spare us many pains.
> And when the ticker tape gave out we didn't touch a thing,
> The office staff could tend to that, we did the ordering.
> *Chorus*
> But now we're in Weihsien
> Nothing's too dirty to do
> Slops, pots or garbage or stirring a vegetable stew
> To shine in this delightful camp, you join the labor corps
> Where, if you do your work too well, they work you more and more.
> For since we've come to Weihsien camp they've worked us till we're dead
> Though now we're called the labor corps, we'll be a corpse instead.
> *Baker*
> Some say that white's a color pure so baking should be chaste

So now you see me plastered up from head to foot in paste.
But since Cordell's supporting us the bakery can go
For now the comfort money's come, why should we raise the dough!
Butcher
I used to take my steak well done. I could not stand it rare,
But now whene're the cows come home, the blood gets in hair.
We call it roast or steak or chops, but when the cookings through
No matter how we cut it up, it all turns into stew.
Stoker
If mama just could see me now, she wouldn't know her boy
My rosy cheeks and golden locks were once her pride and joy
But stoking fires and hauling coal have crusted me with jet
Though ladies may prefer us blondes, alas I'm now brunette.
Officer
I thought I'd take an office job to spare my lily hands
And so I signed with the police and issued my commands
But when police began to count they put me on the shelf
For though I counted everyone I clean forgot myself.
Ladies
You'd think to hear these fellows sing, the men do all the work
But I am here to tell you now, the ladies never shirk.
We clean the leeks, we scrub the floors but then, what really hurts
When they have done the dirty work, we have to wash their shirts.[5]

Set to a blues tune, the 'Weihsien Camp Song' was comical and jolly. In it, the internees marvelled at their change of fate from privileged executives to manual labourers. The jovial and self-deprecating depictions of camp life inherent in such songs also offered a new lens for reflecting on lives that had been disrupted by war. Through such a lens, seemingly insoluble struggles took on a sense of chance or serendipity and therefore seemed less malicious and overwhelming. For many internees, this realization could break the grip of self-pity, stress and depression.

Music of resistance

Resistance to imprisonment existed in many forms at Weihsien Camp. There were a small number of escapes from the camp, for example, while one internee, Father Raymond J. de Jaegher, hid messages in pails of human refuse that were shared with anti-Japanese resistance guerrillas outside the camp (de Jaegher

1969: 238). In addition, however, internees demonstrated resistance by defying camp regulations and by spreading forbidden messages. Music became an important tool through which such defiance and resistance could be displayed.

One of the best-known instances of resistance through music could be found in the underground black market. As starvation threatened the well-being of the internees – especially those who were ill or frail – some internees decided to take matters into their own hands. Among them were several Trappist monks who lived in a section of the camp where mounds of earth were piled against the wall. Sister Ann Colette Wolf fondly recalled several 'black-market heroes' in her biography (1990: 177–8). The monks cleverly used chants, prayers and songs to hide black-market activities from the watchful eyes of Japanese sentries. Standing on the mound, a monk would pry loose a few bricks to create a small hole in the wall through which eggs, peanuts, sugar and money could be passed. If a Japanese guard happened to pass the area, two Trappist friends further down the line would begin a Gregorian chant. At this signal, the monk near the brick wall would quickly cover the items that were being passed through the wall with his long robe. By the time the Japanese guard had reached him, the monk would be kneeling, deep in prayer (1990: 177).

Among such 'black-market heroes', Father Scanlan, a British Trappist, was the most brave and ingenious in using music as a way to defy Japanese guards. Sister Ann Colette Wolf in *Against All Odds* recounts Father Scanlan's early morning singing:

> On one occasion Scanlan was caught by the Japanese guards. He was condemned to two weeks of solitary confinement in a small shed near the officers' quarters. Scanlan was supposed to exist on bread and water. About the sixth night after Scanlan was imprisoned, he arose at 2 a.m. and began chanting the morning prayer in a very loud voice. One of the Japanese officials, disturbed by the loudness, told him to stop chanting. But Scanlan told him the monks always chant their morning Prayer at 2 a.m. and he had to do it. Scanlan was released after eight days in prison. The first time he appeared in the dining room after release, he received a thunderous ovation. Hundreds of people stood up, clapped enthusiastically, and spontaneously sang, 'For he's a jolly good fellow.' (1990: 178)

The internees' appreciation of Father Scanlan's bravery did not stop there. For the camp's first Independence Day celebration in 1943, internees created a song inspired by Father Scanlan's solitary confinement experience:

> Many thanks to my friends, your good wishes
> Flooded my lonely cell yesterday

Oh why can't I swim like the fishes,
So the rain could have washed me away
But confinement has some compensation
I'm not in a rush to be free,
Before it was Tsingtao that fed me
Now my food comes from dining room three.
The scene that I have from my window
A pasture where cattle do browse,
So how can a fellow be lonely
When the girls come to visit the cows.
The Fourth was in honour of freedom
Which is what I have anything but.
Oh, give me eggs when I need them
And I'll gladly sit tight in my hut.

OH, I hope that the time passes swiftly,
And I will be seeing you soon
Then you'll find me right back in the harness
By the light of the silvery moon. (Henshaw 2012: 158)

On other occasions, the internees displayed resistance by ridiculing the camp's policies through musical performances. Sitting in the front rows, the guards were present at all the entertainment events. They may well have been curious about Western-style entertainment, but by attending, they were able to monitor the performances closely. Although the Japanese made it clear that any ridicule of the camp's policies would not be tolerated, the internees sometimes took risks to challenge this proviso. On one occasion, the Entertainment Committee put on a parody based on an English poem. In this parody, a father pursued his eloping daughter. He held out an egg as an inducement for his daughter to return to him. When that failed, he held out two eggs. Watching this, the internees burst into laughter because this plot insinuated and ridiculed the camp's stinginess in providing basic products such as eggs despite the internees' repeated pleas. Watching the laughing audience, the Japanese guards in the audience were seriously offended, and the internees almost lost their right to put on such performances thereafter (Muehlenbein 1962: 166).

Similarly, internees used music to convey forbidden messages to their fellow internees. Although no radios were allowed in the camp, a few internees secretly manufactured radios from scraps, often picking up news from Tokyo. Nicholas Mihailoff was one such internee. Before internment, Mihailoff had worked at the Tientsin British Motor Corporation. In Weihsien, he repaired Japanese radios.

By stealing spare parts, Mihailoff was able to assemble a working receiver. He hid this but passed on the news that he heard from his radio to trusted fellow internees. One Friday night in July 1943, a whisper travelled rapidly around the camp that Sicily had fallen to the Allies. The song leader in charge of the singing group kept singing the tune 'Santa Lucia' over and over again. When the song leader was sure the internees knew the message, he changed the words 'Santa Lucia' at the end of the chorus to 'Goodbye, Sicilia'. Everyone enthusiastically joined in the singing, much to the consternation of the guards (Wolf 1990: 181).

In addition to these planned acts of choral resistance, other incidents of defiance and resistance occurred spontaneously. Although patriotic songs and national anthems were forbidden, sometimes circumstances led the internees to sing their favourite song, such as 'God Bless America'. Ida Talbot noted one such incident in her diary on 4 July 1943. On that Independence Day, a section of the camp's wall collapsed after days of heavy rain. 'People just keep on Massing to see the broken wall and to look out onto freedom. Then people sang "God bless America". It is very touching time, and how we longed with all our hearts that this was all over.' The Japanese were the last ones to know, then they brought over a bale of barbed wire. The collapse of the prison wall on Independence Day looked like an omen of freedom to many. Some priests from America dressed up in blue shirts, white pants and red ties. Some even wore the letter 'V' on their clothing. Sitting on the stage in the assembly hall, they sang patriotic songs. Ida writes, 'At God Bless America, the Stars & Stripes was unfurled. It was impressive. What a day!' (Talbot n.d.)

In *Captives of Empire*, Greg Leck (2006) recounts a similar spontaneous burst of singing. In July 1945, the Weihsien Dramatic Club presented its annual song, dance and skit revue – 'Red, Hot and Blue'. 'The euphoria at this point in time was so great at the final curtain, the entire audience spontaneously arose to sing *God Save the King* and *God Bless America*.'

Each time the internees defied their captors, there were risks. One significant event which risked the wrath of the Japanese guards occurred on 5 May 1945 – the day of the German surrender. A daring internee utilized sound to celebrate this event, tolling a bell in the camp to convey this forbidden message to his fellow internees. As Norman Cliff recollected: 'Just before 11-p.m. the startling sound of a tolling bell customarily used as the signal for roll-call, broke the stillness of the night and aroused the sleeping community. This was followed at a short interval by scurrying feet racing round the alleys, and the raucous sound of agitated Japanese voices and then the wail of a siren' (Cliff 1945). The internees were gathered for a roll-call, standing for more than an hour in the cold of the early morning. The Japanese withheld the internees' food rations for a week before the ringer turned himself in. Peter Fox, hearing the good news of Nazi Germany's surrender over the homemade radio, rang the bell in celebration. In his confession, he stated: 'The bell was rung by me last Saturday night as an expression of joy & thanksgiving for peace in Europe. I regret any unforeseen inconvenience caused to anyone' (Cliff 1945).

The best example illustrating Weihsien's ingenuity in employing sound and music for the purpose of resistance is probably the Salvation Army Band. According to Peter Bazire, in early 1943, upon hearing the news that the Salvation Army was to be moved from Peking to Weihsien, Brigadier Leonard Stranks cycled around and asked people to bring musical instruments to Weihsien. He put some brass instruments between mattresses and tied them together in pairs to protect them. In the spring of 1943, Brigadier Stranks put together the Salvation Army Band soon after their arrival at Weihsien. Brigadier Stranks served as the conductor and he also played the E flat bass. The band practised on Tuesday evenings in the sewing room and played three times a week at meetings or in the open air (Bazire n.d.). Marcy Ditmanson, daughter of Brigadier Stranks, recorded the band's roles in celebrating 4 July 1944:

> We've celebrated the 'Fourth' with a full day's program of athletic, religious and social events, with the whole community, regardless of nationality, either participating in or enjoying the goings-on. We had to have permission, of course, for the celeb(ration). . . . We had a special church service at 11:45, well attended by both Am(ericans) and Brit(ish). The band played. Most of the selections we played, (Am)erican[s] were instrumented in camp: 'Star Spangled Banner', 'O Beautiful for Spacious Skies' 'God Bless America', ... The (base)ball game in the evening was between the Am(ericans) and the (Brit)ish [. . .] At the close of the game we played 'God Bless Am(erica)' and 'My Country, 'tis of Thee'. All the spectators, numbering 5-6 hundred, I suppose, stood at attention as we played the latter piece. It was a most impressive moment. To the Br(itish), of course, we were playing their nat'l anthem; to the Americans one of the best-loved patriotic hymns. (Bazire n.d.)

The next day, Marcy Ditmanson's diary records: 'There have been some repercussions from yesterday's celebrations.' 'My Country, 'tis of Thee' was an American patriotic song, but the Japanese objected to the Salvation Army Band playing 'national anthems'. Brigadier Stranks responded that neither of these songs were national anthems, betting on the guards' ignorance of the history of 'My Country, 'tis of Thee'. However, as 'My Country, 'tis of Thee' shared the same melody as 'God Save the King', Britons in the camp stood to attention in honour of their national anthem when hearing it. In the end, Stranks was warned by Schmidt, head of Weihsien's Disciplinary Committee, not to play any more patriotic airs (Bazire n.d.).

As captives living in a compound enclosed with barbed wire and watchtowers, internees had few options to express their complaints, protests and resistance. As Greg Leck argues, 'Most resistance could only take the form of opportunistic, symbolic, or token acts designed to be a psychological boost. Anything more overt or forceful would gain nothing and only invoke the wrath of the Japanese' (Leck 2006: 347). The Salvation Army Band was ingenious in that it not only cleverly negotiated with the guards to keep performing patriotic songs but also invented a 'Victory Medley'. By jumbling tunes together and omitting the top lines, the band was able to practise a Victory Medley that included the national anthems of all the Allied forces represented in the camp. According to Peter Bazire (n.d.), in the summer of 1945, the Salvation Army Band 'began practicing the national anthems of all the countries represented in the camp, but NOT the top line, so as not to arouse the suspicion of our guards. These tunes were arranged as a medley by a band member'.[6] Mary Taylor Previte, in *Songs of Salvation*, also mentioned this Victory Medley. This was a joyful mix of four Allied national anthems – American, English, Chinese and Russian, sandwiched between triumphant hymns of the church – 'Onward, Christian Soldiers', 'Rise Up, O Men of God' and 'Battle Hymn of the Republic'. This Victory Medley uplifted the spirits of the internees each day they practised. More importantly, it repeatedly showed the limitations of the guards in terms of their knowledge. Consequently, their resistance to the camp's rules as well as the outplaying of the Japanese guards exposed the destructibility of the guards and the Axis Powers behind them.

On 17 August 1945, the Salvation Army Band saw all their covert practice come to fruition. As Mary Taylor Previte recounts, on this day an American airplane flew lower and lower in the skies above Weihsien. Seven parachutes drifted to the ground. Waves of prisoners ran into the fields beyond the camp to look for them. They hoisted the paratroopers' leader onto their shoulders and carried him back towards the camp in triumph:

> In the distance, from a mound near the camp gate, the music of 'Happy Days Are Here Again' drifted out into the fields. It was the Salvation Army band blasting its joyful Victory Medley. When they got to 'The Star Spangled Banner', the crowd hushed . . .
>
> From up on his throne of shoulders, the young, sun-bronzed American major struggled down to a standing salute. And up on the mound by the gate, one

of the musicians in the band, a young American trombonist, crumpled to the ground and wept. (Previte 1985)

Conclusion

In the Weihsien Internment Camp, the approximately 2,000 internees were able to create a distinctive musical culture characterized by faith, resilience and courage. In their religious services, the approximately 1,000 missionaries created an auditory environment of faith where ecumenism shone through in hymns and Masses. Taking advantage of the Japanese guards' authorization of secular musical activities, the internees set up an Entertainment Committee. Under its auspices, they created a wide range of musical productions in the forms of concerts, operas and dramas. This showcased the internees' resilience and creativity under strenuous circumstances. Additionally, the internees were ingenious in availing of music to express their defiance and resistance to their captors.

As this study of the diverse musical activities in Weihsien Internment Camp reveals, music brought the prisoners reprieve from the cruel reality of their captivity and offered a reconnection to the pre-war world representing stability and normalcy. It also provided a space for the internees to process their lives in the camp, and more importantly, to share their efforts to make sense of the Japanese occupation. Living an interned life permeated by hunger, uncertainty, crowdedness and demanding labour, music had the power to draw people together, to forge a communal identity that outlasted their captivity. In a seemingly incongruous way, Weihsien became an endearing place to the makers and audience of musical activities. By October 1945, the internees were awaiting evacuation. They created their last song to the tune of 'The Old Oaken Bucket' to say farewell to Weihsien and to each other:

> How dear to our hearts are the scenes of old Weihsien
> When fond recollection presents them to view
> The court yards, the main roads, the well trodden by ways, paths
> And every loved spot where we stood in a queue
> The beautiful garden, the wide spreading shade trees
> The birds whose gay songs start the day with good cheer
> But foremost among them a holding our mem'ries
> The wonderful people that dwell with us here.
> They're folks that we eat with
> They're folks that we play with

They're folks that we live with
The best of all here.
They're preachers and teachers and doctors and nurses
Professors, musicians, and artists a few
They're blonde and brunette and ones and all in between ones
They're old ones and young ones and wee babies too
They're Catholic fathers and busy Dutch cleansers
They've fashions in headgear and gowns without end
We list to the talk that betrays many nations
But all of them now are just neighbors and friends
They're folks that we eat with
They're folks that we play with
They're folks that we live with
The best of all here.
When we are far away will mem'ries throng
Of Weihsien as we knew it in tale and song?
And as we sit imbibing ice-cold tea
Will we remember soup in kitchens three?
And as we motor o'er country wide
Think of the garbage cans we dumped outside/
No matter where we roam when once we're free
Weihsien will ever be part of you and me.
No matter where we roam when once we're free
Weihsien will ever be part of you and me.[7]

Music, as an essential and shared form of cultural practice, functioned in many ways in occupied countries during the Second World War. Music was an expression of the individual as well as communal identities. Additionally, it was a common language that could either bridge or enlarge sociocultural, political and economic gaps. The study of sonic occupation during the Second World War adds to existing conversations in the field of sound and music studies. Moreover, shifting from an ocularcentric to an auditory focus, this study of music at an internment camp sheds light on the significant role of sound and music in understanding foreign occupation and wartime camps. By contextualized analysis of diverse sounds and music created and listened to by various groups at Weihsien, this chapter is able to reveal the multifaceted employment of music by internees. Without oversimplifying the complex interplay between music and hierarchy, this chapter commends the human spirit, manifested in the faith, resilience, courage and ingenuity of various prisoners, that shone through in musical activities undertaken in the dire circumstances of oppression, occupation and persecution.

Notes

1 www.weihsien-paintings.org (accessed 7 January 2021).
2 Manuel Roxas was a speaker and general when the Philippines was occupied by Japan during the Second World War. After the war, he served as president of the Philippines from 1946 until his death in 1948.
3 Details are taken from the Dramatic Club poster drawn by Jacqueline De St. Hubert. Available online: http://www.weihsien-paintings.org/Christian_deSaintHubert/paintings/p_dramaticClub01.htm (accessed 7 January 2021).
4 Unknown, 'The Weihsien Chorus', collected by former internee Norman Cliff. Available online: http://www.weihsien-paintings.org/NormanCliff/Songs/txt_SolomonLevi.htm (accessed 7 January 2021).
5 Nancy Cochran and music by Solomon Levi, 'Weihsien Camp Song'. Available online: http://weihsien-paintings.org/TerriStewart/Songs/txt_WeUsedToBe---.htm (accessed 1 January 2021).
6 Ibid.
7 'Farewell Song at the Evacuation of Weihsien Internment Camp in October 1945'. Available online: http://weihsien-paintings.org/TerriStewart/Songs/txt_TheOldOakenBucket.htm (accessed 1 January 2021).

References

Bazire, P. (n.d.), 'The Salvation Army Band in Weihsien: 1943–1945': Available online: http://www.weihsien-paintings.org/PeterBazire/text/TheSalvationArmyBandWeihsien.htm (accessed 1 January 2021).

Cliff, N. (n.d.), 'From Norman Cliff's Scrapbooks': Available online: http://www.weihsien-paintings.org/NormanCliff (accessed 6 January 2021).

Cliff, N. (1945), 'Alarm at Weihsien: Incident of 5th May, 1945': Available online: http://www.weihsien-paintings.org/NormanCliff/Diary/BellIncident/BellIncident.html (accessed 1 January 2021).

De Jaegher, R. (1969), *The Enemy Within: An Eyewitness Account of the Communist Conquest of China*, Bombay: St. Paul Publications.

Eldredge, S. (2012), 'Wonder Bar: Music and Theatre as Strategies for Survival in a Second World War POW Hospital Camp', in G. Carr and H. Mytum (eds), *Cultural Heritage and Prisoners of War: Creativity Behind Barbed Wire*, 19–33, New York: Routledge.

Freud, S. (1962), *Civilization and Its Discontents*, trans. J. Strachey, New York: W. W. Norton and Co.

Gilbert, S. (2005), *Music in the Holocaust: Confronting Life in the Nazi Ghettos and Camps*, Oxford: Oxford University Press.

Henshaw, J. (2012), 'Beyond Collaboration and Resistance: Accommodation at the Weihsien Internment Camp, China, 1943–1945', in G. Carr and H. Mytum (eds), *Cultural Heritage and Prisoners of War: Creativity Behind Barbed Wire*, 152–68, New York: Routledge.

Langdon, G. (1966), *Shantung Compound*, New York: Harper and Row.

Leck, G. (2006), *Captives of Empire: The Japanese Internment of Allied Civilians in China, 1941–1945*, Bangor, PA: Shandy Press.

McDonald, G. (1980), *With Lamps Burning*, St Joseph, MN: Saint Benedict's Convent.

McGinnis, K. (2020), 'A Musical Reeducation: Music-Making in America's German POW Camps and the Intellectual Diversion Program', in P. Potter, C. Baade and R. Marvin (eds), *Music in World War II: Coping with Wartime in Europe and the United States*, 226–45, Bloomington: Indiana University Press.

Moore, R. (2016), *Moondani Kyema: 'Embrace the Dawn': My Story*, 2nd edn, Traralgon: Kyema Publishing.

Muehlenbein, W. (1962), Unpublished memoir manuscript, draft one, Saint Benedict's Monastery Archives, St Joseph, MN.

Muehlenbein, W. (1978), 'Midwest China Oral History Interviews' in *China Oral Histories*, 51: Available online: http://digitalcommons.luthersem.edu/china_histories /51 (accessed 6 January 2021).

Muehlenbein, W. (1980), *Benedictine Mission to China*, St Joseph, MN: Saint Benedict's Convent.

Norman, G. (n.d.), 'Poem Written on the Arrival of the Chefoo Group in Weihsien': Available online: http://www.weihsienpaintings.org/NormanCliff/Songs/txt_poem. htm (accessed 6 January 2021).

Nicolini-Zani, M. (2016), *Christian Monks on Chinese Soil: A History of Monastic Missions to China*, trans. S. Senyk and W. Skudlarek, Collegeville, MN: Liturgical Press.

Ocampo, A. (2018), 'Postwar Friendship Between Two Soldiers', *Philippine Daily Inquirer*, 31 January: Available online: https://opinion.inquirer.net/110677/postwar-f riendship-two-soldiers#ixzz5g6hmmSiV (accessed 7 January 2021).

Pander, L. (n.d.), 'Weihsien: March 1943 to October 1945': Available online: http://www .weihsien-paintings.org (accessed 6 January 2021).

Previte, M. T. (1985), 'A Song of Salvation at Weihsien Prison Camp': Available online: http://www.weihsien-paintings.org/Mprevite/inquirer/MPrevite.htm (accessed 7 January 2021).

Previte, M. T. (2005), 'Speech at Weihsien Concentration Camp Liberation 60th Anniversary Celebration', 17 August: Available online: http://www.weihsien-paint ings.org/60YearsAfter/texts/Mary_speech.htm (accessed 7 January 2021).

Previte, M. T. (2019), Unpublished interview with the author, 2 January.

Talbot, I. (n.d.), *Ms Ida Talbot's (Unabridged) Weihsien Diary*: Available online: http: //www.weihsien-paintings.org/ChSancton/diary/Diary/calendar.htm (accessed 7 January 2021).

Taylor, J. (n.d.), 'God's Faithfulness to Nine Generations', *OMF International*: Available online: https://omf.org/us/gods-faithfulness-to-nine-generations/ (accessed 7 January 2021).

This American Life (n.d.), Interview of Mary Taylor Previte, Episode 559: Captain's Log: Available online: https://www.thisamericanlife.org/559/transcript (accessed 1 January 2021).

Vetter, F. (*c.* 1955–58), 'Sister Francetta Vetter: Oral History Tape Interview, Tokyo, Japan', transcript, Saint Benedict's Monastery Archives, St Joseph, MN.

Wolf, A. (1990), *Against All Odds: Sisters of Providence Mission to the Chinese, 1920–1990*, Saint Mary-of-the-Woods, IN: Saint Mary-of-the-Woods.

Part II

Memory, sound and occupation

Introduction to Part II

Jeremy E. Taylor

Part II of *Sonic Histories of Occupation* is entitled 'Memory, sound and occupation'. The three chapters included here address the role of sound in reconciling communities to shared histories of conflict, colonialism and/or occupation, using methodologies that engage with Indigenous knowledge systems, ethnography and community-based research.

In each case, the notion of 'occupation' is interpreted quite differently. Magowan, Donaghey and McNelis, for instance, note the controversies inherent in the application of the word 'occupation' to the Northern Ireland context. Instead, they stress the potential for new technologies such as StoryMap for the 'retelling of occupation as a productive and emergent presence rather than simply rewriting history in two-dimensional terms'. In contrast, Sliwoski draws on the burgeoning research on military bases as sites of Cold War 'occupation' in his chapter on the US naval base in Subic Bay in the Philippines and the neighbouring Olongapo City. For Sliwoski, sound remains one of the untouched topics in such scholarship, despite (as he shows) the constant references to sound in the accounts of Americans and local Filipinos who lived in Subic Bay and/or Olongapo during the time of the base's operations. Hatfield's final chapter in this part – in keeping with a growing body of research on Indigenous peoples in Taiwan – understands 'occupation' as a recurring situation for the Cepo' Pangcah (sometimes referred to as 'Amis People), having been subject to Han Chinese settler colonialism, Japanese colonial control, the arrival of the Nationalist Chinese authorities on Taiwan after 1945 and the continuing presence of private corporations eager to open up Taiwan's Pacific coast to international tourism.

Despite these very different interpretations and uses of the notion of 'occupation', all chapters seek to explore either how sound is deployed as a means of responding to past trauma or how the memory of conflict, invasion or occupation is itself endowed with sonic qualities. For Magowan, Donaghey and McNelis, 'the ambiguity of sound is particularly potent for enabling sonic memories from the past to be connected with, yet simultaneously displaced by and/or resonant with the sonic present'; sound, in other words, offers a means through which the memory of a difficult past and a divided society (or, indeed, divided memories of a shared past) can be managed. For Sliwoski, 'the naval occupation of Philippine land . . . was structured around a military-sonic domesticity', yet such domesticity endowed memory of the base with a 'false polarity' which Sliwoski calls the 'loud town, quiet base' narrative. Occupation has the means, in other words, to change the ways in which we remember the sounds of the past. Hatfield shows how learning to listen to both the Cepo' Pangcah and their country – itself a repository of sounds endowed with memories of invasion and occupation – might help in 'decolonizing' the academic study of sound and occupation.

Part II thus offers new strategies for interpreting sound and the memory of historical conflicts, and for using sound itself as a means of addressing difficult or 'occupied' memories. In this way, these chapters address a number of this volume's core questions, including what the study of auditory environments in different geographic and temporal contexts might contribute to a better understanding of 'occupation', and how the study of the sonic histories of occupation and colonialism might contribute to the development of new research methodologies in sound studies and history.

4

Occupying new sound worlds

Debordering sonic imaginaries in StoryMaps[1]

Fiona Magowan and Jim Donaghey, with Annette McNelis

Introduction

The sight and sound of free-flowing vehicles crossing the border into Northern Ireland conjure a feeling of peacefulness, harmony and freedom. This is how people want to live.

Annette McNelis

This quote harnesses the sonic imagination in a semi-autobiographical narrative by musician Annette McNelis as she takes us on a journey across the border in the north-west of the Irish landscape. After passing through a few villages on her journey from Buncrana in County Donegal to the city of Derry/Londonderry,[2] she pauses at the invisible crossing, where her narrative conveys a sense of elation and freedom, revelling in the absence of lines and checkpoints in the landscape and in the sights and sounds of these debordered mobilities. Through her StoryMap[3] narrative, Annette invites the viewer–listener to relate to this previously 'occupied' space of conflict in new ways.

In this chapter, we explore how concepts such as occupation and debordering resonate in post-conflict Northern Ireland, particularly as reflected in the lived experience of people in post-conflict border areas. We focus on the StoryMap contribution of our co-researcher Annette, who lived through days of razor wire and surveillance tower checkpoints and now deeply appreciates the significance of free movement. This analysis grows out of some of the key questions that this volume asks: What does occupation sound like? How are sound and music implicated in the disciplining of colonized subjects and aural spaces? And what can studies of occupation contribute to developing new research methodologies and approaches to studying sound? This chapter seeks to respond in particular to the last of these questions, with particular reference to StoryMap and its 'decolonizing' research potential. However, in view of the locally contentious implications of the terms 'occupation' and 'colonization', we consider it necessary to adjust our vocabulary. However, this is more than a semantic sleight as we shall see, as a shift towards engagement with 'debordering' shapes the methodological framing in important ways and enriches our engagement with the concept of decolonization itself.

In particular, we take into account questions of how we listen to occupation and, more importantly, why we *must* listen to occupation (as per the Introduction to this volume). Our chapter illustrates that people listen to soundscapes post-occupation both as memories of previous sonic and physical conflicts, and for the release of sonic liberation in post-conflict environments. As we shall see, our co-researchers are involved in an environmental listening that reorients their 'sonic histories' to facilitate new modalities of storytelling. The sonic vibrations that our StoryMap participants experience and narrate are visceral reminders of the political conflict at borders that previously harnessed and restricted not just sound but also movement, as well as the subsequent transformation of human interconnectedness that facilitated a new cosmopolitics of belonging (Stengers 2011; Josephides and Hall 2014) across borders when they were reopened. Such a transformative process can be revelatory as it enhances alternative ways of moving across sonic landscapes, in turn forcing us to rethink what 'occupation' actually refers to. In this volume, occupation is used as a pluralizing concept. And in this chapter, we examine the multiplicity of opportunities that opening up once closed physical and sonic spaces affords for those in post-conflict settings. Through the analysis of the StoryMap, we argue that listening to sonorous environments is a dynamic and multimodal decolonizing process that can refashion the interpretation of routes and intersections criss-crossing the environment at the same time that such sounds intertwine with the more entrenched politics of materiality of rural–urban landscapes.

Decolonizing research practices

The decolonizing of research lies primarily in new forms of researcher–collaborator engagements, particularly around community-based participatory research (CBPR) processes which centre participants' experiences, memories and actions at the core of the research. These exchanges offer both unlimited potential and significant challenges in navigating the demands and expectations of the academy. On the one hand, the particular 'epistemological orientation' (Jacobson and Rugeley 2007: 24) of CBPR can promote unorthodox outputs which simultaneously confound and transcend normative academic expectations. On the other, they 'hold the potential to honour multiple communities while advancing the tenets of decolonization within educational research' (Rogers Stanton 2014: 573). In either case, engagement entails taking risks that push the boundaries of methodological inquiry. Thus, the question as to *who* produces knowledge on sound is key to our chapter, as Story Mapping is taken up through the participants' experiences and memories of their journeys across landscapes that were once conflict zones. The remaking of the landscape is most pertinently revealed by those who have been the victims of its occupation, for they understand the constraints placed on bodily practices and daily interactions within it.

The local context of Northern Ireland throws up particular complications for CBPR since the ubiquitous 'two-traditions' model necessitates a constant sensitivity to contentious issues and terminology that might be perceived as being sectarianly partisan. As a legacy of the (near-)civil war of 'the Troubles' (1969–98), the ongoing conflict is manifested especially at a cultural and *community* level, so *community*-based research comes up against this deeply divided community rubric in a very immediate and visceral sense. Even the 'decolonizing' tenets of CBPR itself come under interrogation here. The concepts (and experiences) of conquest have had clear resonances across the island of Ireland throughout the last millennium. Occupation and colonization have a history extending back to the Anglo-Norman invasion of Ireland in the twelfth century but are perhaps most poignantly exemplified by the English 'plantations' of Ireland from the 1550s onwards. In our own research context in the North, the Plantation of Ulster from the early 1600s onwards continues to have profound reverberations, not least in the city of Derry/Londonderry. As a result, the concepts of 'conquest', 'occupation' and 'colonization' are highly contentious in the contemporary political landscape; their application is usually associated with Irish Nationalist/Republican discourses, which can draw parallels with anti-colonial struggles elsewhere in the world (such as in the United States, Ghana, Kenya, Zimbabwe and Cyprus – even to the extent of having a shared foe in the form of the British imperial project). These discourses are countered by British Unionist/Loyalist perspectives which view Northern Ireland (and, previous to partition in 1921, all of Ireland) as an integral part of the UK, rather than as an English or British colony.

Such opposing discourses are at the root of the national-ethno-sectarian conflict in Northern Ireland, which in turn was the underlying pretext of the murderous violence of 'the Troubles'.[4] Even in the post-conflict context, this oppositional discourse has been 'baked in' to the power-sharing institutions of the Stormont Assembly established in the Good Friday Peace Agreement of 1998. Various measures ensuring representation from both 'sides' of the ethno-national-religious divide result in sectarian identities being foregrounded, in both the legislative body and the executive itself. Some political parties, such as the People Before Profit Alliance (Trotskyist), Alliance Party (Liberal) and Green Party (environmentalist), and one independent member (ex-Alliance Party) are designated as 'other' (eleven members in total), but the vast majority of assembly members designate themselves as either 'Unionist' or 'Nationalist' (with seventy-nine members in this category, including those from the Democratic Unionist Party, Sinn Féin, the Social Democratic and Labour Party, the Ulster Unionist Party and the Traditional Unionist Voice, as well as two independent Unionists). This has significance in legislation on sensitive or contentious issues, which must receive majority support from both 'sides'. This hardening of sectarian divisions has been felt in wider society too, with polarized voting patterns, especially after 2003, and a series of 'culture war' disputes (around symbols and language) dominating the post-conflict political landscape.

In the contemporary context of persisting sectarian 'conflict' in Northern Ireland, therefore, the concepts of 'occupation' and 'decolonization' are not easy to deploy in conflict-transformation analysis, as the terminology is simply perceived as being too partisan. This presents a problem for CBPR into contemporary perspectives of the conflict in Northern Ireland that seeks to embrace the liberatory aspects of 'decolonization'.

Potential controversies around the term 'decolonization' are further evident in the scholarship. Naylor comments that a 'decolonial approach is one that recognizes the differences created by *the conquest* and perpetuated in contemporary unequal relations *between people and states*' (Naylor et al. 2018: 200, emphasis added), while Grosfoguel argues that a decolonizing approach 'forces us to look at the world from angles and points of view *critical of hegemonic perspectives*' (2002: 209, in Naylor et al. 2018: 200, emphasis added). However, in the Northern Ireland context, the 'conquest' that Naylor points to in her description of a 'decolonial approach' is fundamentally contested due to the fact that the multifaceted conflict in Northern Ireland is conceived of as being between competing hegemonies, between competing states (i.e., Ireland and the UK – and one could add Northern Ireland as a 'statelet' in its own right) *and* between competing ethno-religious groupings or 'peoples' (Catholic/Irish vs.

Protestant/British). Such 'decolonial' analysis is particularly complicated in this context and is rejected outright by one of those two polarized and competing hegemonies. So, while the core critiques of decolonization, and especially its methodological implications, resonate with our own research approaches, this unavoidable contentiousness invites exploration of other critical perspectives and methodological framings which can be utilized without the potential for alienation of one 'side' or the 'other'.

Consequently, rather than address decolonization directly, we have sought to employ innovative research methods that invite our participants to re-engage with the past by analysing the contemporary impact of their landscapes upon sense and memory in sight, sound and movement. This deep immersion in sound memories arises from 'the relationship between a specific listener and the music [or sound and their] . . . emotional reactions relating to familiarity, to texts, to previous musical associations, to previous situational associations' (Becker cited in Titon 2009: 504). In turn, this process of audition creates its own link with past experiences in the auditory imagination, bringing an earlier materiality of landscape to articulate with its altered parameters. Emotional responses to occupation and decolonization are thus deeply engrained in relationships with changing sonic memories over time. As Becker notes, '[e]motions relating to music [or sound] are culturally embedded and socially constructed and can usefully be viewed as being about an individual within a community, rather than being exclusively about internal states (1991: 151).' We will demonstrate how StoryMap provides a new methodology for articulating sonic memories and listening to new social imaginaries, enabling the narrator to enter into their own work of debordering. As we shall show in our analysis of Annette's story of border crossing, the cartographical basis of the StoryMap platform lends itself to geographically derived sensorial analyses, especially the critical strands emerging from human geography, anthropology and border studies. Thus, to unpack the complexities of these concepts, we begin first by outlining our own theoretical shift from decolonization to debordering before going on to analyse Annette's sonic border narrative.

From decolonization to debordering

Bordering (and debordering), especially in its 'action-centred' participant form, echoes much of the power relation critique of decolonization. As Werlen states, 'Bordering processes are . . . highly differentiated in respect to the economical, political and symbolic power at one's disposal in processes of world-binding as the practices of *everyday geography-making* (2005: 57). Also of use in our analysis are feminist and intersectional geographical approaches, which 'impl[y] a fresh gaze on borders and processes of bordering, understood as the continual social construction of borders by heterogeneous agents' (Bürkner 2018: 190; see also Stoetzler and Yuval-Davis 2002; Newman 2006; van Houtum and van Naerssen 2002). As Cassidy et al. argue, 'If we are to understand borderings as constructed within everyday life, we must pay attention not only to these social divisions, but also their constitution within *hierarchies of power*' (2018a: 140, emphasis added). These 'action-centred' and feminist engagements with bordering echo the critiques that emerge from decolonization while pointing to a distinct focus on the embodied and affective practices of *everyday* life. Indeed, as we shall see, the StoryMap format responds particularly effectively to the methodological implications that arise from this critique.

A key tension in feminist and action-centred border studies is between the 'intimate' and the 'global' (or between the 'everyday' and the 'geopolitical'), wherein Pratt and Rosner argue that 'the intimate is *not the opposite* of the global but its supplement or even its undoing' (2006, in Cassidy et al. 2018a: 139, emphasis added). This productive tension is also expressed in Deleuze and Guattari's concept of 'deterritorialization', which recognizes that borders are 'parts of "everything" that are both signs *and* lines' (Woodward and Jones 2005: 236, emphasis in original). So, for Deleuze and Guattari, the tension is between borders as 'signs' (i.e. subjectively interpreted/conceived) and 'lines' (cartographical/national boundaries), which could, in feminist terms, be expressed as the tension between the 'intimate' (subjective) and 'geopolitical' (material borders). Almost as if to invoke StoryMap specifically, Deleuze and Guattari write: 'What are your lines? *What map are you in the process of making or rearranging*? What abstract line will you draw, and at what price, for yourself and for others?' (Deleuze and Guattari 1987: 203, emphasis added). The productive tension between the subjective processes of bordering/debordering and the lived material experience of the national boundary or 'cartographical border' generates critical liminality and transformative potential, and the StoryMap format is an excellent medium through which to explore this tension. Like the concept of deterritorialization, this format enables 'ways of thinking about socio-spatial demarcations [that are] sufficiently capable of addressing the violence of everyday life on the border' (Woodward and Jones 2005: 237). Yet, deterritorialization also places explicit emphasis on *transformative potential* which

can be understood as an event of becoming. . . . Bordering describes a vast array
of *affective* and *transformative* material processes in which social and spatial
orders and disorders are constantly reworked. (Woodward and Jones 2005: 239,
emphasis added)

As 'deterritorialization facilitates new, inventive forms of bordering' (Woodward
and Jones 2005: 240), this process in turn entails '*transformation*' (Best 2003:
181, emphasis added) in the everyday practices and experiences that shape
new border imaginaries. Indeed, we have chosen to develop StoryMap as a
research tool because, although it re-inscribes national borders in its default
maps (sourced from OpenStreetMap),[5] it nevertheless holds great potential to
move away from (or beyond) 'methodological nationalism' (Wimmer and Glick
Schiller 2003: 599) and to take the view of participants literally from street
level, thereby realigning the formality of political borders with personalized
practices. Wimmer and Glick Schiller also make the case that '[g]oing beyond
methodological nationalism requires *analytical tools* and concepts not colored
by the self-evidence of a world ordered into nation-states' (2003: 599, emphasis
added). Instead, as Werlen notes, '[a] modern geographical representation of
the world has to take the subject into account by studying how subjects live and
realize the world, particularly *their* world, and not just live *in* a world' (2005: 57,
emphasis in original).

It is commonly acknowledged in the scholarship that the critical insights of
debordering must be accompanied by, and indeed arise from, methodological
innovation. For example, Cassidy et al. contend that 'we must attempt to explore
[borders] through the situated gazes of differentially positioned social actors
. . . embedded *in everyday life*' (2018a: 139, emphasis added). The feminist
emphasis on putting the 'everyday' at the heart of methodology is entangled with
recognition of embodiment. As Cassidy et al. put it: 'Feminists have highlighted
the ways in which bodies are not inactive agents in this process' (2018a: 140).
The queer-feminist emphasis on performativity (Butler 2009: 44) also resonates
in the view that bordering(s) '[a]s a performative process . . . invoke not only
official but also personal memories and understandings of places' (Cassidy et al.
2018b: 175; see also Green 2010).

This performativity is extended by particular kinds of sound-image
engagements with the environment made possible by StoryMap. These digital
audio-visual processes of sonic debordering go beyond textual representations
in literary criticism that have previously recognized the importance of sound in
narratives of conflict and violence. In this regard, Chute has argued that graphic
narratives 'require a rethinking of the dominant tropes of unspeakability,

invisibility and inaudibility' (2008: 93). This approach is also taken up by Brister (2014) in her discussion of audibility as it pertains to Sacco's interpretation of the sounds of occupation represented in comics relating to the Intifada in Palestine. Just as Palestine has been the subject of oppressive physical occupation that has led to 'discursive erasure and silencing in order to gain access to and control territory' (Wolfe 2006: 388), so 'Sacco's mapping of Israeli-Palestinian spaces and recording of the sonic regime of the territories are attempts to disrupt the logic of elimination and to construct an anti-colonial narrative that records occupation' (Brister 2014: 113). His graphic depictions of pain, beatings, screams and grimaces in these comics are a means of documenting 'acoustic occupation' (Titlestad 2004: 584) and are often enlivened with onomatopoeic 'acoustigrams' (Warner 2008), such as the 'Rat-tat-tat-tat' of gunfire (Brister 2014: 114).

Eeva-Kaisa Prokkola's work examines such embodied and performative engagements through a narrative lens, though she appeals for other '*methodological tools* that are sensitive to the particular everyday situations and sites where discourses are negotiated' (2014: 442, emphasis added) and for 'methodological sensitivity in the collection and analysis of individual's stories' (2014: 446). Echoing Prokkola, Varró writes there is a 'need to attend to how narratives . . . are performed and become materialised' (2016: 186), and like Deleuze and Guattari, Prokkola might almost be calling specifically for the StoryMap format when she points to the 'challenge for researchers . . . [in] finding the ways to collect and interpret interview materials in an ethically respectable manner, so that the interview stories are not (pre-)conceptualized by the interviewers and thereby subordinated' (Prokkola 2014: 443).

Debordering sounds

Our StoryMap methodology grew out of our research engagement with participants who had been enrolled on a music facilitation training programme with an international NGO, Musicians Without Borders (MWB). In the Partnership for Conflict, Crime and Security Research (PaCCS)-funded project, 'Sounding Conflict: From Resistance to Reconciliation (2017–21)', we have worked with theatre and arts practitioners, as well as musicians, to explore the effects of sound and storytelling in various protracted-conflict or post-conflict settings. One element of this research has been conducted in Derry/Londonderry, Northern Ireland, in partnership with MWB, which uses music for social change and peacebuilding and which employs a variety of approaches to creativity to assist in healing from the effects of conflict, violence or trauma.[6] Integrating a range of innovative research methodologies (Donaghey and Magowan 2021), we worked with participants on the MWB programmes to understand their emotional responses to immersive sounding and listening exercises. Following the organization's theory of change, we explored creative research methodologies that would help elicit the participants' experiences of the programme.[7] At the end of the programme, we then invited participants to contribute to our analysis by reflecting upon how their perspectives of local conflict have impacted upon and transformed their musicking practices. We invited all participants to send us audio-visual cameos of environmental and historical sonic perceptions of their localities, focusing on familiar neighbourhoods or journeys, with sound commentaries which were then arranged on the StoryMap platform.[8] This tool, developed by the Northwestern University Knight Lab, enables the co-location of audio and visual materials anchored to specific places on a cartographical map. The images of specific sites are embedded with audio recordings of sounds or videos of those places, and the viewer–listener can zoom into a particular site or move between sites across a town or region. The effect is to take the viewer–listener on a journey with the attendant sounds and movements surrounding that area, and the 'slides' of audio-visual and textual content are arranged in a linear narrative, mapped to a linear cartographical 'journey'. This design tool has enabled us 'to map out the logical sequence of [our research] initiative from inputs to outcomes' (Vogel 2012: 3), revealing a range of responses to conflict that were absent from participants' interview responses to their uses of music for peacebuilding during the facilitation programme.

As we shall show in this chapter, recalling previous conflict histories through audio-visual engagements with the materiality of sound can invite new narratives of peace. In this process, the narrator establishes a relational authorship over silences that have marked collective histories of violence locally and their resonances more widely. In sound, image and text, the viewer–listener is thus vicariously invited to reinterpret these sonic memories of past events as part of a contemporary, everyday soundscape of recorded sound bites. This process invites reflection upon the nature of temporalities past and present in the act of remapping. While it might be argued that there is a form of circularity inherent in the practice as the debordering of soundscapes are re-emplaced in digital form, the remapping tool also facilitates new kinds of temporalities to emerge as certain sounds are highlighted over others and the lines of the journey taken on the map (see Figure 4.1) become enlivened by sonic presences. In taking the reader through this journey, we use screenshots of each of the images in the

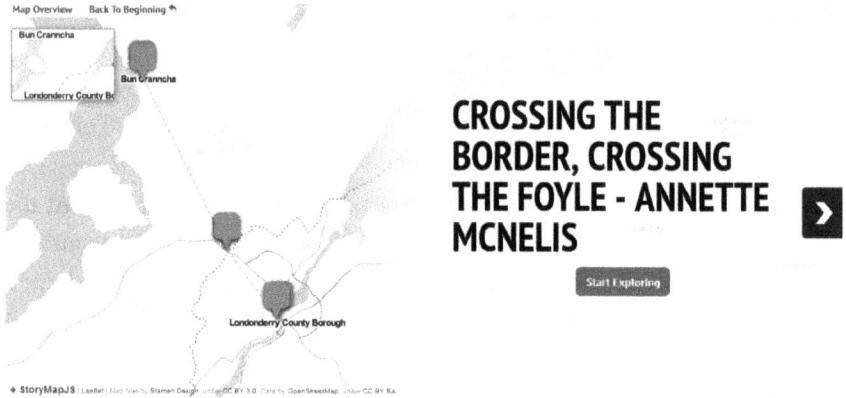

Figure 4.1 'Crossing the Border, Crossing the Foyle', StoryMap by Annette McNelis, 15 May 2018, slide 1.

StoryMap, together with Annette's textual reflections, and describe the sounds that the viewer–listener can hear in situ. Each location is its own microcosm of sound and related images, and the viewer–listener can linger as long as desired in one locale before moving to the next.

StoryMap allows for the retelling of occupation as a productive and emergent presence rather than simply rewriting history in two-dimensional terms as text. It thus overcomes some of the problems of graphic representations of sound discussed earlier relating to comic forms and instead raises wider questions about the nature of integrated textual-visual-sonic imaginaries in the processes of remembering, and how their interpretation can facilitate new kinds of place-making. In generating contemporary soundscapes that open up reflections upon past conflicts, we would contend that StoryMap invites its own form of debordering histories rather than invoking occupation which 'is a matter of seizing, delimiting and asserting control over a physical, geographical area – of writing on the ground a new set of social and spatial relations' (Mbembe 2003: 25–6). It does so, as we shall argue, by expanding the sonic imagination as a dialogical re-engagement with past violence, destruction and decay as generative of spaces that have the capacity to facilitate alternative and hopeful ways of listening to historical sites of injury. In doing so, the format of the StoryMap enables the creative construction of new kinds of sonic-visual patterns to develop and provides a medium for their analysis. Furthermore, the audio-visual semi-autobiographic excerpts that result facilitate comparative analysis of how 'textual sound', more often considered in the context of graphic narratives, is received as a sense of place by its viewer-listeners.

Close attention to sound brings places into play through the intersubjectivity of being-in-the-world as a being-with-others (Heidegger [1927] 1962), enabling the occupation of places through the social imaginary. As Lems notes in her work on migration, '[p]lace . . . is not just where we are. It is something surrounding, yet not immovable, it is something imagined, yet material, and it [is] something that gathers, yet also disseminates' (2018: 213). Kathleen Stewart further posits that '[t]he sense of place grows dense with a social imaginary – a fabulation of place contingent on precise modes of sociality and on tense, shifting social deployments of local discourses that give place a tactile, sensate force' (2006: 137). We shall see how these dynamics of the social imaginary are reshaped through the interplay of sound bites, image and text in Annette's journey.

Sonic border imaginaries from Buncrana to Derry/Londonderry

In this StoryMap, Annette McNelis invites the reader/listener to travel with her from her home in Buncrana, County Donegal, in the Republic of Ireland across the border to Derry/Londonderry in Northern Ireland (see Figure 4.1). Her first photograph is one of a peaceful, rural country setting on a rather wet and grey-looking day, as she reveals latent memories of the Troubles that are awakened by recalling her childhood in Donegal close to the border. In this first photograph, she invites us into 'deep listening' of the landscape to the sound of 'heavy rain in garden', thereby setting up the conditions for an interplay between the auditory imagination, image and recorded soundscapes (see Figure 4.2).

Figure 4.2 'Crossing the Border, Crossing the Foyle', StoryMap by Annette McNelis, 15 May 2018, slide 2.

In her text, she recounts the false sense of security to which she had become accustomed as a young child, believing that the Troubles were much more distant than on her doorstep. However, she vividly recalls the effects of conflict through her father's concern and empathy as a town councillor for those who had been displaced by the violence in Derry/Londonderry as he sought to assist and aid them in providing mattresses for them to sleep on:

> Heavy rain in the garden.
>
> As many of my fellow trainees had grown up in Northern Ireland during the height of the troubles, I had grave doubts about my right to participate on the MwB training course. Having grown up in Buncrana, close to the Border with Derry, I didn't feel my life had been affected that much by the conflict situation.
>
> When we were invited to contribute to this Soundbite Storymap my doubts re-surfaced, but on reflection I realised that the effects of this war had impacted on me much more than I had realised. I suppose it was the normality of it all that had me believing otherwise.
>
> I remember my Father, a town Councillor at the time, coming in to my Granny's house with news that more mattresses had been found for people who had fled Derry. Even as a 9-year-old I sensed that something very serious was happening. This was 1969.

Jackson argues that being-in-the-world is both 'relational' and 'continually at risk' (2005: xiv). This risk is evident as Annette's memories of conflict unfold in realizing her ongoing fear of particular border places, where she recalls violent acts such as brutal murders while, less than 20 miles away across the border, sounds of exploding bombs pervade her auditory imagination and memories of being a student in college in the 1970s (see Figure 4.3).

Karen Blu has discussed the ambiguities of border imaginaries in Native American contexts that felt the effects of the Civil War and which eventually led to the decimation of Native American hunting grounds through encroachment from farming and railroads. She posits that 'names of places, provide openings to multiple interpretations, entries into a variety of imaginings' (Blu 1996: 201–2). In such 'variety of imaginings' and emergent memories, we find 'the space of appearances', which may be alternative re-readings of place – 'where that which is *in potentia* becomes *in presentia* – disclosed, drawn out, brought forth, given presence or embodied' (Jackson 2005: xiv). For Annette, the realization of fear of these sounds of the past means that the border takes on an ominous presence for her in dreams at night-time, pervading the psyche and rendering the anticipation of violence an ever-present potentiality. Indeed, in their research along another

Figure 4.3 'Crossing the Border, Crossing the Foyle', StoryMap by Annette McNelis, 15 May 2018, slide 3.

border county in south Armagh, Hastings Donnan and Kirk Simpson (2007) note that in the 1970s and 1980s, the fear of speaking out about violence in border areas was deeply embedded in the fear of intimidation from neighbours. They analyse how 'speaking with a "softer voice" reflects the reality of the context in which south Armagh Protestants live, a minority who must regulate their behaviours and modify their attitudes so as not to give offence or reveal their fears' (Donnan and Simpson 2007: 9).

> Heavy rain in the garden [sound bite]
> The brutal murder of a young local couple in the early '70s, just outside Muff, left me with a dread of travelling to this village, for years afterwards.
> As a student at the North West Regional College during the '70s I heard bombs explode close by and trips to Dublin via Aughnacloy occasionally triggered bad dreams because of a fear of the unfamiliar Border crossing.
> The impact of the Omagh Bomb on the Buncrana community has been well documented. I organized the music for the town's memorial service to mark the first Anniversary. The experience affected me deeply.
> Listening to the sound of heavy rain recently made me think of the ripple effect of war. Rain can fall, flow then trickle and seep everywhere. Reflecting on my personal experience has made me wonder how far-reaching have been the toxic effects of this war.
> Despite getting too many damp days in Donegal there are times when I love the fresh, clear sound of falling rain. The beauty of where I live can still shine through a heavy downpour, just as the warmth and goodness of ordinary people can brighten communities during difficult times.
> Border traffic [bus sound bite]

> I would be a rich woman if I had pound for every journey I have made into Derry. I used to dread the checkpoints at the Border, especially at the height of the troubles.
>
> As a young teenager I found it particularly worrying when travelling by bus. I found it nerve wracking whenever the bus was boarded by armed soldiers. It was particularly tense if a soldier walked down the aisle of the bus checking between seats and studying the passengers.
>
> When travelling by car there was always the worry that car might be searched, with some random, innocent item in the boot being considered suspicious, resulting in your being taken in for questioning – a scary possibility! Fortunately it never happened to me.

As we continue our journey with Annette from Buncrana towards and across the border to Derry/Londonderry, her memories return to the sense of dread associated with border checkpoints and the fear of armed soldiers boarding the bus when travelling to school to check for suspicious objects or passengers. However, just as places can be ambiguously and multifariously reconstituted, so, too, do sounds allow the re-imagination of places to be otherwise (see Figures 4.4 and 4.5).

As we listen to the sound bite of heavy rain associated with the former journey, the immersive sounds of flowing water 'trickle' and 'seep everywhere' (Figure 4.3). Annette's sensitive reflections upon the inescapable sounds of conflict have the potential to drench the auditory imagination of the listener in multifarious ways, according to local knowledge and experiences of this border area.

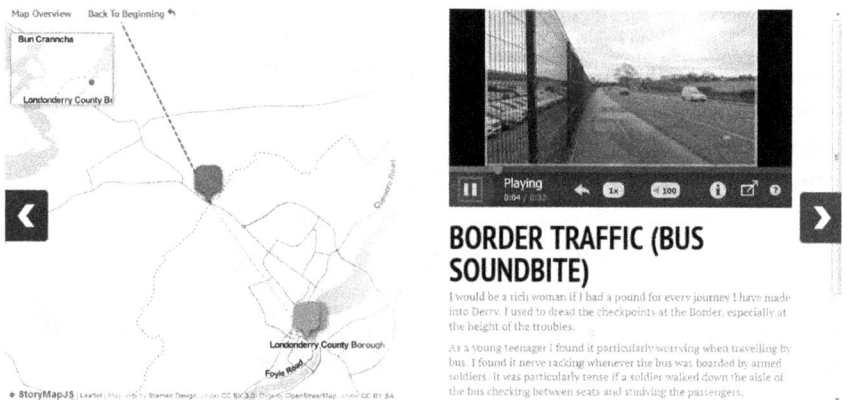

Figure 4.4 'Crossing the Border, Crossing the Foyle', StoryMap by Annette McNelis, 15 May 2018, slide 4.

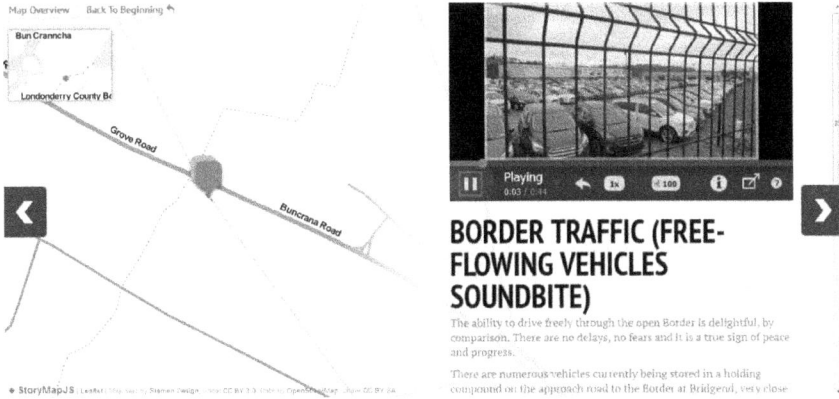

Figure 4.5 'Crossing the Border, Crossing the Foyle', StoryMap by Annette McNelis, 15 May 2018, slide 5.

Border traffic [free-flowing vehicles sound bite]

The ability to drive freely through the open Border is delightful, by comparison. There are no delays, no fears and it is a true sign of peace and progress.

There are numerous vehicles currently being stored in a holding compound on the approach road to the Border at Bridgend, very close to where the checkpoint had been. This could never have been a possibility during the troubles. I like how the image of the stationary cars contrasts with the movement of the free-flowing traffic, which is now the norm of this stretch of road today.

The result of the Brexit referendum came as a huge shock to me. The uncertainty of this situation currently had people on both sides of the Border holding their breath. I have not encountered one person who wants a hard-border situation.

The sight and sound of free-flowing vehicles crossing the Border into Northern Ireland conjure a feeling of peacefulness, harmony and freedom. This is how people want to live.

These reminiscences further prompted memories for Annette. She was a member of the committee that organized Buncrana's 1999 first anniversary of the Omagh bomb. The Omagh bomb of 15 August 1998 was the largest single atrocity causing loss of life in Northern Ireland in which thirty-one people were killed, among whom were unborn twins. More than 250 people were injured. Buncrana lost five young people that day, Oran Doherty (8 years old), Sean McLaughlin (12 years old), James Barker (12 years old), Fernando Blasco Baselga (12 years old) and Rocio Abad Ramous (23 years old). Fernando and Rocio, from Madrid, had been part of a Spanish exchange group who had been staying in Buncrana and who had visited Omagh with the group that day. The full horror of this 'Real IRA' bomb rippled across the political divide and musical spectrum, generating fear among Republican musicians about singing rebel music. As one musician noted, 'I found republican music dropped off *big time* after the Omagh bomb in 1998 – especially up round the North. You were afraid to sing it. None of the pubs wanted it' (interview with Michael, 17 July 2015, quoted in Miller 2018: 356, italics in original). Yet, when taken onto a global stage, the song has provided a platform for protests for justice that are imagined well beyond local borders of fear. In the 2001 Slane Castle concert in Ireland, U2's Bono 'listed out all the names of those who lost their lives in the Omagh bombing [from memory], and shouted "No More" about many acts of violence that occurred during the sectarian violence and warfare' (Respondent in Morley and Somdhal-Sands 2011: 67).

At the Buncrana funeral for the three local victims, thousands of mourners lined the streets, along with leading figures of the time from across the political divide, including Irish president Mary McAleese, Northern Ireland's first minister David Trimble and Sinn Féin's Gerry Adams and Martin McGuiness. The heaviness of loss was palpable as the funeral cortège filed quietly past the lines of bystanders. As noted in relation to archival footage of the funeral, 'The silence was broken only by the cries of despair, sadness and anger as [civilians] followed the final journey of the three young innocent victims' (AP Archive YouTube 2015).

At the twentieth anniversary in 2018, this senseless atrocity brought families, churches, support groups and self-help groups together to remember those who were victims not just of this act but also of similar acts of violence worldwide. A bell, designed to mark the tenth anniversary of the Good Friday Peace Agreement, rang thirty-two times in memory of the victims, with an extra single peal for victims around the globe. In this service, as in the first anniversary event, music has provided a medium of catharsis for those grieving deeply. In this event, the Omagh Community Youth Choir, set up in 1998 by Darryl Simpson, performed his original composition which speaks of hope, love and unity. The chorus invites listeners to

> Come and join us at the water, where the two rivers flow into one
> Where peace and hope come together and our hearts are filled with love for everyone.

Darryl explained how he had established the choir:

> I decided I wanted to do something positive that would bring our community together and in some ways, that was the first time that, I think, the darkness and the sadness that had prevailed over Omagh at that time had released a little bit when all these voices came in together in harmony. (Page 2018)

One of the choir members further remarked that 'It shows that both sides of the community can come together and create something really beautiful from something so tragic' (Philip Hutchinson, interviewed in Page 2018).

Just as Annette recaptures fragments of her own poignant musical memories of this time, we are then invited to listen to the flow of water which, on the one hand, she likens to the 'ripple effect of war'. On the other hand, she tells us that this 'fresh, clear sound of falling rain' can equally evoke the potential for new beginnings and empathetic relations to flourish in her community (Figure 4.2). This reimagining of community returns the viewer–listener to a sense that while the echoes of the past may be presenced by resounding place memories, they are 'haunting[s] that do not [have to] govern lived events' (Jackson 2005: xv). This is evident in Annette's contrasting evaluation of the sounds of free-flowing traffic near to the site of a former border checkpoint. The roar and decrescendo of passing cars embody wider political concerns about pending decisions on Brexit that create another level of anxiety for residents along the border area (Figures 4.5 and 4.6).

Peace Bridge
I always remark to family and friends that if I were a tourist visiting Derry I would think it a beautiful City.
All the regeneration that has taken place along the River Foyle has been so beneficial to the City and the jewel in the crown has to be the new Peace Bridge. There is something very bright and beautiful about the design and the way it winds across the river gives it a familiar, friendly and fun appearance. I always feel it is inviting me on board with open arms and I have crossed it many times. It is such a wonderful thing to see the hordes of people crossing it daily, from both sides of the river.

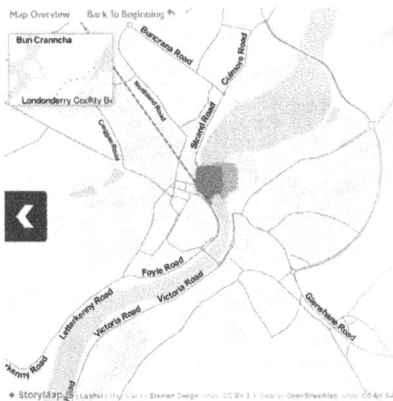

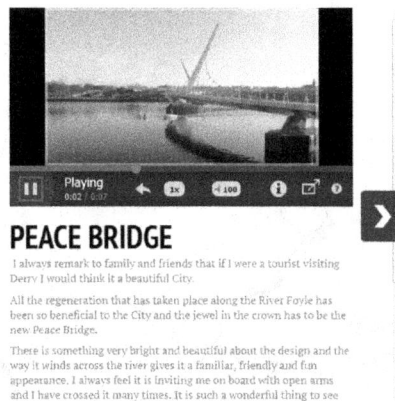

Figure 4.6 'Crossing the Border, Crossing the Foyle', StoryMap by Annette McNelis, 15 May 2018, slide 6.

The views from the Peace Bridge are amazing and the fact that it is a pedestrian bridge keeps the crossing carefree and safe, which must be contributing, in a profound and positive way, to the wellbeing of the people of the City.

As we arrive in Derry/Londonderry, in the final slides of her StoryMap, Annette's journey culminates at the Peace Bridge across the River Foyle (completed in 2011), with the soft hum of engines in the background and the slap-slap of footsteps as a jogger passes by. Here, the flow of sound, image and design coalesce in the gently curving structure of the Peace Bridge with supports like 'sails' on either side, affirmed by the ripple of the river beneath (see Figure 4.7). This flow is both historical and political with the 'sails' symbolizing hope for unity between the Unionist Waterside and Nationalist Cityside. As Annette notes, 'there is something very bright and beautiful about the design and the way it winds across the river gives it a familiar, friendly and fun appearance. I always feel it is inviting me on board with open arms.' In redefining the historical divisions of Derry/Londonderry, she says, the Peace Bridge 'seems to unite both sides of the city in a more personal way, making it beat like one heart'.

Peace Bridge
To me the Waterside and the City have always felt like two separate hearts of the city. Sitting proudly between Craigavon Bridge and the Foyle Bridge, the Peace Bridge seems to unite both sides of the city in a more personal way, making it beat like one heart. I consider the Peace Bridge to be a powerful symbol of peace and harmony – a bridge between the dark past and a bright future.

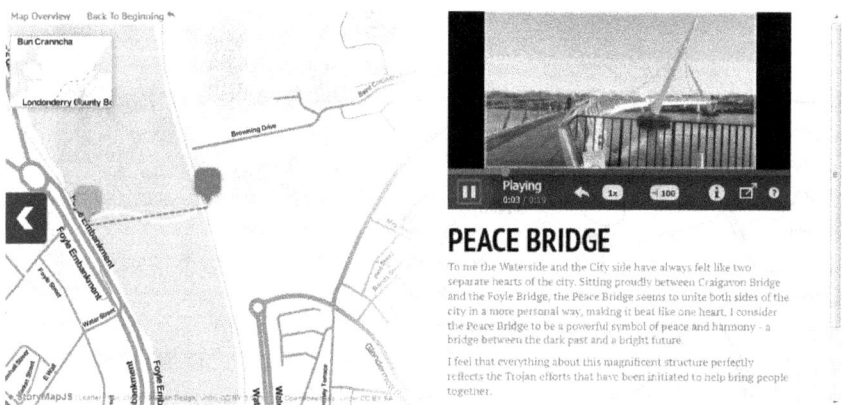

Figure 4.7 'Crossing the Border, Crossing the Foyle', StoryMap by Annette McNelis, 15 May 2018, slide 7.

I feel that everything about this magnificent structure perfectly reflects the Trojan efforts that have been initiated to help bring people together.

All people really want is to be able to go about their lives in peace.

The value of StoryMaps in community-based participatory research

This example demonstrates the potential for StoryMap to reshape our perceptions of the landscape in varieties of sonic forms and, in doing so, it has the potential to respond to the methodological needs of our research in five key ways, as follows:

(1) Visceral layering: StoryMap allows a layering of reflections on top of the 'material' base of the cartographical map, with scope for various multimedia to be employed. It brings a creative tension between subjective bordering processes, sonic imaginaries, memories and the physical border into play simultaneously;

(2) Affective simultaneity: As listener–viewers responding to Annette's journey, we are invited to become recipients of her experience, immersed in a particular space-time moment of the sights, sounds and movements of her travel and border crossings. These come to stand as a means of drawing us into alternative memories of prior conflict zones as 'space[s] of practiced place' (de Certeau 1988: 117) in sounded actions;

(3) Sound narratives: These everyday embodiments of sound, image and movement in turn become non-verbal means of narrativizing place. Although Annette includes short explanatory texts with each map, image and soundclip, it would be possible for those who know the area to narrativize their own journey and the border through complementary and contrasting sound-images of personalized experience. Thus, the experience of the SoundMap is at one level atemporal both for those who have different experiences of the areas and for those with no prior knowledge or experience of the landscape and its history. Yet it creates a sonic template from which viewer-listeners can draw their own comparisons of comparable locales;

(4) Grounded perspectives: In these personalized processes, the platform facilitates bottom-up and participant-led creativity, which is key to effective CBPR;

(5) Mutual transformations: As a method of CBPR the activities and materials generated by participants are the focus not only of analysis but

also of the transformation of engagement between academic facilitators and research participants. Thus, the borderings implicit with 'academic/public *hierarchies of power*' (Cassidy et al. 2018a: 140), which we outlined at the start of this chapter, must also be subject to careful scrutiny and repositioning in order to ensure a mutually transformative give-and-take in the research engagement.

These facilitation research processes are not new but have long comprised the basis of research with Indigenous communities. For example, in her CBPR with Northern Plains Native peoples, Christine Rogers Stanton (2014) provides a set of criteria that highlight key differences between Indigenous and academic modes of learning and engagement. Some of these include the recognition that storytelling is evocative rather than linear; the validation of storytelling is from the teller rather than the academic reviewer; emotional, intersubjective, sensorial and collaborative experiences are given central weight; and the sharing of experiences depends upon levels of perceived safety and well-being (Rogers Stanton 2014: 575, Table 1).[9]

Debordering with Musicians Without Borders?

As well as having important implications for our methodology, an engagement with bordering also fits with our ethical commitment to do 'research *with* and research *for* our research partners', MWB (in addition to 'the "traditional" ethnographic sense of doing research *about*' MWB) (Donaghey and Magowan 2021). Perhaps this engagement with bordering is in some sense nominatively determined – the name *Musicians Without Borders* compels us in this direction – but we do well to take this 'borderlessness' seriously (for a parallel discussion of this concept as it applies to Médecins sans Frontières/Doctors without Borders, see Debrix 1998). As we have seen in StoryMap, the analytical frameworks of bordering are commensurate with the approaches of MWB themselves, enabling our research to complement their practice. Creativity, performativity and artistic expression are at the core of this complementarity, and the subjective processes of bordering are reflected in embodied performance. Ernste writes that 'the bordered body is not just an interface but also a face, an instrument of human *expressivity*' (Ernst 2005: 164, emphasis added; see also Plessner 2003), and Németh asserts that bordering is 'in itself an (inter)active process involving actorship . . . focusing on the representations of borders through *performative acts'* (2017: 52, emphasis added). This recognition of borders as being performed contains transformative potential by emphasizing that 'bordering is not a given condition but an action' (Németh 2017: 52). This is at the core of MWB's peacebuilding ethos and theory of change. More than this, it conceives of the performance of borders as *the* essential aspect of their reproduction and, with a view to peacebuilding activity, recognizes that these 'perceptual borders can often be "stickier"; this is more difficult to eliminate than physical borders' (Németh 2017: 51, see also van Houtum 1999).

Performativity is the key to achieving meaningful social transformation, and art and creativity are the tools to effect that change. As Barrow states: '[a]rt has the ability to provide us with new possibilities for thinking about identity and continuity as changing concepts . . . retaining cultural/spatial traditions while engaging with the diversification of contemporary society' (2013: 1). This 'spatial' artistic emphasis encompasses the materiality of the border (in addition to, and in creative tension with, its subjective reproduction as addressed in performativity). However, the retention of 'cultural . . . traditions' pointed to by Barrow is problematic in the particularly contentious context of Derry/Londonderry where most musics, and especially traditional musics, are bifurcated along the sectarian 'two traditions' social divide. Particular tunes, rhythms and instruments are perceived in this context as belonging to one 'side' or the 'other' (obscuring the historical intermingling – and co-related geneses of particular characteristics of both musical traditions). By misrecognizing prior histories of shared musical transmission and exchange, distinct music cultures have become part of the subjective processes of bordering in Derry/Londonderry. Németh argues that such borders must be recognized, even confronted, to create opportunities for transformation:

> Defining and explaining difference is . . . an important step in avoiding misconceptions and faulty perceptions that may lead to fear and hostility. Consequently, clear demonstrations of difference can help to better define barriers/borders for both audiences and artists, and thus enable borders to be more easily crossed, or indeed disassembled. (2017: 67)

Likewise, Viktorova emphasizes the 'mediating' capacity of boundaries which function to 'establish connections between the spheres they separate'; boundaries and borders are transgressed in the 'unifying mechanism' of 'communication' (2003: 152). For Viktorova the 'setting of boundaries signals the possibility of their transgression' and this exposes 'their artificiality or conventionality', and this is a 'meaningful act' or 'event' (2003: 156). However, MWB explicitly do *not* take this 'confrontational' and transgressive approach to bordering into the musical context of Derry/Londonderry and avoid incorporating any reference to specific musical forms from each part of the community. In contrast, some of MWB's peacebuilding activities in their locations around the rest of the world do incorporate elements of local music practices and instruments into their creative activities, offering participants a sense of ownership over the process. As we can see in Northern Ireland, sectarian contention still infects local politics *and* expressive culture. Indeed, it was this pervasive contentiousness that invited our initial engagement with bordering for this research project, especially as we sought to understand how MWB are able to negotiate musical and creative practices without bringing this 'culture war' into creative spaces, a process which would be detrimental to MWB's peacebuilding aims in Derry/Londonderry. Nevertheless, MWB's peacebuilding mission is reflected in the imaginaries that underlie and emerge from bordering concepts, which brings our argument back to issues of decolonization outlined at the start of this chapter.

Conclusion

(De)bordering and decolonization share an emphasis on imaginaries as reservoirs of transformative potential. Through non-verbal creativity, the imagination, freed from the strictures of the cartographic and ethnic borders and boundaries of identity, is integral to MWB practices, and as evidenced in Annette's StoryMap it facilitates new musical and artistic engagements with self-expression. As Harsha Walia puts it, decolonization is 'the imagining and generating of alternative institutions and relations' (2013: 249), and Bürkner, similarly, argues that 'imaginaries . . . induce alternative practices and emancipation' (2018: 191). Bürkner offers a further parallel with MWB's practice, arguing that 'most imaginaries remain vague or even opaque because for their proponents this generally implies a strategic advantage' (2018: 191). In the Derry/Londonderry context, this ambiguity around borders, especially as expressed musically, is exactly the 'strategic advantage' that leads MWB to use improvisation and instruments from other cultural traditions in the Northern Ireland context, rather than drawing directly upon the rich seam of local musics.

In this chapter, we have sought to address how implicit tensions surrounding the use of the terms 'decolonization' and 'debordering' in relation to the Northern Irish political landscape can be refashioned through alternative sensory and creative engagements with place. Through the use of StoryMap, we have argued that the ambiguity of sound is particularly potent for enabling sonic memories from the past to be connected with, yet simultaneously displaced by and/or resonant with, the sonic present. Annette's story has offered glimpses of how recollections of sound have shaped moments of her life-journey back and forth across the border from times of conflict to peace. In turn, we are invited to listen in to these affective processes of debordering that her journeys have entailed. As a participant in the Music Bridge Programme, Annette has also been trained in non-verbal improvisatory practices that invite expansive creative musical imaginaries and unite participants in deeply shared sonic responses. This debordering of identity and practice in MWB creative activities in Derry/ Londonderry is generative of emotional flow, positivity and hope, each of which is clearly evoked in Annette's projection of the sounds of rain that flow like the River Foyle under the Peace Bridge.

As we have tried to demonstrate, the technological advances of digital media, such as the debordering potentialities of StoryMap, provide new opportunities to reflect critically upon transformations of conflict narratives and corresponding sonic imaginaries over time. By incorporating these innovations into wider scholarship and practice, there is potential to engage directly with the immediacy of aural and emotional dynamics through the lived experiences of sonic memories of the past. In turn, former landscapes of harm and injury can be retuned through everyday sounds of peace, 'occupying space' at the individual level, inviting those in positions of power and influence in policy-making to listen more closely to how sound, music and the arts can offer radical critiques of the past that can lead incrementally to interconnected visions of enhanced global futures.

Notes

1   We are very grateful to PaCCS (the Partnership for Conflict, Crime and Security Research) for funding the five-year 'Sounding Conflict' Project (2017–21, reference AH/P005381/1), which has enabled us to undertake this study. We would also like to thank our partner organization, Musicians Without Borders, particularly the director, Laura Hassler, and the project and training coordinator, Meagan Hughes, as well as Peter O'Doherty and Eibhlín Ní Dhochartaigh of Cultúrlann Uí Chanáin who host the Music Bridge Programme, together with participants, for enabling our collaboration. Finally, we are especially indebted to Annette McNelis for her willingness to share her evocative insights in the StoryMap on the website and as part of this chapter.

2 The city of Derry/Londonderry, the second largest city in Northern Ireland, lies just 2 kilometres from the border with County Donegal and the Republic of Ireland. The city has been a key site in the history of Ireland and was a focal point for conflict during the Troubles.

3 StoryMap is an online digital tool that enables users to employ sound, image and mapping to narrate a series of activities within and between places anywhere in the globe.

4 The death toll was almost 3,600 between 1969 and 1998 (McKittrick et al. 2001: 1552) with a further 158 conflict-related deaths between April 1998 and April 2018 (Nolan 2018).

5 An interesting shortcoming of OpenStreetMap in the context of the StoryMap platform is the naming of Derry/Londonderry as 'Londonderry County Borough' (in the Staman Design map tiles). This may have been an attempt to take an 'official' line in the face of the contested naming of the city. The default map tiles on OpenStreetMap's main home page do slightly better but still manage to misstep by opting for 'Londonderry/Derry', the particular ordering of which is not used in vernacular or official discourse. See https://www.openstreetmap.org/#map=11/54 .9900/-7.3626 (accessed 21 January 2019).

6 The year 2019 marks the twentieth anniversary of Musicians Without Borders who have established music programmes from rock schools in Macedonia and Kosovo to community music training programmes in Palestine, Rwanda, Tanzania and Uganda, as well as in El Salvador and Northern Ireland (see https://www.musician swithoutborders.org/2018/12/20-years-of-peacebuilding-through-music/) (accessed 20 January 2019).

7 For discussion of the Music Bridge Evaluation Programme, see Magowan and Donaghey 2018.

8 To follow the StoryMap on our website, go to Research Findings, Research Outcomes, Derry/Londonderry project under soundingconflict.org.

9 It should also be noted that there are many other linguistic, political, economic and cultural issues of decolonization that also concern Indigenous communities themselves (see, for example, Roche et al. 2018).

References

AP Archive YouTube Channel (2015), 'Ireland: Funeral of 3 Youngsters Killed in Omagh Bombing', *YouTube*, 21 July: Available online: https://www.youtube.com/w atch?v=eNaq-wBHNFw (accessed 20 January 2019).

Barrow, E. (2013), 'Art Beyond Conflict – Social Exchange and Reconciliation Directives', *THIRD TEXT: Critical Perspectives on Contemporary Art and Culture*, September: Available online: http://www.thirdtext.org/domains/thirdtext.com/loc

al/media/images/medium/emma_barrow:art_beyond_conflict_1.pdf (accessed 28 January 2019).

Becker, J. (1991), 'Anthropological Perspesctives on Music and Emotion', in P. N. Juslin and J. A. Sloboda (eds), *Music and Emotion*, 135–60, Oxford: Oxford University Press.

Bell, L. M. (2015), 'The Busker: Writing Occupy, Politics and Protest', *New Writing: International Journal for the Practice and Theory of Creative Writing*, 12 (2): 185–92.

Best, U. (2003), 'Gnawing at the Edges of the State: Deleuze and Guattari and Border Studies', in E. Berg and H. van Houtum (eds), *Routing Borders Between Territories, Discourses and Practices*, 177–92, Aldershot: Ashgate.

Blu, K. (1996), 'Where Do You Stay At?': Homeplace and Community among the Lumbee', in S. Feld and K. Basso (eds), *Senses of Place*, 197–228, Santa Fe, NM: School of American Research Press.

Brister, R. (2014), 'Sounding the Occupation: Joe Sacco's *Palestine* and the Uses of Graphic Narrative for (Post)Colonial Critique', *A Review of International English Literature*, 45 (1–2): 103–29.

Bürkner, H. J. (2018), 'Imaginaries Ready for Use: Framings of the Bordered Intersectionalised Everyday Provided by the EU's Sectoral Policies', *Political Geography*, 66: 189–98.

Butler, J. (2009), *Frames of War: When is Life Grievable?* New York: Verso Books.

Cassidy, K., N. Yuval-Davis and G. Wemyss (2018a), 'Intersectional Border(ing)s', *Political Geography*, 66: 139–41.

Cassidy, K., N. Yuval-Davis and G. Wemyss (2018b), 'Debordering and Everyday (Re) bordering in and of Dover: Postborderland Borderscapes', *Political Geography*, 66: 171–9.

Castells, M. (2012), *Networks of Outrage and Hope: Social Movements in the Internet Age*, Cambridge: Polity Press.

Chute, H. (2008), 'The Texture of Retracing in Marjane Satrapi's *Persepolis*', *Women's Studies Quarterly*, 36 (1–2): 92–110.

Csikszentmihalyi, M. (2002), *Flow: The Psychology of Optimal Experience*, London: Random House.

Debrix, F. (1998), 'Deterritorialised Territories, Borderless Borders: The New Geography of International Medical Assistance', *Third World Quarterly*, 19 (5): 827–46.

de Certeau, M. (1988), *The Practice of Everyday Life*, trans. S. Rendall, Los Angeles: University of California Press.

Deleuze G. and F. Guattari (1987), *A Thousand Plateaus: Capitalism and Schizophrenia*, Minneapolis: University of Minnesota Press.

Derrida, J. (1997), *Of Grammatology*, trans. G. C. Spivak, Baltimore, MD: Johns Hopkins University Press.

Donaghey, J. and F. Magowan (2021), Emotion Curves: Creativity and Methodological "Fit" or "Commensurability"', *International Review of Qualitative Research*, DOI: 10.1177/19408447211002768.

Donnan, H. and K. Simpson (2007), 'Silence and Violence among Northern Ireland Border Protestants', *Ethnos*, 72 (1): 5–28.

Dowler, L. and J. Sharp (2001), 'A Feminist Geopolitics?', *Space and Polity*, 5 (3): 165–76.

Ernste, H. (2005), 'Debordering Subjectivity', in H. van Houtum, O. Kramsch and W. Zierhofer (eds), *B/ordering Space*, 155–70, Aldershot: Ashgate.

Funnell, S. and P. Rogers (2011), *Purposeful Program Theory: Effective Use of Theories of Change and Logic Models*, San Francisco, CA: Jossey-Bass.

Gilmartin, M. and L. D. Berg (2007), 'Locating Postcolonialism', *Area*, 39 (1): 120–4.

Green, S. (2010), 'Performing Border in the Aegean: On Relocating Political, Economic and Social Relations', *Journal of Cultural Economy*, 3 (2): 261–78.

Grosfoguel, R. (2011), 'Decolonizing Post-colonial Studies and Paradigms of Political Economy: Transmodernity, Decolonial Thinking, and Global Coloniality', *Transmodernity*, 1 (1): 1–36.

Heidegger, M. ([1927] 1962), *Being and Time*, trans. J. Macquarrie and E. Robinson, New York: Harper and Row.

Jackson, M. (2005), *Existential Anthropology: Events, Exigencies and Effects*, Oxford: Berghahn.

Jacobson, M. and C. Rugeley (2007), 'Community-based Participatory Research: Group Work for Social Justice and Community Change', *Social Work With Groups*, 30 (4): 21–39.

Josephides, L. and A. Hall (2014), *We the Cosmopolitans*, Oxford: Berghahn.

Lems, A. (2018), *Being-Here: Placemaking in a World of Movement*, New York: Berghahn.

Magowan, F. and J. Donaghey (2018), 'Sounding Conflict: From Resistance to Reconciliation', Musicians Without Borders Music Bridge and Training of Trainers 2017 Report.

Mbembe, A. (2003), 'Necropolitics', *Public Culture,* 15 (1): 11–40.

McKittrick, D., S. Kelters, B. Feeney and C. Thornton (2001), *Lost Lives: The Stories of the Men, Women and Children who Died as a Result of the Northern Ireland Troubles*, New York: Random House.

Morely, V. and K. Somdahl-Sands (2011), 'Music with a Message: U2's Rock Concerts as Spectacular Spaces of Politics', *AETHER: The Journal of Media Geography*, 7 (Winter): 58–74.

Naylor, L., M. Daigle, S. Zaragocin, M. Marietta Ramírez and M. Gilmartin (2018), 'Interventions: Bringing the Decolonial to Political Geography', *Political Geography*, 66: 199–209.

Németh, A. (2017), 'The Immigrant "Other" and Artistic Expression: (de)bordering via Festivals and Social Activism in Finland', *Journal of Cultural Geography*, 34 (1): 51–69.

Newman, D. (2006), 'Borders and Bordering. Towards an Interdisciplinary Dialogue', *European Journal of Social Theory*, 9 (2): 171–86.

Nolan, P. (2018), 'The Cruel Peace: Killings in Northern Ireland since the Good Friday Agreement', *The Detail*, 23 April: Available online: https://www.thedetail.tv/articles

/the-cruel-peace-killings-in-northern-ireland-since-the-good-friday-agreement (accessed 18 October 2018).

OpenStreetMap main page, zoom to border area around Derry/Londonderry: Available online: https://www.openstreetmap.org/#map=11/54.9463/-7.3859 (accessed 21 January 2019).

Page, C. (2018), 'Omagh Bomb: Bell Tolls to Mark 20th Anniversary', *BBC News* website, 15 August: Available online: https://www.bbc.co.uk/news/uk-northern-irel and-45144511 (accessed 20 January 2019).

Plessner, H. (2003), *Gesammelte Schriften* (Collected Writings), Vol. I-X, Frankfurt: Suhrkamp.

Pratt, G. and V. Rosner (2006), 'Introduction: The Global and the Intimate', *Women's Studies Quarterly*, 34 (1–2): 13–24.

Prokkola, E. K. (2014), 'Using Narrativity as Methodological Tool', *ACME: An International E-Journal for Critical Geographies*, 13 (3): 442–9.

Roche, G., H. Maruyama and A. Virdi Kroik, eds. (2018), *Indigenous Efflorescence: Beyond Revitalisation in Sapmi and Ainu Mosir*, Canberra: ANU Press.

Rogers Stanton, C. (2014), 'Crossing Methodological Borders: Decolonizing Community-Based Participatory Research', *Qualitative Inquiry*, 20 (5): 573–83.

Stengers, I. (2011), *Cosmopolitics II*, Minneapolis: University of Minnesota Press.

Stewart, K. (2006), 'An Occupied Place', in S. Feld and K. Basso (eds), *Senses of Place*, 137–65, Santa Fe, NM: School of American Research Press.

Stoetzler, M. and N. Yuval-Davis (2002), 'Standpoint Theory, Situated Knowledge and the Situated Imagination', *Feminist Theory*, 3 (3): 315–33.

Titlestad, M. (2004), 'Listening to Bloke Modisane: Considering Acoustic Regimes in Colonial and Postcolonial Writing', *Social Identities*, 10 (5): 575–88.

Titon, J. T. (2009), 'Ecology, Phenomenology, and Biocultural Thinking: A Response to Judith Becker', *Ethnomusicology*, 53 (3): 502–9.

van Houtum, H. (1999.), 'Internationalisation and Mental Borders', *Journal for Economic and Social Geography*, 90 (3): 329–35.

van Houtum, H. and T. van Naerssen (2002), 'Bordering, Ordering and Othering', *Tijdschrift voor economische en sociale geografie*, 93 (2): 125–36.

Varró, K. (2016), 'Recognising the Emerging Transnational Spaces and Subjectivities of Cross-border Cooperation: Towards a Research Agenda', *Geopolitics*, 21 (1): 171–94.

Viktorova, J. (2003), 'Bridging Identity and Alterity: An Apologia for Boundaries', in E. Berg and H. van Houtum (eds), *Routing Borders Between Territories, Discourses and Practices*, 141–60, Aldershot: Ashgate.

Vogel, I. (2012), *Review of the Use of 'Theory of Change' in International Development*, London: DFID: Available online: http://www.theoryofchange.org/pdf/DFID_ToC _Review:VogelV7.pdf (accessed 20 January 2019).

Walia, H. (2013), *Undoing Border Imperialism*, Oakland, CA: Institute for Anarchist Studies.

Warner, M. (2008), 'Phew! Whaam! Aaargh! Boo!: Sense, Sensation, and Picturing Sound', *The Soundtrack*, 1 (2): 107–25.

Werlen, B. (2005), 'Regions and Everyday Regionalizations. From a Space-centred Towards an Action-centred Human Geography', in H. van Houtum, O. Kramsch and W. Zierhofer (eds), *B/ordering Space*, 47–60, Aldershot: Ashgate.

Wimmer, A. and N. Glick Schiller (2003), 'Methodological Nationalism, the Social Sciences, and the Study of Migration: An Essay in Historical Epistemology', *International Migration Review*, 37 (3): 576–610.

Wolfe, P. (2006), 'Settler Colonialism and the Elimination of the Native', *Journal of Genocide Research*, 8 (4): 387–409.

Woodward, K. and J. P. Jones III (2005), 'On the Border with Deleuze and Guattari', in H. van Houtum, O. Kramsch and W. Zierhofer (eds), *B/ordering Space*, 235–48, Aldershot: Ashgate.

Yuval-Davis, N. (2011), *The Politics of Belonging: Intersectional Contestations*, London: Sage.

Zarzycka, M (2011), 'War in Silence?: Photographs, Sounds, and the Ethics of Reception', *Afterimage*, 39 (1–2): 15–17.

5

Loud town, quiet base

Olongapo City, Subic Bay and the US Navy, 1950–70

Kevin Sliwoski

Introduction: Locating the sonic

Sound is scarce within US military records. Sound is largely absent also in the growing critical scholarship about military bases. Although scholars such as Cynthia Enloe ([1990] 2014), Catherine Lutz (2009), Katherine T. McCaffrey (2002), Jana K. Lipman (2009), Trevor Paglen (2009), David Vine (2011), Kenneth T. MacLeish (2013) and Erin Fitz-Henry (2015) write critically about foreign occupation and US military bases, their focus on sound is as a passing reference. When sound is present in records or scholarly works, it is rarely explicit and demands the researcher to read and to listen obliquely to the text. Music and sound scholars, however, have developed a growing subfield within music studies on the sonic impact of the US military and the sound experiences of US service members. Suzanne Cusick (2008), Jonathan Pieslak (2009), Martin Daughtry (2015) and Lisa Gilman (2015) have studied the recent US wars in Iraq and Afghanistan through the lenses of sound, listening, trauma, violence and occupation. Others, like David Suisman (2015) and Jessica Schwartz (2012), focus on the ways in which US militarization has been mediated and experienced through sound.

These critical studies of war, sound and violence have expanded the scope of music and sound studies, and introduced new questions, subjects, materials and interpretations related to sound. These scholars have risen to anthropologist David Vine's suggestion of a bifocaled approach to studies of empire and militarization, which he defines as 'subjecting U.S. Empire and its actors to the same kind of ethnographic scrutiny most often reserved for imperialism's victims' (Vine 2011: 233). A bifocaled approach has scholars treat the experiences of local populations, American service members and state institutions equally and ethnographically. Vine argues that critical nuance is missing from studies of war and militarization, and sound studies scholars have made important interventions within that discourse. Jim Sykes cautions about issues of representation in the emerging literature on sound and war within music studies. He writes that 'the sounds of everyday life are absent or placed in a sharp dialectic with the sounds of war' (2018: 3). Sykes worries that focusing on the producers and the machines that generate the sounds of war risks alienating the people and sounds that are part of war but are not part of a military. This has also been a concern for scholars who write on US empire and militarization, such as Maria Hohn and Seungsook Moon (2010) and Setsu Shigematsu and Keith L. Camacho (2010).

The expanding scholarship on military bases, war, sound and occupation intersects constructively with the growing critical literature on US–Philippine colonial history. Many scholars write about the complexity of perspectives and forces related to the historical military relationship between the United States and the Philippines. Sharon Delmendo, for example, argues that US–Philippine history is a 'study of two nationalisms' (2004: 16) developed in proximity to each other, while Vernadette Vicuna Gonzalez points out the hypermasculine 'doubled subjectivity' (2013: 3–4) of US service members in the Philippines as tourists and soldiers. These studies address the military history between the United States and the Philippines but also ask questions about how systems of asymmetrical power became institutionalized. Other scholars such as Mary Talusan (2004), Stephanie Ng (2005), Lucy Mae San Pablo Burns (2012) and Christine Balance (2016) have looked to music and performance to understand the legacies of colonial history between the Philippines and the United States. These scholars demonstrate the wider scope of US–Philippine history and show how Filipinos used musical performance to understand, undermine and translate the experiences of US colonialism and occupation. Taken together, these works provide examples of how to engage with military and sonic histories of the Philippines and show the importance of considering many historical viewpoints to counter, upend and criticize accepted narratives of Philippine history, US occupation and US military bases in the Philippines.

Out of all the installations the US military established in the Philippines during the twentieth century, none experienced the full range and concentration of occupation-related sounds than Naval Base, Subic Bay and its neighbouring city, Olongapo. Subic Bay is located at the south-eastern point of Zambales Province, on the large northern island of Luzon in the Philippines. When the United States took possession of the Philippines after the 1898 Spanish-American War, it inherited a nation constructed on 300 years of colonial and occupational rule, and a small naval installation at Subic Bay. The Philippines gained legal independence from the United States through the Treaty of Manila in 1946. One year later, the United States and the Philippines signed the Military Bases Agreement Act (1947), granting the United States nearly unrestricted use of several military installations in the Philippines, notably Naval Base, Subic Bay and Clark Air Base. The Military Bases Agreement Act contained a land-lease clause that granted the United States a ninety-nine-year rent-free lease for the land housing the bases (*Agreement Between the United States of America and the Republic of the Philippines Concerning Military Bases* 1947; see Figure 5.1).

By the 1960s, US Naval Base, Subic Bay was a 262-square-mile (680 square kilometre) naval reservation that at times housed approximately 40,000 US service members, families and contract employees, and hosted millions of sailors and marines taking shore leave when in port. The base shared a border with Olongapo City, a city of 60,000 people. Olongapo had been legally part of the US naval station after the Second World War and stayed under military jurisdiction until 1959. Even after it became Philippine sovereign territory, the city's culture,

Figure 5.1 An aerial view of the Subic Bay US Naval Station, 1953. Photo by Michael Rougier/The LIFE Picture Collection via Getty Images.

economy and politics remained tethered to the base's growth. Subic Bay became important to the US military during the Korean War (1950–3), when the massive post-war drawdown of troops made many in government insecure about the US geopolitical position in the Pacific. The 1950s brought significant changes to the naval reservation at Subic Bay, with huge construction and infrastructure projects, new units and more personnel as the base became the new home for the US Seventh Fleet. Naval Base, Subic Bay became one of the largest and most strategically important repair, supply and logistics hubs for the US Navy. Subic Bay was at its busiest between 1964 and 1973, during the peak years of the Vietnam War (1955–75). After the Gulf of Tonkin Incident (1964), the United States began committing huge numbers of combat troops to Vietnam. Subic Bay was the nearest major support installation compared to other bases in Japan, Guam or Taiwan, and millions of people passed through the base while base workers repaired ships and service members took leave.

The build-up of personnel, materials and infrastructure during this time meant that Subic Bay was a noisy place, even though sound is rarely directly present in the historical record. This was also a period when Filipinos and Americans negotiated new geopolitical relationships since the Philippines was no longer a colonial possession. Subic Bay, however, was hosting more Americans than ever before. The US Navy never left, and the base did not close until 1991.

The history of Naval Base, Subic Bay during the 1950s and 1960s is a useful historical case to examine the relationship between sound and occupation – and what sound tells us about occupation – because the United States and the Philippines were still defining their postcolonial relationship; definitions of occupation were fluid and ill-defined. The 'loud town, quiet base' narrative that hangs over the history of the US Navy at Subic Bay as the focus of this chapter conveys American attitudes towards the Philippines, demonstrates lingering colonial structures and shows how sound can shape occupation and empire. By focusing on military history through sound and using the military base as a research site, I ask questions about US militarization and draw attention to the ways in which the US military tried to rebrand its presence overseas and on how it tried to minimize its role as an occupying force.

Self-noise and oblique listening

Although the US Navy's presence at Subic Bay spanned a century, the US military's shift to operations in the Pacific during the mid-1950s to the late 1960s transformed the base's reputation and physical layout. It is important to give this military base a full-body auscultation at this specific moment in time; to listen to its pulse and all its vital organs: its infrastructure, its environment and its people. This kind of close study and close listening to people, place and institution is a useful method to draw out more details when studying overseas American occupation and militarization. It can also help to better identify and define contemporary forms of occupation. To do so requires oblique listening, a sonic methodology that emphasizes listening between the cracks and below the surface to multiple perspectives. Oblique listening is a method for researching and writing sonic histories by listening critically to texts, performances and interviews for the sonic even when it is not explicit. Oblique listening challenges scholars to find different sources – like military records – to write sound narratives beyond familiar musical, performative and ethnographic perspectives. This is what Martin Daughtry (2015: 3) works towards in his writing on the belliphonic, 'the spectrum of sounds produced by armed combat', and similar to what Christine Balance (2016: 26) calls disobedient listening, which she uses to 'unsettle dominant discourses on race, performance, and US popular music'. Kyle Devine (2015: 368) also advocates for oblique approaches in his push for a political ecology of music, 'how the stuff of musical culture is made and possessed, dispossessed and unmade'. These scholars have worked to expand the boundaries of music and sound research, and they demonstrate several ways to be oblique listeners and researchers: by introducing new spaces, rehearing accepted or familiar narratives and including new or different materials and individuals.

Classified and unclassified US naval records from the 1950s and 1960s detail the real and perceived contrasting sound worlds of the American base and the adjoining Filipino municipality of Olongapo City. The naval base and its affiliated materials, people and infrastructure were represented as quiet and orderly, a reflection of the public image that the navy tried to uphold. Reports like a 1951 'Noise Survey and Repair Procedures for Submarine Noise Reduction' suggest the navy was concerned with reducing its sonic footprint and being sensitive to allied nations by reigning in its sonic emissions (Department of the Navy Bureau of Ships 1951). A closer reading of the survey reveals the navy's interest in submarine noise reduction was not altruistic but was driven by a desire to design a more lethal and efficient fleet. The survey's authors explain that 'the effectiveness of our submarines depends on their ability to remain undetected by the enemy' and advise that 'a constant awareness of possible noise sources and methods for eliminating them is necessary in order to keep the submarine as quiet as possible' (Department of the Navy Bureau of Ships 1951: 1).

The manual covers the science of sound including vibrations, noises, frequencies, reflections, sine waves, harmonics, infrasonic and ultrasonic, and the authors present practical solutions for underwater noise reduction based on these scientific principles advising a reduction goal of 20 decibels per case (Department of the Navy Bureau of Ships 1951: 2–6, 21). Sailors and submariners were encouraged to trace and measure excess 'structure-born' vibrational noise with a vibration meter, a sound-level meter outfitted with a vibration pickup instead of a microphone or hydrophone (Department of the Navy Bureau of Ships 1951: 12–13). The authors also warn about the effects of 'self-noise', the noises internal to a sonar or listening ship that can disrupt or interfere with outward-facing sonar hydrophones. In these contexts, American sailors and submariners were asked to be critical listeners, to observe the ship's and their own 'self-noise', and to actively reduce the noise of their ships. These suggestions point to the intimate sonic relationships between ships and sailors and to the presence of sound in naval life (Department of the Navy Bureau of Ships 1951: 2–6, 12–13, 21).

The survey authors, however, do not consider the potential sound effects of a docked submarine. The navy's policing of 'self-noise' did not extend beyond the confines of a ship at sea or combat-related work. The focus is on deployed vessels and submarines. Sounds in other contexts are not considered. Docks, piers and quays of different ports that serviced docked ships and submarines were loud, busy spaces filled with ships under repair, workers, machine shops and other materials. Submarines and their crews added to that sound space, yet a submarine in port for repairs was not considered a sonic actor in the same way a deployed vessel was. The navy's concern was to reduce ship or submarine noise at sea, not in port, even though upgrades, adjustments and additional listening surveys could only take place in shipyards like Subic Bay (Department of the Navy Bureau of Ships 1951: 23).

The navy's indifference to the impact of its self-noise at Subic Bay demonstrates persistent colonial attitudes and further shows how sound and occupation overlap. Paying attention to the navy's self-noise adds expanded dimensions to US–Philippine history and shows that Subic Bay and Olongapo City were sonically complicated places where Americans and Filipinos grappled with different legacies, experiences and definitions of occupation. In this chapter, I repossess the term 'self-noise' and use it to mean the collective sound of an institution, group, individual or process, and its intentional and unintentional effects on another group or institution. The loud town, quiet base narrative is about the self-noise of the US Navy and of the Philippines. Using oblique listening to focus on the politics of self-noise and daily life at Subic Bay leads to a deeper understanding of how Filipinos and Americans encountered and confronted forces of occupation and colonialism.

While the naval base and the navy's reputation are documented as a spectrum of sonic contradictions, Olongapo, in contrast, was categorized as loud, dirty, disorderly and congested. Although Olongapo was at times all of those things, the city does not sonically exist beyond such reductive descriptions. Olongapo's sound world was tied to its use as an entertainment destination for US sailors arriving in port after the monotony of a months-long Pacific cruise. Olongapo was known for 'fancy ladies and the musical napalm of the bars', 'the faded thin walls of the teetering shacks', where 'poverty festers like the open street sewers' (*USS Ranger Cruise Book* 1967). This word choice illustrates how US sailors perceived Olongapo's bar and music culture. Sailors remembered the music, the space and the people as lively, hot, chaotic, exciting and all-consuming, washing over listeners, dancers and drinkers and immersing them in an explosive musical experience. The clubs and bands provided a soundtrack of release and abandon, of rest and relaxation. Women's bodies, music, poverty and cleanliness are themes that were reproduced in cruise yearbooks by sailors on different ships throughout the 1950s and 1960s. There is little space in these narratives for Olongapo to exhibit sonic or other kinds of social or cultural diversity. Instead, Olongapo was a superficial experience for sailors on liberty, and their impressions of its people and spaces were often clichéd and exoticized, filtered through a history of occupation and colonialism (Figure 5.2).

The US Navy's sonic observations of its neighbour did not include any proportional self-examination of the base's self-noise. There was no commentary from the navy's administration about the sound experiences of US sailors or the sonic impact of the navy in the Philippines. Nor was there a willing awareness to examine ways the navy might be adding to or disrupting the overseas sound world it was a part of. Interviews, cruise books, newspapers and naval documents, however, show that Subic and Olongapo's real and imagined sonic reputation was constructed in part by the presence of the US Navy. Sailors of the USS *Coral Sea* remembered how 'the peaceful sound of tropical stillness is occasionally shattered by gunfire from the rifles of *Coral Sea* Marines and sailors' (*Cruise of USS Coral Sea* 1963: 125). In this description, US Marines are sonic disrupters, filling the jungles around the naval reservation with lead casings, gunpowder and the reverberant cracks of rifles.

Figure 5.2 Street scene, Olongapo, 1972. Photo by Robert Alexander/Getty Images.

The navy's contrasting sonic representations of Americans and Filipinos was a mindset inherited from previous generations of US military and political leaders during the American colonial period in the Philippines. Sound in this context reflects ideas about cleanliness. Anne McClintock writes how cleanliness was at the centre of the British colonial project. McClintock pulls apart images and advertisements of bar soap and clean white linens, used to emphasize the differences between British colonizers and British colonial subjects (McClintock 1995). The British were clean, white and civilized, while the colonized were dirty, brown and uncivilized. Many Americans viewed the Philippines and individual Filipinos in a similar manner; the US doctrine of 'benevolent assimilation' towards the Philippines was intended to uplift, modernize and clean up 'little brown brothers', to help the Philippines become a modern nation in the image of the United States (Rafael 2000: 76–81). In connecting sound to McClintock's stance on cleanliness, sound and hygiene become parallels: loud is to dirty as quiet is to clean; colonizers are imagined to be quiet while the colonized are imagined to be loud or noisy. Karin Bijsterveld argues there is a similar class-based distinction between a 'quiet' intellectual class and a 'loud' working class (2003: 183). For the post-Second World War US Navy and the American government, control over sound was how the United States rebranded its relationship with the Philippines and a source the United States used to try to create boundaries with the Philippines. The US Navy attempted to use or manipulate sound to maintain hierarchies of power in Subic Bay.

Olongapo sounds

While debates over the politics of occupation were performed by senators, diplomats and protestors throughout the 1950s and 1960s, US sailors and citizens of Olongapo City tried to make sense of their everyday sonic relationships. The sonic differences between the base and the city were often contrasted in terms of volume. When I asked veteran navy submariner Jim Pope about the sounds he heard at Subic Bay, he outlined a binary of sound and silence that reflected the physical divisions between town and base. An Iowa native, Jim grew up poor and started providing for his parents and siblings in his early teens as a farmhand and janitor. He enlisted in the navy in the 1950s, completed training and sailed to the Philippines in the late 1950s, the start of his twenty-seven-year military career. Jim was a submariner and later became a sonar technician. In our conversation, he was reflective and discerning in talking about sound and silence (Pope 2017). When I asked him about Olongapo, he offered clear and immediate memories of the city as noisy and chaotic. Off-base, Jim recalled 'drunken brawls and fights and that kind of stuff. . . . That was going on all the time. Shore patrol wagon honking away and running to some brawl some place . . . it was always Americans involved' (Pope 2018). The sailors of the USS *Hancock*, who documented their 1960 port of call through Subic and liberty in Olongapo, echoed Jim's observations: 'The air is filled with dust, new smells, and excitement. Shouts and cheers echo from the cock pit; raucous laughter and coy giggles from the clubs mix with grunts and cackles from farm-like back yards and the spirited shrieks of seemingly countless children' (Allen 1960: 70). These sailors describe a dense acoustic environment filled with many sounds that reflect aspects of Filipino culture and demonstrate how familiar the sounds of daily life in Olongapo were to US sailors.

These two accounts detail several things. The well-known and lively bar and music scene in Olongapo was also the setting for chronic public noise created by Americans. Nightclubs were places for live music and loud Americans. Jim described how the familiar sirens of shore patrol vehicles were a ubiquitous presence in Olongapo during the evenings. And he described the diversity of sounds in the city beyond the live bands and street musicians. Olongapo sounded congested and overwhelming. Humans, animals, structures and numerous genre cover bands together created a complicated sonic tapestry that filled the space and the ears of US sailors. Many of these sounds were of Filipino cultural origin – the *carabao*, wandering children, fighting cock pits and street vendors. Although Olongapo was loud because of the city's design and congestion, it was also chaotic because of US service members filling its spaces. Millions of sailors and marines took liberty at Subic every year throughout the 1960s, and the gate leading off-base would regularly see a daily minimum of 5,000 sailors pass through back and forth. In 1967, for example, 2,586 ships docked at Subic Bay at a rate of approximately 216 per month (*Command History of the United States Naval Station Subic Bay* 1967: 32).

I also interviewed US Navy veteran David Ball who was stationed at Subic in the 1960s and 1970s. He did not recall the base leadership or his own command ever expressing concern about sailors being excessively loud. A diver, corpsman and submariner, David filled many roles during his naval career. He lived and worked at Subic Bay during two sets of orders, lived off-base and travelled widely. The Philippines interested him and his wife, and he recounted numerous detailed narratives of his time overseas. He described how the shore patrol was strict in regulating behaviour during liberty but not overly concerned about sound. Raised voices would attract the shore patrol, but only because yelling preceded fighting. Otherwise, loud American voices were keynote sounds in Olongapo (Ball 2018).

Olongapo's reputation for fun, filth and music was well known in the 1960s, and that legacy endures to this day. However, that description is reductive and obscures the range of activities and infrastructural projects led by the US Navy in collaboration with local Philippine leadership that added to this sound world. The navy's influence and jurisdiction might have been legally limited to the base by the 1960s, but its cultural, economic and sonic reach extended beyond the base's borders. By 1960, the US Navy had made numerous gestures of goodwill towards the Philippines and had returned full jurisdiction over Olongapo back to the Philippine government. The base's Public Works Center (PWC), however, was part of the connective tissue that linked and influenced on- and off-base life. One of the PWC's flagship programmes in the 1960s was construction procurement and contracting in conjunction with the base's Process Plant Section. The base experienced a construction boom in the 1960s to expand the base's facilities in support of combat operations in Vietnam. When the navy contracted part of its construction and materials needs off-base, they also parted with the accompanying sonic afterlife of heavy construction and material processing. Base newspaper *Subic Bay News* detailed how 'heavy boulders blasted by means of explosives from mother rock are hauled in by dump trucks to undergo the crushing process', which would later be carried by trucks through Olongapo to the base (Alinea 1967b).

It is not surprising that the US Navy contracted many of its industrial services off-base, as military leaders struggled to control the base's public image. The on-base process plant was known for 'Belching smoke, emitting dust and giving out jarring noise' (Alinea 1967b). By moving some of the dirty and noisy industrial work off-base, the navy demonstrated its commitment to supporting the local Filipino economy and created a more sonically peaceful work and home life on base for its sailors and military dependents. The other way to read this is that the navy dumped the unwanted, dirty or ugly aspects of industrialization off-base for the local Filipino population to deal with. Large numbers of Filipinos depended on the formal and illicit economies the base propped up, and the United States controlled and influenced aspects of the local economy, another manifestation of an inherited colonial relationship. The navy's leaders at Subic Bay wielded power and fashioned economic and sonic life on and off-base to the specifications they found acceptable.

In some instances, however, naval leaders at Subic Bay were eager to emphasize the sonic impact of the navy in Olongapo. In a politically calculated 1968 piece titled 'Fleet's Work and Music Promote Closer Relations', US Navy journalist Bob Rainville explained the positive effects of sailor–civilian interactions. US sailors worked with Olongapo City citizens to help build up the Boys Town Community Center, a space and programme for the struggling community's children. Sailors served as instructors in farming and building, and helped lay foundations for new facilities (Rainville 1968: 5). A navy band from the USS *Coral Sea* 'played popular music for the boys and the school children', and 'performed before students at the National High School and Bajac-Bajac Elementary School in Olongapo City' (Rainville 1968: 5). In a performance reversal, the US Navy Band played for Filipinos instead of the Filipino bands performing for US sailors on liberty.

The performance, however, was a political device used to demonstrate to the local Filipino community the positive aspects of a continued friendly relationship with the US Navy. This was the politics of occupation mediated through music, through the sonic. Sailors at Subic Bay were regularly a part of community outreach events and disaster relief efforts to be good partners to their Filipino hosts. These actions could also disguise the shape of naval and sonic occupation; they were attempts at geopolitical sleight-of-hand, to misdirect and mask American dominance at Subic Bay and in the Southwest Pacific. Sound and music were tools used to elicit positive emotional responses instead of critical political ones from Filipino communities abutting the naval base.

The 1968 performance concluded with the ceremonial presentation of a school bell, offered by Lieutenant Commander John A. Baxter, chaplain on the USS *Camden*, to the mayor of Castillejos, Rodrigo Trimorand, and to the elementary school's principal Gerardo Beltran (Rainville 1968: 5). This was a public display of intercultural exchange that happened around a musical and sonic symbol. Alain Corbin (1998: 4, 218) argues that bells hold emotional power and transmit 'auditory messages' of power, ownership, control, time and regulation. The 1968 bell presentation and the bell itself was an act the navy hoped would symbolize the selfless and generous sailors who represented the navy and the United States. The bell was also a reminder of the existing power relations between the United States and the Philippines and between the naval base and the city. Although the bell was intended as a gesture of goodwill between two allied nations, it could also represent the US Navy's dominance over the local economy and culture, a sonic reminder of occupation, an extension of the base's sonic presence. The navy did not merely occupy a cordoned-off stretch of coastal Philippine land but made its presence known and felt inland away from the base, as a physically, sonically and culturally occupying force.

Subic: Sound and silence

By 1968, when US troop levels peaked in Vietnam and support operations in the Philippines were at their busiest, the navy's leadership at Subic Bay enacted policies and restrictions to assert more control over noise, movement and security on base and the immediate surrounding areas. In response to a series of criminal activities on base, increased congestion and more local hiring, power-driven, two-wheel vehicles were strictly prohibited between sunset and sunrise on base, with minimal exceptions granted (*Subic Bay News* 1968: 2). The number of motorcycles and motorbikes on base was apparently a cause for concern, but the navy's restrictions also affected the sound world on base. The restrictions meant a quieter, more orderly and more controlled after-dark culture on base. Because of increased support operations, the base was also a site of perpetual construction and accompanying environmental and sonic disruptions. The waters of the bay grew more quiet in the late 1960s as the anchorage boundaries were restructured in response to piracy against US ships. The base's transportation command had spare vessels patrol the bay, but by the late 1960s those ships were running salvage operations off the coast of Vietnam. By 1966, the western portion of the bay was a restricted zone. This series of policies was designed to contain noisy disruptions and behaviour by sailors and Filipinos, and between Philippine and American sovereignty. As Olongapo's neon lights flickered awake and the bands began their sets, the base was supposed to become dark and quiet.

Subic's leadership also made efforts to distinguish the sound worlds of families stationed overseas and the sailors passing through Subic for liberty, refuelling or repairs. David Ball remembered how the navy used cattle cars to transport sailors from the piers across the base to Magsaysay Gate, the main point of access for sailors venturing out into Olongapo. He described how cattle carriers were attached to semi-trucks, and that coming back from town, 'there were lots of drunks on there, lot of fights on there. People were thrown off. Talk about noise – that was noise' (Ball 2018). David's experience details how the navy herded sailors like cattle to control their bodies and their ability to make sound, to make sure their noisy and unruly behaviour did not intersect and violate the transplanted suburban family neighbourhoods. The navy wanted to preserve its on-base military-sonic domesticity, the totality of sounds and music within suburban-style housing and family recreation areas on base.

To solidify the division between family life and bachelor life, the base command opened Grande Island in March 1966 as a rest and recuperation site for US service members. Newly repurposed, and capable of hosting several thousand sailors, the island resort offered food, beaches, a golf course, a movie theatre and other leisure activities. The navy planned for Grande Island to establish better long-term relations with the local Philippine government by siphoning off the flood of noisy sailors that visited Olongapo. This was the same year the navy's land lease for Subic was shortened to twenty-five years and when the navy began constructing a fuel pipeline from Subic to its neighbouring inland installation, Clark Air Force Base (Anderson 1991). There were many reasons to maintain a positive relationship with the local community with so many political and sonic changes occurring. Although the navy's policies were a reaction to crime and geopolitics and not necessarily sound, the outcome affected all those elements.

Community, recreation and family life at Subic Bay were marked and organized around sound. A 1967 story in *The Admiral's Log*, the school newspaper of Subic Bay's George Dewey High School, detailed a performance by the USS *Bryce Canyon*'s navy band. The nineteen-piece band 'brought down the house with its outstanding interpretations of Herb Alpert's Tiajuana Brass selections' and their 'clowning antics and various skits' (*The Admiral's Log* 1967). Earlier that year, the China Seas EM (Enlisted Mens) Club was 'converted from a temporary building to a semi-permanent structure' (*Command History of the United States Naval Station Subic Bay* 1967: 3). And a year later, in 1968, the base's go-kart track was reopened, 'basketball, volleyball and deck shuffleboard courts were built between barracks', new skeet shooting ranges were added and 'a total of 32 USO shows were presented at Naval Station Theater and NAS Cubi Theater'

(*Command History of the United States Naval Station Subic Bay* 1968: 3, 1, 8). All these events describe a dynamic indoor and outdoor musical and recreational sonic culture on base. Sailors and civilians heard live music and other acts throughout each year, while the base's Special Services Division took steps to make entertainment and recreation permanent parts of base culture by building new spaces and expanding older ones. The base was in many ways like any other domestic American suburb, with sports fields and courts, stages and community centres, parks and theatres. The base was not a silent, sterile place as so many technical and administrative naval documents suggest but was instead home to American service members, their families and other civilians who engaged in all manner of sonic activities. The sound and culture of the naval occupation of Philippine land for these individuals and communities were structured around a military-sonic domesticity, a manufactured pastoral suburbanization coexisting with military industry and logistics.

In addition to the base's family and domestic sound worlds, Subic Bay was marked by the sounds of industry and labour. Although most naval documents and navy leaders did not emphasize the impact of sound, other people experienced the base's industrialism acoustically, and were aware and familiar with that kind of sonic power. In a 1967 *Subic Bay News* article, reporter Romeo C. Alinea wrote a detailed report about the workers at Ship Repair Facility (SRF) 23, a blacksmiths shop. Alinea described how 'this group makes known its presence and its work by the sound and hot fumes it evolves' and that the 'neatly arranged furnaces burn like inferno, aggravated by the resonant sounds of pounding hammers on iron bars atop anvils' (1967a). The article was a propaganda piece that highlighted the contributions of the shop's fifty-three Filipino base workers. Alinea used the clamour of the shop as a device to demonstrate the exceptional and humble work ethic of the workers, who, without complaint, wielded fire and endured smashing metal to support the navy's missions: 'Friendly fire after all retains its God-given usefulness and noise is not a nuisance per se in this place' (Alinea 1967a). This article takes the reader into this shop and shows what it sounded like and how it fit into the overall industrial work area. One hears the 'pounding hammers', the 'welding and chipping' and the massive 'electric driven hammer' (Alinea 1967a). It was one of many machine shops located in that area of the base. Alinea writes how the 'deafening sounds' were not deterrents to the shop's output. The Filipino workers are heroic in this narrative, doing difficult work in difficult conditions. It is a sweaty, masculine space, full of strong men wielding hammers and tongs to manipulate the earth's natural elements.

The navy's efforts to assert political and economic control had a corollary effect on the base's sound, on the base's social and cultural life and on raw decibel measurements. In these examples, we can hear how sound is wrapped up in politics and see how it becomes politicized, a battleground for power. On-base life was not louder or quieter than off-base – it was simply different. The base did not have the congestion and traffic that distinguished Olongapo, and base residents enjoyed considerably more open space than their Filipino neighbours. Sound on base was largely relegated towards the bay itself where the dockyards and the repair facilities were located, with some exceptions. Exceptions included how the US Navy tried to sustain positive US–Philippine relations through celebrations on base. In December 1969, for example, the navy hosted a Fil-Am Fiesta – a celebration 'designed to promote friendship and understanding between American servicemen and their Filipino hosts' (*Command History Report* 1969: 27). The event was endorsed by Olongapo mayor Amelia Gordon and included a parade, events, performances and exhibitions featuring Americans and Filipinos, all raising money for Philippine charities. Local Filipinos were invited to tour three US ships and one Philippine ship (*Command History Report* 1969: 28). The navy's narrative account of this event is rich in sonic detail: we can hear the boxing matches, cock fights, bingo games, film screenings, carnival, parade, arcade, sporting events, singers and bands – a blend of American and Filipino cultural activities. This was a massive event, and Subic Bay hosted approximately 100,000 Filipino guests, tripling the base's population. This large event dismantles the imagined quiet culture of Subic Bay used to distinguish the base and therefore the United States and Americans from Olongapo and Filipinos. The history and legacy of US colonialism and military occupation in the Philippines continued to exist into the 1960s and was regularly mediated through the ways the United States and the US Navy sought to differentiate themselves from Filipinos. Distinguishing base from town and American from Filipino was another facet of pre-Second World War US colonialism that continued to exist at Subic Bay, influencing the way in which naval leaders asserted control over sounds and spaces.

A home port away from home

The United States built its relationship with the Philippines on control – control of space, control of bodies, control of institutions and control of sound. The US colonial government used the Philippines as a laboratory to test social policies and ideas before importing them back for domestic use. Alfred McCoy shows how the incubation of modern policing, surveillance and intelligence gathering in the Philippines projected US authority and control, tactics later incorporated into the modern American security state (McCoy 2009). The Philippines was also a place where Americans developed understandings of race and gender, a process that continued at postcolonial Subic Bay. Paul Kramer writes how the politics of racial recognition defined American colonial institutions in the Philippines and how race needed to be a malleable social construct to represent Filipinos as racially dark, savage or barbaric (Kramer 2006). Writing in counterpoint to McCoy and Kramer, Nerissa Balce (2017) and Benito Vergara (1995) demonstrate how colonial photography visually reinforced perceived racial and sexual differences between Americans and Filipinos. Both show how American perceptions of the Filipino population were carefully curated. American control and occupation of the Philippines was enforced through military measures, but also through cultural, political, economic, visual and, later, sonic factors.

The methods of control used by the United States in the Philippines were mediated through stages and forms of occupation. The Philippines was subjected to three colonial governments and occupations: Spain, the United States and Japan. For many years, the Philippines was a geopolitical token, traded and possessed. When the Philippines became an independent nation in 1946, occupation was recent history. A year earlier, in September 1945, US Marines maintained a military occupation of Subic Bay from the US Army, who assumed control of it after defeating the Japanese (Anderson 1991: 76). Thus, even with independence, Philippine land was occupied by the US military. Vague phrasings written into the Military Bases Agreement Act concealed latent sovereignty issues regarding military occupation, debated in the mid-1950s and throughout the following decades. The crux of these debates was that both the United States and the Philippines interpreted the indeterminate language regarding the titles to mean that they were each uniquely the possessor of lands used by US forces (Ma 2001). The history of American occupation was a persistent issue even in an independent Philippines, as the two countries debated sovereignty and extraterritoriality (Ma 2001).

The post-Second World War base leases negotiated between the United States and the Philippines demonstrated the extent of continued American power in the Philippines. As the US State Department and Defense Department negotiated agreements for US military outposts in the Philippines, US colonial and military occupation narratives were extinguished, and rent-free property leases replaced the previous generation's overt tactics of military and governmental occupation.

On paper, these legal agreements appeared to overwrite the historically asymmetrical relationship of military occupation and colonialism between the United States and the Philippines, and were established through legitimate diplomatic efforts by representatives of both governments. These documents used language that emphasized mutual security concerns in the region, a collaboration between two Allied nations. The arrangements between the United States and the Philippines were for 'mutual security', 'common defence', 'mutual interests', 'mutual protection', 'military necessity' and 'international security' (Military Bases Agreement Act 1947). This agreement and other treaties, however, were written upon a fraught history, and functioned as palimpsests more than clean slates, as traces of the colonial past seeped through the freshly inked signatures.

The 1947 agreement favoured the United States and granted the US military complete autonomy over the land leased to them by the Philippine government, including jurisdiction over Olongapo City. The agreement ensured that Subic Bay would become a nexus for re-negotiating power dynamics and defining overseas American culture and lifestyles in the following decades. Critics of overseas US base leases argue that these arrangements were negotiated under unequal terms, and that overseas bases enacted colonial and imperial dynamics under a new banner, a more subtle, legal approach to occupation, what Mark Gillem calls a 'mortgaged empire' (2007: 26). This arrangement differed between countries with US bases, such as South Korea, Japan and Guam, but there was always a legal architecture in place that allowed the United States to lease the land for overseas bases essentially rent free. Host nations in return received the benefits and privilege of a security relationship with the United States. There were variations on this arrangement, and in the case of the Philippines, the United States provided annual military, defence and other kinds of monetary aid packages. In this way, the United States was still 'paying' for the right to station troops overseas. The Philippines, however, received substantially less economic aid than other US allies in the region, such as Thailand and Australia (Ma 2001).

Issues of occupation and sovereignty were complicated further from the 1950s onwards, as the United States was forced repeatedly to give legal and symbolic concessions concerning Subic back to the Philippine government. There was negotiation and exchanges of power, and for the United States, a significant loss of control and influence. What matters is the distinction between whether this arrangement was the legal occupation of land by the US military or a US military occupation. If it is the former, then referring to it as an 'occupation' may not be appropriate. Another label – such as occupation-adjacent – might be more useful. The diplomatic complications between the United States and the

Philippines over Subic Bay point to the importance of what Jürgen Osterhammel describes as networks of 'maritime enclaves', a colonial form alongside extraction and settlement ([1995] 2005: 9–10). Global powers fought over the Philippines for its strategic and sheltered maritime ports, which provided access to Asian markets and coveted trade routes in the Pacific.

Maritime expansion and trade networks led to naval enclaves or harbour colonies and later developed into strategic global positions. Osterhammel writes that 'the military base was the only colony type that was adaptable to modern circumstances on a long-term basis' ([1995] 2005: 10). He argues that military bases as a form of colony manage to persist and outlive other forms of colonialism, suggesting that military bases have unique functions within colonial endeavours and possess a distinct militarized role and definition. In the case of Subic Bay, the presence of the US military (specifically the navy) cannot be separated easily from decades of US colonialism and occupation. Militarized overseas maritime enclaves (and airfield and army enclaves) continue to be used by the United States to execute global policy. This network of bases has been called a 'base nation' (Vine 2017) or 'bases of empire' (Lutz 2009). Whatever this network is called, once established, bases like Naval Base, Subic Bay become home ports away from home for millions of US sailors and civilians, a port in a friendly host nation, often glad to support US troops. US sailors were happy sailing to 'the P.I.' (i.e. 'the Philippine Islands') and anticipated the sounds of the city and the base that awaited them there.

Conclusion: Listening to militarism

Although sound is a fixture of overseas US military culture, it is routinely neglected. The US Navy's disavowal and manipulation of its record of self-noise in the Philippines perpetuated stereotypes and assumptions about the differences between US Naval Base, Subic Bay and the neighbouring Olongapo City. Sound was an element used to make distinctions between these two connected places. An oblique analysis of military records, cruise yearbooks, newspapers and interviews demonstrates how sound was a politicized factor and influenced debates about the role of the US Navy in the Philippines. Sound is relevant within the context of US–Philippine occupation narratives, because the sonic (and music) was often how the politics of occupation and sovereignty was enacted or performed by different groups of people. Clubs, bars, industrial shops and other spaces were sonic contact zones where Americans and Filipinos negotiated the legal and cultural effects of occupation.

Sound can occupy space and consciousness, reality, imagination and memory. In the case of Naval Base, Subic Bay, sound collapsed spatial boundaries. It penetrated and permeated daily life on either side of the base's gates. A sonic narrative about the US military in the Philippines helps construct a filled-in history of Subic Bay and Olongapo City, places where Americans and Filipinos interacted within a militarized culture. The presence of the navy produced concentrated, intense sonic events, while around those events, people found quiet, introspective moments. The loud town, quiet base narrative, then, is a false polarity, born of US colonial governance and reinforced by later generations of Americans serving in the navy. The navy's own records reveal how busy and noisy Subic Bay was, a counter to the image and brand the navy wanted for the base. The arguments and memories from sailors that depict Olongapo as a noisy space, meanwhile, fail to consider that the city might have been noisy for them, but quiet for others. Nor is there awareness that the US Navy and its sonic infrastructure was the reason why Olongapo was sonically dense. Jim Sykes writes that the sound studies literature on war has suggested a problematic universal: that 'peacetime is quiet and wartime is noisy' (2018: 10). Sykes writes that peacetime in many places might be noisy rather than quiet and that clear distinctions between the audible quotidian can vary from place to place. This was true at Subic Bay, where the loud–quiet standard varied culturally between Americans and Filipinos.

Sound is part of occupation and empire, and sounds can vibrate and resound across occupied space. Bruce Smith suggests that 'the shape of empire replicates the shape of sound', and I would argue the reverse is also likely to occur – that the shape of sound can replicate the shape of empire (1999: 288). Sound can fill in geographies of empire, assuming its shape while pushing out of its borders. Adding to Smith's argument, I contest that while state-controlled empire has geographic limits, sound is far-reaching and can spill over physical borders and transmit other cultural or social facets of empire or occupation. The sounds of empire are mutable, immediate and more readily experienced in an imperial context than other aspects of empire. Where colonial schools or other institutions take time to set up, the sounds of empire are immediately present, whether mediated through the military, diplomacy or politics. At Subic Bay, the sounds of empire manifested in shipyards, machine shops and family housing units, and in bars, music halls and outdoor markets.

A sonic perspective of the US military occupation of the Philippines demonstrates a history of fuzzy dialogics. Using sound as an amplifier to examine daily life and interactions around base and town shows that simple definitions of occupation and imperialism fail to describe the complexity of daily life and geopolitics at Subic Bay. Sound makes occupation a fungible descriptor of US–Philippine relations and complicates stock narratives and assumptions about the shape of US imperialism. The academy's emphasis on limiting US–Philippine history to reductive narratives of colonialism or occupation obscures the more sinister role of global US militarism, which disguises itself within such histories. The fuzziness of occupation and narrative stasis requires an oblique approach to better discern the role of global US militarization. By listening around and in-between, the scope of American occupation and militarism in the Philippines becomes clearer.

Occupation, exploitation and colonialism are intrinsic elements of US–Philippine history, and of the history of Subic Bay. More fundamentally, however, the history of these two nations is a story of the global reach and excesses of US militarism. US occupation and colonialism in the Philippines were side effects of the larger project of global military dominance. Twentieth-century American technocrats and military leaders used the tools of industrial warfare and set up a global network of military bases without deeper philosophical and ethical considerations as to what followed in the wake of unrestricted militarism. Sound was not a serious concern, yet, a global military cannot escape its own self-noise, and those unintentional resonances are there for us to listen to, frequencies for criticism. There are many ways to listen to and for occupation, but we must listen because occupation is merely a symptom of encroaching militarism and the militarization of daily life. Listening obliquely to the colonial self-noise of US military occupation at Subic Bay shows that the scope of occupation and militarism extends in every direction, affects every sense and leaves traces in even the most unexpected places.

References

Agreement Between the United States of America and the Republic of the Philippines Concerning Military Bases, 26 March 1947. Library of Congress: Available online: https://www.loc.gov/law/help/us-treaties/bevans/b-ph-ust000011-0055.pdf (accessed 7 January 2019).

Alinea, R. C. (1967a), 'Amid Noise and Fire, SRF's Blacksmiths Shop (23) is Tops', *Subic Bay News*, 24 February. Folder Subic Bay, P.I.—US Naval Base, 1967, Box #1585, Shore Establishment, Naval History and Heritage Command, Washington, DC.

Alinea, R. C. (1967b), 'Big Boost To PWC's Participation in the Bases Construction Boom', *Subic Bay News*, 28 April. Subic Bay, P.I.—US Naval Base, Philippines, CH

1967, Box #1585, Shore Establishment, Naval History and Heritage Command, Washington, DC.

Allen, R. C., ed. (1960), *1960 Hannah, USS Hancock CVA-19, Carrier Air Group 11, 1960 Westpac Cruise*, Tokyo: Daito Art Printing, Co.

Anderson, G. (1991), *Subic Bay: From Magellan to Mt. Pinatubo*, Dagupan City, Philippines: Lazer.

Balance, C. B. (2016), *Tropical Renditions: Making Musical Scenes in Filipino America*, Durham, NC: Duke University Press.

Balce, N. (2017), *Body Parts of Empire: Visual Abjection, Filipino Images, and the American Archive*, Ann Arbor: University of Michigan Press.

Ball, D. (2018), Unpublished interview with the author, 11 April.

Bijsterveld, K. (2003), "'The City of Din'": Decibels, Noise, and Neighbors in the Netherlands, 1910–1980', *Osiris*, 18 (1): 173–93.

Burns, L. M. (2012), *Puro Arte: Filipinos on the Stages of Empire*, New York: New York University Press.

Command History of the United States Naval Station Subic Bay, Philippines as of 31 December 1968: Part I—Chronology of Outstanding Events, 3,1,8 (1968). Folder Shore Establishment, Subic Bay, Naval Station, Philippines, 1968, Box #1589, Naval History and Heritage Command, Washington, DC.

Command History of the United States Naval Station Subic Bay, Philippines as of 31 December 1967, 3 (1967), Folder Shore Establishment, Subic Bay, Naval Station, Philippines, 1967, Box #1589, Naval History and Heritage Command, Washington, DC.

Command History Report, 1 January to 31 December 1969, Part II: Basic Narrative, 27 (1969), Box #1590, Folder Shore Establishment, Subic Bay, US Naval Supply Depot, Philippines, Naval History and Heritage Command, Washington, DC.

Commander Fleet Air Philippines and Commander Naval Air Bases Philippines: Staff Study Of US Naval Air Station Cubi Point, P.I. (1956), NAS Cubi 37, NRHS 313-08-006, Box #11, General Correspondence and Reports, 1945–1959; Commander, US Naval Forces, Philippines; Records of Naval Operating Forces, Record Group 313; NARA-Pacific Region (SF), 6.

Corbin, A. (1998), *Village Bells: Sound and Meaning in the 19th Century French Countryside*, trans. M. Thom, New York: Columbia University Press.

Cruise of USS Coral Sea (CVA-43), April 3, 1963–November 25, 1963 (1963), Washington, DC: Department of the Navy Library.

Cusick, S. G. (2008), "'You Are in a Place That Is Out of the World…'": Music in the Detention Camps of the "Global War on Terror"', *Journal of the Society for American Music*, 2 (1): 1–26.

Daughtry, J. M. (2015), *Listening to War: Sound, Music, Trauma, and Survival in Wartime Iraq*, New York: Oxford University Press.

Delmendo, S. (2004), *The Star-Entangled Banner: One Hundred Years of America in the Philippines*, New Brunswick, NJ: Rutgers University Press.

Department of the Navy Bureau of Ships (1951), *Noise Survey and Repair Procedures For Submarine Noise Reduction*, Washington, DC: Department of the Navy Library.

Devine, K. (2015), 'Decomposed: A Political Ecology of Music', *Popular Music*, 34 (3): 367–89.

Enloe, C. ([1990] 2014), *Bananas, Beaches, and Bases: Making Feminist Sense of International Politics*, 2nd edn, Berkeley: University of California Press.

Fitz-Henry, E. (2015), *US Military Bases and Anti-Military Organizing: An Ethnography of an Air Force Base in Ecuador*, New York: Palgrave Macmillan.

Gillem, M. (2007), *America Town: Building the Outposts of Empire*, Minneapolis: University of Minnesota Press.

Gilman, L. (2015), *My Music, My War: The Listening Habits of US Troops in Iraq and Afghanistan*, Middletown, CT: Wesleyan University Press.

Go, J. and A. L. Foster, eds. (2003), *The American Colonial State in the Philippines: Global Perspectives*, Durham, NC: Duke University Press.

Gonzalez, V. V. (2013), *Securing Paradise: Tourism and Militarism in Hawai'i and the Philippines*, Durham, NC: Duke University Press.

Hohn, M. and S. Moon, eds. (2010), *Over There: Living with the US Military Empire from World War Two to the Present*, Durham, NC: Duke University Press.

Kramer, P. (2006), *The Blood of Empire: Race, Empire, the United States and the Philippines*, Chapel Hill: University of North Carolina Press.

Lederer, W. J. and E. Burdick (1958), *The Ugly American*, New York: W. W. Norton and Company.

Lipman, J. K. (2009), *Guantanamo: A Working-Class History Between Empire and Revolution*, Berkeley: University of California Press.

Lutz, C., ed. (2009), *The Bases of Empire: The Global Struggle Against US Military Posts*, New York: New York University Press.

Ma, L. (2001), 'Treaty or Travesty? Legal Issues Surrounding the US-Philippines Military Base Agreement of 1947–1992', *The Journal of American-East Asian Relations*, 10 (1–2): 92–121.

MacLeish, K. T. (2013), *Making War at Fort Hood: Life and Uncertainty in a Military Community*, Princeton, NJ: Princeton University Press.

McCaffrey, K. T. (2002), *Military Power and Popular Protest: The US Navy in Vieques, Puerto Rico*, New Brunswick, NJ: Rutgers University Press.

McClintock, A. (1995), *Imperial Leather: Race, Gender, and Sexuality in the Colonial Contest*, New York: Routledge.

McCoy, A. (2009), *Policing America's Empire: The United States, the Philippines, and the Rise of the Surveillance State*, Madison: University of Wisconsin Press.

Ng, S. (2005), 'Performing the "Filipino" at the Crossroads: Filipino Bands in Five-Star Hotels Throughout Asia', *Modern Drama*, 48 (2): 272–96.

Osterhammel, J. ([1995] 2005), *Colonialism: A Theoretical Overview*, Princeton, NJ: Markus Wiener Publishers.

Pieslak, J. R. (2009), *Sound Targets: American Soldiers and Music in the Iraq War*, Bloomington: Indiana University Press.

Pope, J. (2017), 'Author', *James Pope*, December 2020: Available online: http://www.popejim.com/index.php/author.

Pope, J. (2018), Unpublished interview with the author, 4 January.

Rafael, V. (2000), *White Love and Other Events in Filipino History*, Durham, NC: Duke University Press.

Rainville, B. (1968), 'Fleet's Work and Music Promote Closer Relations', *Subic Bay News*, 13 December. Folder Subic Bay, Philippines, 1968. Box #1585, Shore Establishment, Naval History and Heritage Command, Washington, DC.

Schwartz, J. (2012), 'Resonances of the Atomic Age: Hearing the Nuclear Legacy in the United States and the Marshall Islands, 1945–2010', PhD diss., New York University, New York.

Shigematsu, S. and K. L. Camacho, eds. (2010), *Militarized Currents: Toward A Decolonized Future in Asia and the Pacific*, Minneapolis: University of Minnesota Press.

Smith, B. (1999), *The Acoustic Worlds of Early Modern England: Attending to the O-Factor*, Chicago: Chicago University Press.

Subic Bay News (1968), '2 Wheel Vehicles Restricted at Night', 15 November: 2. Subic Bay, P.I.—US Naval Base, Philippines, CH 1968, Box #1585, Shore Establishment, Naval History and Heritage Command, Washington, DC.

Suisman, D. (2015), 'The Oklahoma City Sonic Boom Experiment and the Politics of Supersonic Aviation', *The Public Historian*, 37 (4): 111–31.

Sykes, J. (2018), 'Ontologies of Acoustic Endurance: Rethinking Wartime Sound and Listening', *Sound Studies*, 4 (1): 35–60.

Talusan, M. (2004), 'Music, Race, and Imperialism: The Philippine Constabulary Band at the 1904 St. Louis World's Fair', *Philippine Studies: Historical and Ethnographic Viewpoints*, 52 (4): 499–526.

The Admiral's Log (1967), 'Navy Band Scores Hit', XI (III) (22 November). Folder Shore Establishment, Subic Bay, Naval Station, Philippines, 1967, Box #1589, Naval History and Heritage Command, Washington, DC.

USS Ranger Cruise Book (1967), Washington, DC: Department of the Navy Library.

Vergara, B. M. (1995), *Displaying Filipinos: Photography and Colonialism in Early 20th Century Philippines*, Quezon City: University of the Philippines Press.

Vine, D. (2011), *Island of Shame: The Secret History of the US Military Base on Diego Garcia*, Princeton, NJ: Princeton University Press.

Vine, D. (2017), *Base Nation: How U.S. Military Bases Abroad Harm America and the World*, New York: Skyhorse Publishing.

Young, R. (2016), *Postcolonialism: An Historical Introduction*, London: Wiley Blackwell.

6

Registering sonic histories in a multiply occupied place

Sound and survivance in Mangota'ay, Taiwan

DJ Hatfield

Not those voices but these: Learning to hear

'No, not that frog sound. Something more like this', said Mangota'ay Pangcah visual and performance artist Rahic Talif as he began to discuss my recording of frogs in a culvert beside the Siuguluan River, which enters the Pacific Ocean near his home village of Mangota'ay, one of the Cepo' Pangcah communities.[1] He had told me his version of the history of the 1877 Cepo' Incident, a massacre after which Qing armies annexed Cepo' Pangcah Country into the empire. To those who know the story, this particular frog sound resembles the keening of elderly women upon hearing the demise of the community's youth, whom the Qing army ambushed at a banquet. I hadn't recorded the right sound. Rahic reminded me that more than recording, my work around Cepo' and along Taradaw ('The River', as Cepo' Pangcah call the Siuguluan River) entailed an aural pedagogy, learning ways of listening and responding to the multiply occupied places of Pangcah Country. I still had to learn to connect frog sounds – these frog voices, not another – to history.

In this chapter, I attend to the ways that Cepo' Pangcah create sonic histories. Indigenous sonic practices, such as registering traces of the Cepo' Incident in frog voices, create resonant figures. Just as the frogs have found spaces to survive in new circumstances, Indigenous practices of registering histories in sound assert that Pangcah relationships to the land endure even under continuing settler-colonial occupation and its attendant social transformations of Pangcah life.

Like frog voices, which resound within settler infrastructures, Indigenous assertion remains entangled with settler occupation; after all, the frog voices resemble the laments of elderly women in the wake of a massacre. If we know how to listen, the frog voices register this incident. Yet this sound is never just any frog voices but a specific species of frog singing in a particular frequency and rhythm at a particular time of year. Moreover, drainage ditches, such as those nearby the old bridge spanning the Siuguluan and near the site of the massacre (now on the campus of Jingpu Elementary School in Cawi'), provide additional habitat and concrete vaults that amplify frog voices. In this fashion, the frog-registered narrative maintains a presence, sounding within settler landscapes. Repeating annually, does it remind us that settler colonialism is, as Patrick Wolfe (2006) argues, structure and not event? Does it matter that hearing these frogs as a memory of the 1877 Cepo' Incident requires a pedagogy in listening?

In asking these questions, I attend to problems of registration. As I argue, the ways that Cepo' Pangcah people register voices create resonant figures through which people grapple with, and develop stances on, their relationship to settler-colonial occupation. In turn, these resonant figures inform local notions of history and community. Moreover, as they animate these figures in intercultural settings, Cepo' Pangcah people assert enduring relationships to their country, bidding settler people to view themselves as guests. Registration – the ways that sounds become particular types of voices – is crucial to this process in which sounds, like frog voices, become media for Indigenous histories and, in turn, survivance.

To develop my argument I will first briefly introduce Taiwanese Indigenous history. Bringing this background into conversation with critical Indigenous studies, I will then move to questions of voice and registration, with particular reference to communicative practices in Cepo'. With this background in place, I will compare and contrast how the sounds of settler infrastructures, the natural world and musical practices register voices. In my conclusion, I will draw from this comparison to ask how we might learn to listen differently, changing our stance on multiply occupied places such as Cepo'.

Much of this chapter necessarily requires a self-reflexive method in which I work through my own experiences of learning to register frog voices, school chimes and riparian sounds as particular figures of Cepo' Pangcah histories. As a settler ethnographer from North America engaged in long-term collaboration with Pangcah visual and performance artists, I must question how I listen; engaging with oral history and interpreting narrative and musical works alongside my collaborators are steps towards deepening my relationships with the resonant figures which my collaborators and consultants in the field animate as they listen, sing and tell stories. In this chapter, I narrate this process of learning to listen as a means to rethink how we might understand the role of registration in the formation of sonic histories that often remain tacit, part of a broader sense of place. And yet, I also examine how figures from these histories might also be employed to confront settler assumptions that present relationships of occupation can – and should – continue indefinitely into the future.

Historical background

Today the 'Amis/Pangcah are one of sixteen officially recognized Taiwanese Indigenous peoples. Like other Taiwanese Indigenous peoples, Pangcah speak an Austronesian language and are descended from Austronesian peoples who resided on Taiwan millennia before the arrival of Sinophone settler colonists around 400 years ago.[2] Today, recognized Taiwanese Indigenous people comprise around 2.3 per cent of the population; with a population of over 200,000 the 'Amis/Pangcah are the largest Taiwanese Indigenous group.

Both vernacular and official Sinocentric histories of Taiwan portray Pangcah Country on Taiwan's Pacific coast and the East Rift Valley as a frontier settled long after the western plains, a distant backwater awaiting development. Only in the 2000s, following Taiwan's transition to a multicultural democracy, have alternate histories portraying the Pacific coast as a vibrant, outward-facing place appeared. These histories point to Taiwan's kinship with the Pacific and Southeast Asia as a means to re-imagine (and rebrand) Taiwan as other than, and beyond, China. Indigenous people tend to approach this national re-imagining ambivalently. In spite of these symbolic gestures, most of Pangcah Country faces pressure from corporations eager to develop the Pacific coast for tourism.

Pangcah understandings of place and history sometimes employ tropes of underdevelopment, but also point to the ocean as a place of ancestral journeys and continued sustenance. Most Pangcah oral histories begin with the arrival of the sister and brother pair Dongi and Rarakan (in some versions, Nakaw and Sra), who landed on Taiwan after surviving a flood, and continue with descriptions of ancestral journeys throughout Taiwan and the Pacific. For coastal 'Amis/Pangcah, whose communities sit on a narrow shelf between the Coastal Range and the Pacific Ocean, fishing and gathering along the *riyar* (ocean) remain important cultural and subsistence practices. The Cepo' Pangach communities, situated around the mouth of the Siuguluan River, also relied on Taradaw as a major means of communication, travelling along it to trade, procure resources and create alliances. Both lagoon and river also drew the attention of other groups, including European merchants who found the lagoon at Cepo' a useful landing site. For the past 500 years, the Cepo' Pangcah communities (Tidaan, Mangota'ay, Laeno and Cawi') have weathered the arrival of Portuguese, Spanish and Dutch colonial merchants, navies and priests; Sinophone settler colonists and Qing imperial armies; Japanese colonial police, schools and industries; and the current Republic of China (Taiwan) government which arrived in the 1940s.

Qing campaigns to assert control over Cepo' in the late 1870s responded to ongoing Western and Japanese colonial pressures. British gunboats had already forced the Qing to sign unequal treaties beginning in 1842, with the treaty that ended the First Opium War (1839–42). In 1871, the Japanese Imperial Navy, wanting to demonstrate sovereignty over Okinawa, occupied part of present-day Taitung County, on Taiwan's south-east coast, after locals kidnapped the crew of an Okinawan ship. Once British diplomats had negotiated a settlement between the Japanese and the Qing court, British engineers and surveyors assisted in the construction of lighthouses and garrisons. The strategic location of Cepo' and its complex relationships with Sinophone merchants made it an important site for a garrison in the Qing campaign to extend effective sovereignty over Taiwan's east coast.

With the Cepo' Incident in 1877 and the defeat of their community, Cepo' Pangcah would begin to be absorbed within a state system. The Qing occupation was brief, however. Only during the Japanese colonial period (1895–1945) would Pangcah encounter apparatuses of modern states such as public works, wage labour, compulsory education, liquor and tobacco monopolies and taxation. Nonetheless, earlier occupations have left traces around Cepo'. Through registering these traces in frog voices, school chimes or song, Cepo' Pangcah assert that they remain, even when residing in urban centres such as Taypak (Taipei) or Takaw (Kaohsiung).

Acoustemology?

In turning to registration I move away from the question of 'what occupation sounds like' towards questions of how Cepo' Pangcah record and inflect occupation in sounds, quotations of sound in discourse and practices of listening. In this regard, my work shares with the work of anthropologist Steven Feld (1996) and other scholars' (e.g. Faudree 2012; Helmreich 2007; Idhe 2007;

Samuels et al. 2010) concerns about how we sense and know the world through sound. This shift to 'how' questions (and away from 'what' questions) might best be indicated in Feld's (1996) move from R. Murray Schafer's (1977) concept of soundscape towards 'acoustemology'.

I am inspired by Feld's discussion of knowing and sensuous participation in the world through sound; however, I must admit that I have been sceptical of acoustemology as Feld defines it (1994, 1996, 2015) because of its avoidance of power relations, particularly colonial occupation, as constitutive. Acoustemology projects a kind of ecological holism upon Indigenous people and their ways of knowing through sonic practices. In this regard, Feld's work is driven by impulses similar to that of Schafer (1977): it desires a world undisturbed by the forces that it assumes have rent a previous acoustic ecology, rather than examining the complicated processes through which Indigenous people have wrestled with dispossession and create decolonizing practices. What if, in contrast, we began with a consideration of how colonial occupation resonates across Indigenous places? After all, the category of 'Indigenous' is always defined in relationship to occupation, to dispossession from, as well as a relationship to, Country.

Settler colonialism and occupation

Occupation for Indigenous peoples connotes more than political arrogation or military violence – although these are components of settler-colonial occupation. Rather, occupation in settler-colonial contexts involves ongoing forms of cultural disintegration and ethical dislocation. As Patrick Wolfe (2006) and others (Coulthard 2014; Kauanui and Wolfe 2012; Kauanui 2016; Simpson 2014) have argued, settler colonialism is structure, not event. In other words, settler colonialism is a congeries of processes, an ongoing project aimed at the elimination of Indigenous peoples. Regardless of the forms such processes take, they aim to sever relationships that Indigenous people articulate through place. Settler occupation accompanies processes of elimination. Culturally, it abets transformation of land from the status of a subject with whom Indigenous people maintain ethical relationships to a resource that may be exploited through settler industry (Coulthard 2010; Simpson 2017).

In contrast to settler objectification of land as resource, Yellowknives Dene political theorist Glen Coulthard (2010) has called attention to what he calls 'grounded normativities', perduring relationships to (and through) Country as ethical ground and guarantor. Coulthard argues that however curtailed the land base may become under colonial occupation, place still remains resonant as Indigenous people continue to maintain lives in relationship to land. Scholars working on the Pacific have amended this notion of place to include ocean as an ethical subject (see, for example, Diaz 2011) – a useful move for Pangcah and other maritime peoples. We may observe such relationships to land/ocean in Cepo' as members of the Mangota'ay, Laeno and Cawi' communities continue to converse with and draw sustenance from the ocean and river mouth in spite of military police harassment under martial law (1949–87) and increasing tourist development pressures today. Cepo' people still hear and speak to *riyar* (ocean), *sra* (land) and Taradaw (the River) as they maintain Pangcah lives.

In keeping with this stress on land as an ethical subject, much recent work in critical Indigenous studies has attended to the ways that place-based strategies of resistance offer alternative models to settler economies and nation-state forms (Alfred 1999, 2005; Corntassel 2012; Coulthard 2010; Simpson 2017). Ethnomusicologists and other scholars working on Indigenous musics and media have shown how a wide variety of sounds and sonic practices inform protest (Barker 2015; Gibson and Dunbar Hill 2000; Martineau 2015), maintain kinship (Fisher 2009), assert modernity or a place in global popular culture circulation (Jacobsen 2017; Tsai 2010), encourage language revival (Barrett 2016; Faudree 2013) and create alliances (Christen 2006). In these works, sound figures as both an element of political mobilization and, more importantly perhaps, an element of everyday strategies of survivance (Steinman 2015; Vizenor 1999).

In other words, listening and sounding in their witness to occupation might also inform decolonizing strategies. Such a strategy emerges from listening to frog voices as a memory of the 1877 Cepo' Incident and resonates with the name some survivors of the incident gave their community when they returned from the mountain refuge of Cilangasan: *Mangota'ay* ('murky' may refer to the turbid waters surrounding the mouth of Taradaw; however, it also encodes a desire to leave memories of the incident murky, letting one's heart remain murky until the day when the waters settle and one can again remember and see clearly). This murkiness inheres in a soundscape where frogs maintain memory for those who learn to listen.

Memories inhering in the soundscape bring to mind the Peircean distinction between index and symbol as developed in research on ritual (Rappaport 1999; Seligman et al. 2008), music (Turino 2007) and interpretation (Tamen 2001). Indices are sign relationships in which the sign makes immediate and co-present its object, often participating in its activity or agency. As these meanings are often embodied, depend on habit and are rarely cognized, they often have the effect of grounding a community in shared practices, a 'shared subjunctive' that affords mediation across social boundaries (Seligman et al. 2008; Turino 2007). In his work on interpretation, literary theorist Miguel Tamen (2001) contrasts indexical meaning as 'participation' with another type of meaning he calls 'symbolic reduction'. Following Tamen, we could argue that sounds that participate in occupation do not mean or symbolize occupation; rather, they establish its presence. What value I might assign to such sounds remains orthogonal to their action, which is broadly indexical, part of the structure of occupation. This kind of registration contrasts with what Tamen (2001) calls symbolic reduction, in that reduction isolates the sign as one of a series of tokens, for example, a sound that is 'another instance of occupation'. Drawing from this work, we can understand registration as one way that listening and sounding practices engage with other voices, developing in this process a variety of stances. Some of these registrations relate to sounds as diffuse indices of occupation. Others may reduce sounds to particular instances of occupation in rhetorics of comparison, accommodation or refusal. The point of this distinction is not so much to categorize as to be aware of shifts in registration, the places where murky, diffuse indices of occupation become clear (and vice versa). How we interact with sounds as voice thus shifts the significance of sounds and sounding through their specific registers.

Like other 'Amis/Pangcah peoples, Cepo' Pangcah have a bountiful tradition of dance and vocal musics. These musics have been the focus of tourism and colonial representations of indigeneity from the Japanese colonial period onward (Wang 2008). Notably, ritual dance musics mediate between external power (including settler power) and Pangcah communities and have been at the centre of anxieties concerning official multiculturalism and tourist-oriented development. In these and other cases, Pangcah employ musical practices in their relationship to colonial occupiers as well as other outside agencies, in attempts to absorb them, rendering them guests (*lafang*) with ethical obligations to their communities (Hatfield 2020). In other words, dance enrols outsiders and mediates difference through ritual action (see Seligman et al. 2008).

How might sonic practices create 'shared subjunctives' (Seligman et al. 2008) but also complicate this account of ritual action, giving us a better purchase on how sound studies might contribute to our understanding of occupation? To answer this question, we can first examine the role of sonic practices in the creation of a broad indexical framework that conveys the diffuseness of occupation and, second, look at the way that sound figures in forms of symbolic reduction. Pangcah people employ sonic practices to situate some actors and institutions as tokens ('another example of colonial occupation') while asserting their participation (embodied, indexically) in the continued life of the *niyaro'*. In this fashion, these sonic practices situate the *niyaro'* as an encompassing indexical framework while reducing the claims of settler institutions.

Quotations of voices

In Sowal no 'Amis the sounds of frogs, waves or school chimes generally remain within the category of *soni*, sounds that may be made both unintentionally and without meaning, as opposed to *ngiha*, sounds made by intentional beings and which are inherently meaningful, even if they have no semantic content. *Ngiha* encompasses both non-linguistic sounds and linguistic utterances in song, storytelling and speech.

To pull *soni* into discourse requires enregisterment such as quotation. Quotations of *soni* and *ngiha* follow the same pattern, the addition of the aspectual particle *sa* or its derivatives *saan/sanay* or *haan/hanay*, which function as quotatives. Both particles register voices, sounds and states in a form of direct discourse: they double or parody the sound or voice ('she said/she was like') rather than incorporate it indirectly ('she said that'). *Saan/ haan* interrupts the speaker's voice with mimetic figuring of the quoted voice. Thus, in narrative and in song, the quotatives *sa cingra/ha ira* create dialogic texts combining sounds (particularly ideophonic usages) and speech, a multiplicity of *nghia or soni*.

Moreover, Sowal no 'Amis also employs a panoply of ideophones to register the sound of actions and states. For example:

Rok-rok sa ko keter no faloco' no hongti
'Burble burble', went the king's heart as it boiled with anger

Awa-ay ko ka-olah-an, cedi cedi sa ko losa' no mako
No one loves me. 'Shimmer shimmer', go my tears

Ma-piw-piw sa i lalan, awa-ay ko kihar i Taitong
'Shimmy shimmy' along the road, I am carefree in Taitung.

The use of quotatives as adverbial and aspectual phrases in Sowal no 'Amis suggests a sonorous registration of action and states. While some of these examples register visual or tactile experiences to establish aspect, it is notable that the paradigmatic usage of *sa/saan* is quotation, as if qualification of actions and states requires direct discourse. While these ideophones may take verb affixes, such as *ma-* or *ka- -an*, to become undergoer or locative voice verbs, for example *ma-piwpiw sa i lalan* (shimmying one's hips along the road) or *ka-tatala'-an no 'orad* (a furious downpour), people more frequently use these ideophones to quote actions and states, treating them as voices.

Registration as direct discourse amplifies the resonance of experiences even as it clears space to establish stance. One way of thinking of registration, then, is as a kind of animation (in the Goffmanian sense). By voicing sonic features in both spoken and sung discourse, 'Amis people animate sonic others and thus stand in a variety of agentive or evaluative relationships with them (Fox 2004: 37–41). This process of animation is one means for Pangcah people to register colonial occupation in a critical fashion.

What did you expect to hear?

I often wonder what tourists expect when they visit coastal Pangcah communities. What a surprise that everything looks, to the untrained eye, just like any other rural Taiwanese (here meaning settler) village: the same concrete houses, the same corrugated metal rooves and motorized doors. Perhaps village streetscapes are too bland in their everydayness to register. Sound, however, does key those who visit or reside in Cepo' to features of the environment and habitation specific to coastal Pangcah communities. At all hours and seasons, one can hear the ocean and river, sometimes backgrounded by other sounds but often present as a source of information about whether it will be a good day to go diving, fishing or gathering and what tools to use. As a sonic and ancestral presence, the ocean provides a set of metaphors that inform musical practice, including dance steps and melodic contours. Before dawn, one can hear the stroke of boat engines, dogs answering barks from across the village and the earliest rooster calls. An occasional truck rumbles along Route 11. If the weather and moon are right for catching fish in the lagoon, one can also hear the sound of small tractors and scooters as men and women head down with their nets. After dawn, as they return, the clack of aluminium doors opening and shouts of '*Talacowa Kiso?*'[3] tell one that another day has begun. Children head to school, and the school chimes begin to peal. Most evenings, the sound of television broadcasts, singing with friends in courtyards or in coin-operated karaokes, and conversation weaves together. After everyone has closed their houses and gone to sleep, Cawi' remains sonically dense with the sounds of frogs, insects, birds and – holding all of it in its constant movement – the ocean and river.

Rain pattering on corrugated metal rooves and the clatter of aluminium doors may have once sounded hopeful when these materials symbolized modernity, but these sounds are now taken-for-granted features of villages rebuilt on far-ocean fishing money during the 1970s and 1980s, much of the construction promoted by a settler government committed to 'life improvement' in Indigenous communities. Programmes of life improvement included prohibitions on speaking Sowal no Pangcah in schools as well as projects for urbanizing Indigenous villages. Most people older than forty years of age can remember living in thatched-roofed structures and punishments for speaking their mother tongue in public.

As it is for other Taiwanese people, for Pangcah the sound of occupation resounds through language and popular musics. The engagements of Pangcah with colonial states and industries appear in lexical items and motifs that by now often escape explicit recognition of their alien provenance; the musical motifs may now sound traditional. It is not so much that these borrowed musical motifs and words no longer resonate more than they contrast with the sounds of later occupations, the Japanese melodies of *enka*-inspired songs contrasting with songs brought by the Chinese Nationalist Party (KMT) after the Japanese surrender in 1945, these songs contrasting with more recent musical conversations with hip hop and K-Pop.

Linguistically, the borrowed terms form a veritable catalogue of modernity. Nearly all, of course, are borrowed from Japanese and, in many cases, Japanese loanwords from Western languages. These terms sound out the diffuse character of occupation, a diffuseness that might leave us deaf to occupation, regarding it as unexceptional. This diffuse character is also a feature of the lived environment as, for example, one hears in local elementary schools or corrugated metal rooves.

To register occupation in sonic practices, then, means to remember and to cultivate modes of audition that preserve relationships to the ocean, river and land that together comprise Cepo'. It is also to make sound in ways that register a gap between the appearance of a normal village and the histories of occupation (including ongoing forms and threats of colonial violence) that condition that normality. It is to register a kind of refusal.

Diffuse sounds of multilayered occupation: School chimes

From the morning and into the late afternoon, elementary schools on either side of Cepo' Lagoon mark school periods with Westminster Chimes and a song adapted from the Second Movement of Dvořák's 'From the New World'.

The song is called 'Homesickness' (*nian guxiang*) in Mandarin Chinese, likely a reference to the afterlife of this movement as the song 'Going Home' as adapted by Dvořák's student William Arms Fisher. The use of both songs derives from Japan. 'Going Home' often plays in Japan on the 5.00 pm chimes, which serve as a test of emergency announcement broadcasts and a gentle reminder to children to return home. In Taiwan, the electronic chime version of 'Going Home' echoes through school compounds and out into surrounding neighbourhoods as schoolchildren head home for supper.

Perhaps nostalgia and a connection with high culture explain its use in school chimes in Taiwan, a country where even garbage trucks play Beethoven and Bądarzewska (and where warblers have come to imitate the melody of Bądarzewska's 'The Young Maiden's Prayer') (van Tongeren 2016). As an index of the school day, moreover, 'Going Home' iterates other features of the school as a component of occupation in Cepo': like the name for elementary school, *kongkoan*,[4] the song borrows from Japanese practice. School chimes resound across different historical occupations, as Japanese sonic practices continue in the contemporary school system. Today, elementary schools in Indigenous districts broadcast popular songs by Taiwanese Indigenous singers; passing beside Gangkou Elementary, one can sometimes hear students practising traditional Pangcah songs. We are no longer in the days when the KMT strove to recover the lost metropole and enforced a monocultural Chinese nationalism, but a multicultural Taiwan where students can study their mother tongue at elementary school, at least for one hour a week. However, the framing of Pangcah language or music within the tones of 'Going Home' or the Westminster Chimes marks the school as a representative of Taypak (i.e. the settler government) within the community's midst, resonating across the space of the community.

Nonetheless, the use of 'Going Home' as the late afternoon bell dates no earlier than the 1970s. Before then, the elementary school in Laeno used only hand rung bells. When asked whether schools had musical chimes during the late Japanese colonial period and the early post-war period, a variety of respondents whom I asked from Indigenous and settler communities around Taiwan underscored that Taiwan was a poor country in the early post-war period. Cepo' lacked electricity until well into the 1970s.

'Going Home' thus registers in ways distinct from the actual conditions of its adoption in Taiwan, even among those who remember that the bells are not a simple continuation of elementary school practice from the Japanese colonial period through the martial law period to the present. Most people hear 'Going Home' as a memory of the Japanese colonial period. Yet, the actual borrowing of this song for school bells happened under the KMT, during the martial law period in which the KMT government sought recognition as 'Free China' and often sought to displace or erase signs of Japanese colonialism. Like the case of 'The Young Maiden's Prayer' on Taiwan's musical garbage trucks, the song was likely transferred from Japan along with the broadcast technology, a kind of resonant accident. Heard as an index of the elementary school's Japanese colonial origins, the song registers several gaps: the first, between decolonizing claims made by the KMT and the reality of continued colonial dispossession; the second, between time as known in land- and ocean-based practices in Cepo' and the time of schools and other colonial institutions.

The school chimes resonate across the space of the entire village. As I sit in my friend's house in Cawi', I can hear them broadcast from across the lagoon, echoing from Gangkou Elementary as well as from Jingpu Elementary School just 100 metres or so down the road. This extension of the sound beyond the school across the *niyaro'* participates in a generalized settler dominance of time and activity, layering clock time, *toki*, over the sounds of river and ocean which index a time organized by daylight, moon and tide. The time of the school is that of governing and disciplining bodies. Nevertheless, the school chimes layer over the ocean and river rather than displacing them entirely. The voice of *riyar* may thus always call us to be other than docile subjects of national institutions.

Tela' to ko 'aresing: Sound registering a change of heart

Sound may also effect a shift in registration, as its voice continues in the narrative. As such, quotation often registers sound as an agent, a voice that compels one to act differently. For example, I had been out recording sounds of Taradaw early one June morning in 2017. Rahic, with whom I was collaborating on a project to document riparian soundscapes, had earlier told me that my recordings had captured the force and murky quality of the river but lacked a feeling for clear, still water. Conditions upriver from Mangota'ay that morning were right, with the sun glinting off the south wall of the canyon as it burned away the morning fog. I recorded the sound of dew as it dropped from leaf to leaf.

When I shared my recording later that day, Rahic became animated as he told me a story that quoted dew falling in the mountains. Rahic's Grandfather had served as a police officer in the Japanese colonial administration. In the early 1930s, Japanese officials, anxious to suppress the remnants of the Wushe Uprising (1930), sent many police officers upland. On the mission, Rahic's Grandfather trekked upriver along Taradaw towards the 'Cold Mountains' (*kasi'enawan a lotok*; the Central Mountain Range). As Grandfather entered a narrow gorge, he felt homesickness. He lit his pipe, smoking as he walked through the gloom of the canyon, wading through the river or scrambling over rocks. It was in the afternoon. Soon the sun reflecting from the walls of the canyon filled it with light. He was not far from his destination. Far above him, near the rim of the gorge, the enemy, Iwatan or Tayen hostile to the Japanese, smelled the tobacco smoke as it drifted upwards:

> 'Who is this enemy we smell, coming near us?' asked the Iwatan. They mobilized their youth to intercept the intruder. Just then, as Grandfather walked through the shimmering canyon, '*tela' saan ko matela' no aresing*', a drop of the coldest dew fell from the leaf of a tree far above him. '*Tela'tela'tela' saan*', it fell from leaf to leaf and into a pool of water where the creek rested, radiating outward, '*to:ng, saanay. Tela' tela' sa*', the dew fell on Grandfather's face and on his chest. At that moment, Grandfather's heart cooled (*mafasaw ko faloco' ira*).
>
> 'Aya! What am I to do, *tela*' went the dew as it fell, cooling my heart. Why am I going to attack the Iwatan? They are people, not my enemy,' said Grandfather.

However, the Iwatan had already discovered him. Soon they were blocking his way. Grandfather had no way to communicate with them except through song. He began to sing of his journey and of the dew:

> *Aya, Widang-aw! Ma-tela'tela' saan to ko aresing*
> *Ma-fasaw no tela' no aresing ko faloco' ako, widang!*
> *saan ko A-Kong*
> 'Aya, My friend! *Tela' tela*' went the dew,
> The *tela*' of the dew cooled my heart, friend,' said Grandfather.

The Iwatan conveyed him to their village. Grandfather was certain that he would be decapitated, but he thought: 'These are people. They are not my enemy.' He slept in their village that night following a banquet. Although he thought, 'Tomorrow morning my head will be gone', he awoke the next morning to the sound of early morning rain dripping from the straw rooves of the village houses. He knew this sound from rainy days in his youth. His hosts brought him a basin of water to wash his face. The cold water reminded him of the dew: 'Aya! What am I to do? These are not my enemies. Why must I do the bidding of the Japanese to attack them?' Warning the village of the Japanese advance, Grandfather left his mission to wander with them, befriending Iwatan, Manuwan and Tayen in the mountains.

Rahic quotes the sound of dew as a way to depict Grandfather's transformation. Underscoring the importance of this quotation in direct discourse, he animates the speech and song of his Grandfather. In Rahic's telling, dewfall's sound indexes the moment of transformation and iconizes Indigenous life (the architecture of thatched-roof houses). Just as the sound of dew falling from the thatched rooves in the Iwatan village resembles the sound of rain on thatched rooves in Mangota'ay, the Iwatan are 'people' and not 'enemy'.

In telling the story, Rahic provided a means to situate the sound of dew within a Pangcah sonic memory. Narrative registration of dewfall encodes a memory of Pangcah responses to occupation, a call to conscience when one might saddle too close to colonial power. An environmental sound becomes available as an alternative history, complete with its own ethical imagination. Punctuating the diffuseness of occupation, sound abets ethical transformation.

Singing of the rapids

Other practices register differently configured landscapes and engage in types of assertion. For example, the *milalik*, a Cepo' Pangcah song associated with travel along Taradaw, produces a sense of place distinct from ordinary contexts of road travel and settler administrative hierarchies. Because the song, like most traditional Pangcah songs, has only vocables as lyrics, improvised additions to the lyrics as well as different versions of the song layer this sense of place with assertions concerning the meanings of Taradaw and its history for social relationships today.

'*Milalik*' is the active voice, subject focal verb form of *lalik*, a cognate of *likir* and *likid*, which means to tumble or speed down a rapidly flowing river. Thus, *milalik* has the connotation of someone shooting the rapids. When asked about this song, most people who can sing it will point out the context of river travel. Rafts once served as the main means of transportation across the Coastal Range, plying Taradaw from Cepo' to Ruisui and down again. Where now white-water rafts convey tourists from Ruisui downward to a restaurant and gift shop beneath the New Canghong Bridge, rafts manned by Cepo's youth once carried goods downriver to the *niyaro*'.

One afternoon, a white-water rafting boat guide and his mother, Meilice, took me on a zodiac raft from the lagoon upriver. We surmounted the first rapids and stopped to hear the birds calling above the rush of the river and falling creeks. Meilice sang the *milalik*.

The melodic contour of *milalik* moves the voice from the dominant upward to the tonic and again upward a major fourth before cascading downward to the tonic an octave below. Most of the movement contrasts upward and downward stepwise movement, with occasional skips over a fourth or a fifth. Although the song is in vocables with improvised lyrics, these added lyrics generally encourage the crew on its journey, naming features of the landscape along the way. In keeping with this convention, Meilice's improvised lyrics, chanted in monotone, animated the part of a leader of a raft crew telling his fellow youths: 'Be strong! We are bringing home wood, logs and bamboo to build houses in our village. Be strong!'

Aware that I was recording, Meilice added her interpretation of the song in relation to local social organization. 'Our people', she said, 'depend on shared labour (*mipaliw*).' In the past, before the road was built, the most important organization for collective endeavours, such as transporting building materials, was the age set organization, which is still active today. The age set organization mobilized youth for the work. Part of this mobilization, the song encouraged the young men to overcome their fear of the rapids. As an environmental activist who fished the lagoon a few times a week, Meilice placed Taradaw within the networks of shared labour (*paliw*) that she highlighted in her remarks. That summer, she also mobilized a group of people who fished the lagoon as 'netizens' who would share labour for environmental assessment, shellfish population management and clean-up work. Her *milalik*, performed on a zodiac in the midst of Taradaw, was meant to enrol me in this ethical relationship to the river.

If Meilice focuses on the age set organization and practices of shared labour, Rahic holds a special affection for *milalik* as a song through which he communicated to Taradaw during a fierce typhoon in which a landslide nearly swept him away. He also articulates in his *milalik* a critique of geographies of occupation.

Rahic's version of *milalik* creates textural contrasts of soaring glissando movements on phrases with skipping motion and nearly staccato articulation on the stepwise falling motion of each verse's cadence. At times, his articulation in these cadences resembles sighing or relaxing after a period of exertion. On several occasions of listening, recording or performing *milalik* with Rahic, I have noticed how his lyrics range from humorous, teasing lines about being cast overboard and mistaking a raftmate's penis for an eel (humour is always a good way to stare down fear, explains Rahic), to those describing the hardships of travel through the rapids. He also sings lyrics that describe Taradaw in historical terms as *narakatan no mato'asay*, the road the old people (ancestors) walked. In these lyrics, Rahic grieves that today Taradaw has largely been forgotten, left to tourists. Following the pattern of the song, Rahic's *milalik* usually ends with an exhortation to the listener: 'Take what we give you as materials to build a beautiful *niyaro*'. However, he extends his vision metaphorically, voicing, along with the river, a sense that no one walks Taradaw any longer.

I suspect that this acquaintance with Taradaw is distinct from the experience of driving to Ruisui along the road above the river. Today the river belongs mostly to tourists. The sounds of outboard motors dominate the Siuguluan River today, participating in a settler transfer of Taradaw to adventure tourism. But Taradaw can still call to us in song. When we *milalik*, do we hear an echo of a life now diminished, of habits transformed by settler governments and their hierarchy of central places? *Milalik* maintains the resonance of a riparian economy that once linked Pangcah communities in the Rift Valley and the Pacific coast. We hear echoes of this system in the family resemblances of ritual musics along the river; yet, the reality of settler occupation has meant that Pangcah today are less oriented to the river than to the routes and networks that link them to Hualien, the major administrative centre, and to schools, stores and township offices in Fongbin or Changbin. *Milalik* reminds us, if we allow it, that this hierarchy of places is a relatively recent feature, an adjunct of the settler state. *Milalik* conjures a world in which Taradaw was central.

Complicating this awareness is our knowledge that the Siuguluan River was always a mediating space. Ruisui had long been an outpost of settler merchants, and the Coastal Range and Rift Valley were home to groups whose relationships with Pangcah were sometimes friendly but often hostile. Nonetheless, *milalik* creates a kind of 'shared subjunctive' (Seligman et al. 2008) in which singers and listeners reclaim Taradaw as a mediating (and life-giving) space, the centre of a Pangcah world.

This use of *milalik* as an assertion is even more notable when we listen to an example of its appearance in inter-ethnic contexts, such as the production of contemporary Indigenous popular music, the audience for which includes people from other Indigenous groups and the settler population, as well as Pangcah people. In his 2013 album, *Cepo'*, Mangota'ay Pangcah singer-songwriter Anu Kaliting Sadipongan performed a version of *milalik* with lyrics co-written with Arik, also of Mangota'ay. The most distinctive quality of Anu's version is that there are fixed lyrics throughout. Anu sings only the first phrase of each verse in vocables. In this version with lyrics, Mangota'ay Pangcah relationships to *riyar* and Taradaw are spelled out for a possibly unfamiliar audience. However, rather than the resonance of riparian trade and travel, ancestral journeys and occupation echo throughout Anu's version. The first of the song's five stanzas establishes the narrative through reference to the legend of Dongi and Rarakan, the sister and brother who became ancestors of Pangcah following a devastating flood (Anu 2013). Moreover, the Anu version begins, tellingly, with the sound of the ocean, which alone occupies the first thirteen seconds of the recording. Above this sound, we hear the first verse sung by an elderly woman. A bass drone, tuned to the tonic, enters at the end of the phrase '*siya siya sa ko tamokis to lafii*' (the whitecaps (across which Dongi and Rarakan travelled on a tiny raft) soughed all evening). The drone continues, shifting after four beats to a minor third and then, four beats later, back to the tonic.

From the first verse's description of floating in the troubled ocean, longing to set one's eyes on a place to land, the lyrics turn to the couple's first sight of Cepo' and their settlement there. As the second verse begins, synth notes begin to fill the background. Anu's voice enters on the second line of the second verse, in which the couple land at Cepo', becoming the ancestors of Pangcah people. As his voice doubles the elderly woman's, a guitar vamp and drums enter. The elderly woman's voice drops out of the mix, and Anu's voice comes to the centre.

The lyrics then describe Taradaw and *riyar* as the source of life for Cepo' Pangcah and assert that the village's laws and ritual continue from the ancestors to the present day. This last phrase, '*rayray tahaanini*', transmitted or passed down to this moment, forms a caesura for the first three stanzas, after which the last two stanzas take up the history of the 1877 Cepo' Incident and the movement of Pangcah people across the Coastal Range to the Rift Valley and to the north and south of Cepo'. The song concludes with a description of Pangcah people cultivating the land and remembering their ancestors 'to this very day' *tahaanini*. In order to underscore this transmission of ancestral presence, Anu repeats this last phrase, '*tahaanini, tahaanini*'.

In this fashion, the two sections of the song establish the song's resonance for an inter-ethnic audience. For listeners who read a paraphrase of the lyrics into Mandarin in the album's liner notes or – more likely – on the subtitles of the video to 'Cepo'' (as Anu's version of *milalik* is titled), the song sounds out a Pangcah history of relationships to the land and struggle against Qing armies, a metaphor for forces now bent on wresting the land from Pangcah people, such as corporate developers and their allies in the settler state. In Anu's version, the song locates ancestral presence as a source radiating forward and outward '*tahaanini*' in which Anu and other Cepo' Pangcah struggle to maintain their stewardship of the ocean and river which has from the time of the ancestors sustained them. Hence, the resonance of Anu's version differs from Rahic's or Meilice's versions, in which a discursively unelaborated but sensed memory of Taradaw opposes settler place hierarchies in the present. Registering in the lyrics present threats on Cepo' as analogous to the Qing invasion in 1877, it is a call to struggle as well as an assertion of Pangcah sovereignty 'to this very day'. In this sense, Anu's version engages in a kind of symbolic reduction, showing developers to be yet another occupying force.

Apart from the lyrics, the mix, in which Anu's voice enters as a doubling of an elderly woman's voice and eventually fades into the ocean, suggests the traditional provenance of the song, as if Anu learned the song from the elderly woman. The video (Lekal 2013) underlines this narrative, showing an elderly woman sitting on a bench overlooking the ocean and a little boy who learns the song by singing along. At the conclusion of the video, Anu – in the video the boy now grown into a youth – returns to this place where he learned the song. This narrative, of course, is anachronistic: Anu co-wrote the lyrics. The video and mix both situate Anu's singer-songwriter practice within a deeper, more traditional pedigree than competitions and record labels in Taiwan's capital city of Taipei. However, Anu's version of *milalik* does more than assert tradition. The lyrics animate a song of travel along Taradaw, understood among Cepo' Pangcah as constituting their relationship to place, making this song speak as an assertion of continued Pangcah presence in Cepo' and in other communities where the descendants of Dongi and Rarakan dispersed. That one can find these communities even in Taypak might be a hidden subtext of Anu's *milalik*.

Conclusion

In a different colonial context – that of Korean survivors of the Japanese comfort women system – ethnomusicologist Joshua Pilzer (2012) discusses both the difficulties and ethical imperative of listening. Contrasting discursive frameworks that promote ready grasp of information to listening's more difficult task, he cautions:

> Voices do not stay still, nor do they stay quiet. They talk back, and most of us have been unwilling to listen, preferring instead the silence of still images, which we can more easily invest with our own thoughts and agendas. (Pilzer 2012: 26)

We can expand Pilzer's caution to cover registration more broadly than conversions to still images, infographics or memes. The moving – I would say animated – quality of voices produces a particular resonance, often dissonant, as we attempt to situate these voices within a historical account. As I have tried to demonstrate here, however, this resonance is productive. Through registration, sounds of occupation become voices with which one can grapple, developing stances and strategies.

In my work around Cepo' I have often been reminded that I need to learn how to hear the ocean and river, knowing through their sounds whether it is a good day for spearfishing or setting nets, remembering through them the layers of occupation that have made the *niyaro'* that Cepo' Pangcah live in today, *niyaro'* that are not merely colonially occupied spaces but an Indigenous place which sounds its history in complicated relationships with, and refusals of, colonial structures. Trusting neither my ears nor my microphones, I still know that I must employ microphones and editing to sound out narratives people relate to me, sometimes in gestures to sounds that I haven't learned to locate or interpret, sometimes as responses to listening to my recordings. These sounds include many that are colonial imports or impositions, but that is the point – we cannot understand Indigenous place apart from the multiply occupied spaces in which it registers Indigenous presence and refusal. In this regard, practices of listening to occupation may alert us to ways that, as anthropologist Daniel Fisher (2016: 50) has argued in his work on Aboriginal radio request programmes in northern Australia, Indigenous people 'register "aboriginality" in ways that sidestep indexical relationships between a single, stable expressive form and any given social identity'. Occupying the voice of the occupier through registration, those who teach me to listen in Cepo' give voice to a history that includes a future.

Apart from the question of what occupation sounds like, then, sound studies scholarship working on occupation can approach practices of registration and animation through which people shift voices, stances and understandings of occupied places. An approach to animation, which sets out by examining how voices are registered and mediated, also suggests that we more closely attend to the perlocutionary effects that result from registration: does it, as in a narrative of dew falling in the mountains, produce caution about boundary maintenance? Does the voice, as in the *milalik*, interpellate us into a world where Taradaw still defines relationships among Pangcah and other groups? Does it, as in Anu's versioning of *milalik*, bid settlers to come to terms with an assertion that they are but guests in Pangcah Country? Through such questions, sound studies may contribute to understandings of occupation and, more importantly, decolonizing strategies.

Notes

1   This chapter grows from a set of collaborations with Cepo' Pangcah artists, environmentalists and language activists Rahic Talif, Meilice (Chen Hsiu-hua), Canglah Pelo, Uding, Anu Kaliting, Sumi, Sapad Kacaw and Iyo Kacaw, as well as

people in communities across 'Amis/Pangcah Country along Taiwan's east coast. I would like to thank these collaborators, the Asian Cultural Council and the Fulbright Foundation who have supported my work, as well as Cepo' Arts Center, Tsai Meng-wu, Suming Rupi, Aki Rupi, Stanley Chang, my age mates and, most importantly, the *to'as no niyaro'*, the elders and ancestors who teach and give life. This chapter is dedicated to the memory of 'Atolan 'Amis leader and vocalist Haru (Pan Ching-Tian).

2   These settlers from southern Fujian, in what is now China, came as labour under the stimulus of Dutch franchise colonialism on the south-west coast of Taiwan.

3   '*Talacowa Kiso?*', Where are you going?, is a typical Pangcah greeting.

4   '*kongkoan*' is a loanword from Japanese (*kōgakō* – a colonial-era Japanese term for 'elementary school') to which a Pangcah ending has been added. Common Pangcah words for government and government functionaries, such as *seifu* (government), *sonciyo* (village mayor), *kenciyo* (county magistrate) and *tayhin* (policeman), are also derived from Japanese.

References

Alfred, G. T. (1999), *Peace, Power, Righteousness: An Indigenous Manifesto*, Oxford: Oxford University Press.

Alfred, G. T. (2005), *Wasase: Indigenous Pathways of Action and Freedom*, Toronto: University of Toronto Press.

Anu Kaliting Sadipongan (2013), 'Cepo' ', [Song] on *Cepo'*, Wind Records, TWW-1301 [CD], Taiwan.

Barker, A. J. (2015), '"A Direct Act of Resurgence, A Direct Act of Sovereignty": Reflections on Idle No More, Indigenous Activism, and Canadian Settler Colonialism', *Globalizations*, 12 (1): 43–65.

Barrett, R. (2016), 'Mayan Language Revitalization, Hip Hop, and Ethnic Identity in Guatemala', *Language and Communication*, 47: 144–53.

Christen, K. (2006), 'Tracking Properness: Repackaging Culture in a Remote Australian Town', *Cultural Anthropology*, 21 (3): 416–46.

Corntassel, J. (2012), 'Re-envisioning Resurgence: Indigenous Pathways to Decolonization and Sustainable Self-Determination', *Decolonization: Indigeneity, Education and Society*, 1 (1): 86–201.

Coulthard, G. (2010), 'Place Against Empire: Understanding Indigenous Anti-Colonialism', *Affinities: A Journal of Radical Theory, Culture, and Action*, 4 (2): 79–83.

Coulthard, G. (2014), *Red Skin, White Masks: Rejecting the Politics of Recognition*, Minneapolis: University of Minnesota Press.

Diaz, V. M. (2011), 'Voyaging for Anti-Colonial Recovery: Austronesian Seafaring, Archipelagic Re-thinking, and the Remapping of Indigeneity', *Pacific Asia Inquiry*, 2 (1): 21–32.

Faudree, P. (2012), 'Music, Language, and Texts: Sound and Semiotic Ethnography', *Annual Reviews in Anthropology*, 41: 519–36.

Faudree, P. (2013), *Singing for the Dead: The Politics of Indigenous Revival in Mexico*, Durham, NC: Duke University Press.

Feld, S. (1994), 'From Ethnomusicology to Echo-Muse-Ecology', *The Soundscape Newsletter*, 8: 9–13.

Feld, S. (1996), 'Waterfalls of Song: An Acoustemology of Place Resounding in Bosavi, Papua New Guinea', in S. Feld and K. R. Basso (eds), *Senses of Place*, 91–135, Santa Fe, NM: School of American Research Press.

Feld, S. (2015), 'Acoustemology', in D. Novak and M. Sakakeeny (eds), *Keywords in Sound*, 12–21, Durham, NC: Duke University Press.

Fisher, D. (2009), 'Mediating Kinship: Country, Family, and Radio in Northern Australia', *Cultural Anthropology*, 24 (2): 280–312.

Fisher, D. (2016), *The Voice and its Doubles: Media and Music in Northern Australia*, Durham, NC: Duke University Press.

Fox, A. (2004), *Real Country: Music and Language in Working-Class Culture*, Durham, NC: Duke University Press.

Gibson, C. and P. Dunbar-Hill (2000), 'Nitmiluk: Place and Empowerment in Australian Aboriginal Popular Music', *Ethnomusicology*, 44 (1): 39–64.

Hatfield, DJ (2020), 'Good Dances Make Good Guests: Dance, Animation, and Sovereign Assertion in 'Amis Country, Taiwan', *Anthropologica*, 62 (2): 337–52.

Helmreich, S. (2007), 'An Anthropologist Underwater: Immersive Soundscapes, Submarine Cyborgs, and Transductive Ethnography', *American Ethnologist*, 34 (4): 621–41.

Idhe, D. (2007), *Listening and Voice: Phenomenologies of Sound*, Albany: SUNY Press.

Jacobsen, K. (2017), *The Sound of Navajo Country: Music, Language, and Diné Belonging*, Chapel Hill: University of North Carolina Press.

Kauanui, J. K. (2016), '"A Structure Not an Event": Settler Colonialism and Enduring Indigeneity', *Lateral*, 5 (1): Available online: http://csalateral.org/issue/5-1/for um-alt-humanities-settler-colonialism-enduring-indigeneity-kauanui/ (accessed 10 September 2020).

Kauanui, J. K. and P. Wolfe (2012), 'Settler Colonialism Then and Now', *Politica and Societa*, 1 (2): 235–58.

Lekal Sumi (2013), 'Cepo'', [Music Video], 5 minutes 51 seconds: Available online: https ://www.youtube.com/watch?v=rJrB5D4y2Ek (accessed 10 September 2020).

Martineau, J. (2015), 'Rhythms of Change: Mobilizing Decolonial Consciousness, Indigenous Resurgence, and the Idle No More Movement', in E. Coburn (ed), *More Will Sing their Way to Freedom: Indigenous Resistance and Resurgence*, 229–53, Halifax and Winnipeg: Fernwood Publishing.

Pilzer, J. D. (2012), *Hearts of Pine: Songs in the Lives of Three Korean Survivors of the Japanese 'Comfort Women'*, Oxford: Oxford University Press.

Rappaport, R. A. (1999), *Religion and Ritual in the Making of Humanity*, Cambridge: Cambridge University Press.

Samuels, D. W., L. Meintjes, A. M. Ochoa and T. Porcello (2010), 'Soundscapes: Toward a Sounded Anthropology', *Annual Reviews in Anthropology*, 39: 29–45.

Schafer, R. M. (1977), *The Soundscape: Our Sonic Environment and the Tuning of the World*, Rochester, VT: Destiny Books.

Seligman, A. B., R. P. Weller, M. J. Puett and B. Simon (2008), *Ritual and Its Consequences: An Essay on the Limits of Sincerity*, Oxford: Oxford University Press.

Simpson, A. (2014), *Mohawk Interruptus: Political Life Across the Borders of Settler States*, Durham, NC: Duke University Press.

Simpson, L. B. (2017), *As We Have Always Done: Indigenous Freedom through Radical Resistance*, Minneapolis: University of Minnesota Press.

Steinman, E. W. (2015), 'Decolonization, Not Inclusion: Indigenous Resistance to American Settler Colonialism', *Sociology of Race and Ethnicity*, 2 (2): 219–36.

Tamen, M. (2004), *Friends of Interpretable Objects*, Cambridge, MA: Harvard University Press.

Tsai, F. L. (2010), 'Playing Modernity: Play as a Path Shuttling across Space and Time of A'tolan Amis in Taiwan', PhD diss., National Tsing Hua University, Taiwan.

Turino, T. (2008), *Music as Social Life: The Politics of Participation*, Chicago: University of Chicago Press.

van Tongeren, M. (2016), 'Taiwanese Bush Warblers Imitating Garbage Trucks: A Mutual Affair?' *Journal of Sonic Studies*, 12: Available online: https://www.research catalogue.net/view/286848/286849/0/0 (accessed 10 September 2020).

Vizenor, G. (1999), *Manifest Manners: Narratives on Post-Indian Survivance*, Lincoln: University of Nebraska Press.

Wang Y. (2008), *Tingjian zhimindi: Heize Longchao yu zhanshi Taiwan yinyue diaocha, 1943* (Listening to the Colony: Kurosawa Takamoto and the Wartime Survey of Formosan Music, 1943), Taipei: Guoli Taiwan daxue chuban.

Wolfe, P. (2006), 'Settler Colonialism and the Elimination of the Native', *Journal of Genocide Research*, 8 (4): 387–409.

Part III

Auditory responses to occupation and colonialism

Introduction to Part III

Jeremy E. Taylor

Part III of *Sonic Histories of Occupation* is entitled 'Auditory responses to occupation and colonialism'. The chapters here examine how the circulation of sounds through media, art, music and technology under colonialism and/or foreign occupation has created new identities, modes of expression and aural spaces. The chapters all explore the role of sound in the territorial expansion of various empires – Russian, Soviet, American and British – as well as auditory responses to such sonic imperialism on the part of local populations.

Dimitri Smirnov's analysis of the work of the Kyrgyz writer Chingiz Aitmatov in Chapter 7, for instance, details references to the sounds of 'railway imperialism' – from trains to station loudspeakers – in Russian and Soviet Central Asia in Aitmatov's fiction. The 'noisy' expansion of Russian (and later Soviet) control in Central Asia was exemplified by such mundane features of the occupied soundscape as public address systems or the screeching sounds of passing trains. By bringing such sounds into his literature, Aitmatov writes in a tradition of intellectuals who have tried to incorporate the sounds of the railway into their critiques of colonialism and occupation.

For Skelchy, the central question of Chapter 8 is 'how sound was engineered and experienced through a wider sensory world shaped by US colonialism in the Philippines', with this chapter specifically considering the ways in which sound was incorporated into the design of the colonial hill town of Baguio in the Philippines. Drawing on the emerging literature on sensory history, Skelchy shows how the 'colonial reconfiguration of Baguio's auditory environment' was central to the (re)creation of this town in the early twentieth century, as US planners sought to create a Simla-inspired upland space in which colonial officials could find respite not just from the heat of Manila but also from its supposed noise.

Tan's chapter adopts a quite different perspective – and material sources such as newspapers and gramophone records – to demonstrate the ways in which 'hybrid' music cultures developed in the cosmopolitan port cities of colonial Malaya. As she shows, 'the soundscapes of colonial Malayan port cities articulated the merging of diverse cultures and the creation of new mixed identities' – including those that were at odds with the image of the 'Anglicized Malayan' that had been imposed on the region under British colonial rule.

All three chapters in this section bring together sound and space – even while they analyse the links between the two from very different disciplinary approaches (comparative literature, sound studies, historical ethnomusicology) and by utilizing very different types of sources. In doing so, however, they address two of the core questions raised by this volume as a whole: How does occupation give rise to distinctive auditory environments and music cultures? And how are sound and music implicated in controlling and disciplining colonized or 'occupied' peoples and aural spaces? As Part III as a whole shows, colonialism and foreign rule did indeed impose new sounds and soundscapes on local populations. Yet local groups also displayed agency in either recording their opposition to such sounds or using technologies and media that arrived alongside foreign rule to develop new modes of sonic self-expression.

7

The sonic occupation of Central Asia

Sound culture and the railway in Chingiz Aitmatov's *The Day Lasts More Than a Hundred Years*

Dimitri Smirnov

Introduction: Listening to the railway in Central Asia

Following more than a century of prolonged conflicts and shifting alliances, in the second half of the nineteenth century the Russian Empire succeeded in conquering the last remaining areas to its south that separated it from Persia, Afghanistan and China. By bringing the khanates of Khiva and Kokand and the emirate of Bukhara under its political control, the Russian Empire was able to considerably expand its sphere of influence in Central Asia. The military campaigns during this time period also paved the way for the political reorganization of previously occupied territories, as demonstrated by the cases of the Turkestan and Steppe governor-generalships or other regions that were integrated into the empire after the subjugation of the three Kazakh *zhuz* (hordes) during the eighteenth and nineteenth centuries. The reasons for the annexation of the southern borderlands were manifold and ranged from economic considerations about the exploitation of natural resources and human labour to the Russian Empire's geopolitical and strategic ambitions of positioning itself as a major military force in the region, and the Tsarist idea of a civilizing mission in Central Asia and the quest to demonstrate Russia's status as a great imperial power.[1] Russian expansion into Central Asia had a lasting impact even after the Russian Revolution of 1917 (ending the Tsarist Empire) and the establishment of the Soviet Union, during which formerly colonized peoples were unable to gain independence from the multiethnic Soviet state (Carrère d'Encausse 1994a, 1994b; Radjapova 2005), leading to what has been referred to as the region's 'second colonial experience' (Brower 2003: 153).[2]

The conquest of Central Asia by the Russian Empire and, later, Soviet rule over the region was accompanied by a reconfiguration of the soundscape. Newly introduced auditory environments exemplify the effects that these imperial constructs had on the population of Central Asia and their cultures. Listening to occupation thus reveals continuities in the different oppressive political systems that shaped the history of Central Asia for over 200 years. Acts of listening to occupation can also be observed in a medium such as literary texts. Through the lens of fiction, the political significance of sounds under occupation can be amplified and made explicit. As this chapter will demonstrate, in Soviet literature, certain sounds that emerged within the soundscapes of Central Asia a century before are taken up to critically reflect not just on Russian expansion in the nineteenth century but also on how the Soviet Union continued this history of occupation and how it upheld imperialist attitudes and forms of governing. The case of Central Asia is instructive for observing the transitions between different systems of occupation that are in many ways antagonistic to each other, but still share important features in controlling and disciplining colonized peoples. Tracing the sounds of occupation shows how these periods of political rule are connected to each other. There are emblematic sounds that illustrate both the legacy of occupation and the reinstatement of imperial power constellations under new circumstances. One feature that is characteristic of the occupation of Central Asia under both Russian and Soviet rule and that decidedly influenced auditory environments and soundscapes is the railway.

Among the many changes within Central Asia that were introduced through the Russian colonial project, the introduction of the railway was one of the most incisive features of the occupation by the Russian Empire in the nineteenth century and at the beginning of the twentieth century. The Russian Empire pursued a so-called railway imperialism, not only consolidating its territories but also expanding territorially through the establishment of a railroad system (Schenk 2014: 114). In the Soviet Union, the railway continued to grow in importance in Central Asia as the example of the Turkestan-Siberian Railroad shows. Built between 1926 and 1931, and becoming one of the most important railway projects in Central Asia and the Soviet Union in general, the Turkestan-Siberian Railroad 'was to bring not only trains to the Kazakh steppe, but revolution' (Payne 2001: 10), on the basis of a massive push for industrialization (Rees 1995). In the Soviet Union as a whole, the railway became inextricably linked to the Gulag prison system, whether as a means of transporting prisoners to the camps (Applebaum 2003: 159–80) or as a building project reliant on forced labour: the Salekhard-Igarka Railroad, or 'Dead Road', Stalin's unfinished railroad venture, and the Baikal-Amur Railroad are two notorious examples in this regard.

Closer to the dissolution of the Soviet Union, in 1980, the Kyrgyz author Chingiz Aitmatov published his first novel, *The Day Lasts More Than a Hundred Years* (*I dol'she veka dlitsya den'*), choosing the Soviet lingua franca Russian instead of Kyrgyz, which dominated his early literary career in the 1950s and 1960s. Aitmatov's novel is exemplary of a new aural sensitivity that is characteristic of literature in the twentieth century (Cuddy-Keane 2000: 71). The reasons for this new aurality and its manifestations in literary texts can be found in the introduction of new sound technologies and the growing industrialization that had made them possible towards the end of the nineteenth century (Cuddy-Keane 2005: 383; Morat, Tkaczyk and Ziemer 2017: 4–5; Schrage 2011: 273). In the context of colonialism, however, the same sound technologies were exported 'to discipline the bodies of natives, principally to exploit their labor but also to tattoo authority on colonized bodies via their ears' (Smith 2007: 56). In this way, sounds could reproduce and reinforce colonial structures and dichotomies, such as the opposition between 'civilization' and 'wildness' (Hendy 2013: 161–2). In *The Day Lasts More Than a Hundred Years*, there is a heightened attention to the auditory regime of the Soviet Union, with particular focus on how technologization impacts aural spaces under occupation. On a general level, the novel highlights an array of topics and themes that relate to Central Asia under Soviet rule. The opposition between the Soviet political system and traditional ways of life is particularly pervasive throughout the novel. The process of Russification, for example, is one of the chief issues negotiated in the novel. The sentiments and ideas expressed in the text even became so influential that some of the novel's terms are now being used in areas beyond literature, as can be seen in the case of the *mankurt* (a figure from a legend which is told in the novel). Bhavna Dave notes that in Kazakhstan, '[m]ankurt is a widely used metaphor to convey the loss of ethnic identity and native language, and has become synonymous with being Russified' (2007: 50).[3] Aitmatov's novel thus lays open political tensions which existed in twentieth-century Central Asia by contrasting native identity, Indigenous traditions and folkways with the political regime and its version of modernity. Through this opposition, the text develops nativist undertones (Ashcroft, Griffiths and Tiffin 2007: 143–4) that are used to promote pre-colonial traditions and values and enable a critique of imperial cultural hegemony. The process of reclaiming an Indigenous culture that was deemed 'primitive' within the Soviet Union, and the Russian Empire before it, is an important aspect of the novel. This critical perspective is also established through themes such as the conflict between languages (Caffee 2013: 30–6), a focus on folk legends and myths and the repressive measures taken against their circulation, the contrasting of urban and rural life and, not lastly, the impact of technological innovations (Mozur 1995: 120–2). The railway is one of the motifs that help to convey the central conflicts of the novel.

The following paragraph is taken from the novel and is repeated multiple times throughout the text. It is featured at the beginning of the novel, stands at the opening of many chapters, is the last closing paragraph at the very end of the novel and is used to indicate shifts between different storylines. The passage may be different in some regard each time it is repeated, but the reader always unmistakably recognizes it as a variation of the same opening paragraph:

> Trains in these parts went from East to West and from West to East . . .
> On either side of the railway lines lay the great wide spaces of the desert – Sary-Ozeki, the Middle lands of the yellow steppes.
> In these parts any distance was measured in relation to the railway, as if from the Greenwich meridian . . .
> And the trains went from East to West, and from West to East. (Aitmatov [1980] 1988: 12)

The importance of the railway within the novel is foreshadowed through the frequent repetition of this passage: here, the centrality of the railroad is emphasized by ascribing it the status of a universal geographical guideline, and it is depicted as the most important point of orientation in the steppes (which is where most of the novel's story takes place). However, the railway is of significance not only in relation to (the control over) space. It also plays 'an important part making the rhythmic patterns which govern and regulate modernity' (Revill 2013: 52) and thus has to be considered in terms of sound (Marcus 2017). It is no coincidence that Aitmatov chooses to highlight the attributes of trains (and the railway in general) that relate to listening, namely by focusing on their sonic properties, the sounds they produce. As this chapter will show, the amount of references to the auditory perception is striking when the events of the novel involve trains, railroads or railway stations, and sounds often serve to emphasize the political conflicts that pervade the text.

Only recently has the railway been taken up again as an object of investigation within sound studies. Michael Bull summarizes the multidimensionality of the railway as follows: 'Trains like other technologies are subordinate clauses in the march of cultural history deriving their meanings from power, economics, cultural and perhaps more personal experiences. At various times we have listened to and understood the locomotive through the prism of leisure, noise pollution, industrialization, imperialism, progress and so on' (2019: xxvi). In the case of Aitmatov's novel, it appears as if the sounds of the railway indeed literally echo the imperial heritage of the Soviet Union, which goes back to the occupation of Central Asia by the Russian Empire. While the railway itself is a prominent trope in postcolonial fiction which has been examined in a variety of publications (Spalding and Fraser 2012; Aguiar 2011), the sound dimension of trains has gone relatively ignored in this context. Recent research in the field of sound studies and ethnomusicology can stimulate a much-needed debate on the importance of sound in the formation of empire which could also be extended to literary studies: 'As a colonizing force in the rise of empire, . . . sound productions became a key tool in imposing other forms of discipline and order. At the outset, sound's presence was anything but orderly. Occupations were inherently noisy and chaotic. . . . In its participation in social order, however, sound production quickly assumed a role in organizing human behavior' (Radano and Olaniyan 2016: 2). Radano and Olaniyan's characterization of occupation as 'noisy' will guide my analysis of the novel as special attention will be paid to the sounds which are foregrounded in the text in connection to the railway. This analysis consists of a close reading of relevant passages from the novel and takes into account, first, sonic phenomena, places, events and other elements presented through the narrative and, second, the way they are presented, that is how the narrative is structured. The latter includes a consideration of narratological concepts (such as focalization) and rhetorical and stylistic features of the text. The close reading examines how these textual characteristics are put in relation to each other to create descriptions of sound that further highlight the political themes of the novel. In accordance with a postcolonial narratology that emphasizes a context-sensitive approach (Birk and Neumann 2002: 116), studies about the history of Central Asia will be used as additional sources to contextualize Aitmatov's novel and its references to the railway. Furthermore, critical literature from the field of sound studies complements the observations about sound in *The Day Lasts More Than a Hundred Years*. My goal is to show how Aitmatov's novel reflects what I tentatively call the 'sonic occupation' of Central Asia. The basic assumption is that occupation and the aural are firmly interrelated and that one has to take into account changes in sound culture – that is, the auditory environment in its wider social and cultural context (Chignell 2009: 103) – in order to gain a fuller understanding of the extent of occupation. The sounds of occupation also influence other forms of cultural production, such as literary texts, and by examining Aitmatov's novel as an example, it can be demonstrated how auditory regimes and changes in the auditory environment due to occupation are perceived, creatively interpreted and challenged in different media. Over the course of this chapter, it should become evident that the way in which the sounds of the railway are presented in the novel lets the reader perceive them as a disciplining force and a means of oppression in their own right.

Since '[w]hat is audible about empire is part of a larger working logic' (Radano and Olaniyan 2016: 6), it will be necessary, as a first step, to give an overview of the introduction of the railway in Central Asia under the Russian Empire. This will serve to contextualize the changes in the sound culture in relation to the social and economic effects that the railway had within the region. The main focus of the first part will be on the historical region of Turkistan (as it has come to be called since the Russian conquest) because part of it later became the Kazakh SSR, which is where most of Aitmatov's *The Day Lasts More Than a Hundred Years* is set. Besides the railway, Aitmatov addresses other issues that also reach back to the occupation by the Russian Empire: Russification, for instance, did not start with the Soviet Union[4] and was already well under way during the period of Russian imperial rule. The second part of this chapter will consist of an analysis of the literary sounds – in the sense of what Sylvia Mieszkowski tentatively calls a 'literary sound studies' (2014: 9, 23–32) – that are related to the railway in the text.[5] Through such an examination of examples from the novel, this chapter will demonstrate how sonic occupation becomes manifest in *The Day Lasts More Than a Hundred Years* and how the effects of the railway on the sound culture of Central Asia extended well into the twentieth century and the Soviet Union.

The railway in Central Asia under the Russian Empire and in the Soviet Union

Similar to other colonial systems around the globe (cf. Das 2015; Dvořáček and Záhořík 2018; Biermann 1995; Baillargeon 2020; Gamst 2006; Ishiguro 2017: 131–3), the railway in Central Asia was an important imperial tool under Russian rule. It served economic and military purposes, and was also a major factor in the colonization of the region.

Plans to establish a railway system in Central Asia emerged in the 1870s. The construction of the Transcaspian Railway started in 1880, and it reached the city of Samarkand in 1888, connecting it to Krasnovodsk Bay. In 1899, the route was extended to Tashkent, as part of the Samarkand-Andijan Line. By 1906, the

Orenburg-Tashkent connection was completed after six years of construction work (Schenk 2014: 84–8; Poujol and Fourniau 2005: 63–8; Brower 2003: 79–80; Abdurakhimova 2005: 141). The growth of the railway system can be summarized as follows: 'By 1880, just before the construction of the Transcaspian Railway, Russia had built 21,000 kilometres of railways, and 70,000 kilometres of railways were built in 1906' (Poujol and Fourniau 2005: 65).

Economically, the railway was intended to facilitate colonial exploitation by the Russian Empire: 'The introduction of the railway . . . was a direct consequence of the policy of making the colonies profitable' (Poujol and Fourniau 2005: 65). Cotton, for example, was one of the most important commodities for the Russian Empire, and the textile industry heavily relied on shipments from Turkistan:

> [T]he share of cotton from Turkistan rose from about 30 per cent to more than 60 per cent in a very short period (from 1908 to 1912). In 1915 more than 350,000 tonnes of cotton were shipped to Russia, compared to 11,000 tonnes by 1877, that is before the construction of the railway and the introduction of American species of cotton. (Poujol and Fourniau 2005: 69)

By building railroads, the Russian Empire ended the economic isolation of Central Asia and integrated the region into the global trade market for the empire's benefit (Brower 2003: 79–80).

The military was also a deciding factor for the establishment of the railway, as the railway was an important means of moving troops faster than ever before from the imperial centre to distant regions. For instance, the Russian Empire sought military security to counter British power in Central Asia against the background of the so-called Great Game (Schenk 2014: 88). The empire also needed to maintain a military presence to put down rebellions in Turkistan and for its campaigns to subdue Turkmen nomads, for instance, in the western deserts of Central Asia (Brower 2003: 80–2).

Trains as more convenient means of transportation were also largely responsible for a large influx of Russian settlers in Turkistan. These settlers received preferential treatment from the colonial authorities in the distribution of land, further contributing to ethnic conflicts (Brower 2003: 130–40). The native population, which consisted to a great extent of pastoral nomads – approximately 80 per cent in 1897 (Tabyshalieva 2005: 87) – were forced to settle in order to keep up with the Russian colonizers and to be able to earn a living (Abdurakhimova 2005: 140). Furthermore, the nomadic way of life was considered primitive, and there were campaigns for the sedentarization of the Indigenous peoples as part of a Russian *mission civilisatrice*, which also pushed the process of Russification (Schenk 2014: 88, 91; Brower 2003: 128). The Russian presence and the railway also made certain occupations obsolete, such as muleteers and travel guides, since the railway presented a more comfortable and much faster means of transportation compared to travelling by camel (Poujol and Fourniau 2005: 66–8).

The railway epitomized the conflict between the traditional pastoral societies and technological modernity. From an imperial perspective, there was on one side the cattle and livestock of the nomads and on the other the so-called iron horse of the empire. The railway was, thus, an incisive innovation which confronted the Indigenous population with new economic, social and cultural problems.

In the Soviet Union, the railway remained a part of the civilizing mission which was described earlier, as can be seen in the example of the massive project of the Turkestan-Siberian Railroad. Among other things, '[t]he colossal struggles involved in . . . acclimating nomads to industrial work while "Sovietizing" peasant seasonal workers . . . cast Turksib in the role of an instrument of civilization in a supposedly uncivilized outback. Turksib's builders, very aware of this civilizing role, constantly made reference to the need to uplift backward natives, reform individualistic managers, and "reforge" insufficiently proletarian workers' (Payne 2001: 5). The building of the Turkestan-Siberian Railroad also furthered ethnic conflicts as the Russian workers 'sought to exclude Kazakhs from the ranks of proletarians' based on 'prejudice, mockery, and vicious pogroms' (Payne 2001: 10). While the blatant contradictions within the Soviet ideological programme cannot be addressed within the scope of this chapter,[6] it can be said that the railway was still an instrument of occupation under the Soviet regime and had an immense impact on the lives of the Indigenous population. The railway also prolonged the imperial history of the region, reinforcing racist mindsets in the context of the opposition between modernity and 'primitivity'.

There is another aspect to the railway in Central Asia which has been disregarded in the academic literature about the region, however – the dimension of sound and its importance in regard to these new means of transportation. Besides being a relevant factor for the subjugation and domination of different regions within Central Asia, trains and railway stations introduced Turkistan to an entirely new auditory environment in the nineteenth century. The pioneering work of scholars of sound studies such as Emily Thompson (2004), Mark M. Smith (2001) and Karin Bijsterveld (2008) has demonstrated how industrialization and technologization created a whole new spectrum of sounds and how both processes influenced the ways of hearing and listening. 'The steam whistle', Thompson writes, 'which announced the arrival of both railroad and factory, constituted the acoustic signal of industrialization' (2004: 120), while Smith goes so far as to call the sound of trains on the railroad the 'rumble of modernity' (2001: 96). The sounds of the railway were also perceived as a nuisance at many points due to different factors: '[W]ith industrialization . . ., new kinds of noises began to offend. The sound of the railroad, for example, became a new source of complaint. The noise of its steam whistle was disturbing not only for its loudness but also for its unfamiliarity' (Thompson 2004: 117). While the idea of the noisy technological innovation of the train might represent a culturally pessimistic 'trope of industrial capitalism in the form of the railroad puncturing rural quietude' (Smith 2012: 44), the negative connotations of the railway do correspond to the perception of trains in Central Asia in the twentieth century when the railway was even at times 'held to be a creation of the Devil' (Poujol and Fourniau 2005: 66) by the Indigenous population. In Central Asia, trains and railroads produced entirely new sounds and unusual noises, at unprecedented volume levels, drastically altering the auditory environment. With the help of the railway, the Russian Empire did not just conquer space and time but also the soundscape.[7]

In Aitmatov's *The Day Lasts More Than a Hundred Years*, these sounds, which are so closely associated with industrialization, become entangled with political oppression; additionally, the array of sounds is extended in correspondence with technological renewals in the field of the railway in the Soviet Union. Loudspeakers, for instance, add to the auditory environment of the railway station, and Aitmatov's novel explicitly references the public address system (as the next section of the chapter will show).

While most researchers and critics focus on the science fiction subplot and space flight when it comes to the technological themes of the novel, the railway is a pervading motif in *The Day Lasts More Than a Hundred Years*. Besides the passage quoted in the beginning of this chapter, in which the centrality of the railroad is emphasized, the railway is integral to many more aspects of the novel. For example, the protagonist Yedigei works at a way station, just like his friend Kazangap, who dies at the beginning of the text and whose burial is the main driving element of the plot. Even the former and alternative title of the novel markedly points to the railway: *Burannyj polustanok*, which can be translated as *Blizzard Stop* or *Blizzard Station*. The following analysis will elaborate on two episodes in the novel in which the railway is of major importance, concentrating on the sonic dimension of the narrated events, the literary means of presenting the railway as an oppressive force and how different sites of sonic occupation become manifest in *The Day Lasts More Than a Hundred Years*.

The railway station as a site of sonic occupation

As mentioned previously, the central plot element of the novel is the burial of Kazangap, an old friend of the protagonist Yedigei. Besides extensive renderings of folk myths and legends, the novel also consists of Yedigei's recollections of his own life leading up to Kazangap's death. Probably most important are his memories of his experiences with the family of Abutalip, his wife Zaripa and their two sons Ermek and Daul. In one of the memories, Yedigei travels to the city with Zaripa, whose husband Abutalip died during his imprisonment after his arrest by the secret police. When they go to the train station to claim a notice which informs them of Abutalip's death, Yedigei thinks about his deceased friend and about what is to become of Abutalip's children. While he waits for Zaripa in the square in front of the station, he notices people getting off a train and loud music coming from the public loudspeakers:

> He was amazed what bored, drab faces people had, how featureless, how unconcerned they looked, how tired and cut off from one another. Added to which, the radio music on the public address sounded as if it were suffering from a throaty cold, filling the whole station square with its monotonously flowing dull noise and adding to the general misery. What sort of music was this? What a programme! (Aitmatov [1980] 1988: 219–20)

In this passage, the culturally pessimistic trope of the train as the emblem of modernity and technologization can be noticed. In line with the opposition of traditional ways of life and the Soviet political system within the novel, the train is rendered in a negative light through how the effects of this mechanical means of transportation are presented: specifically, the isolation and apathy of the passengers who leave the train. At this point in the text, the reader also notices how the music coming from the loudspeakers in the square matches the alienated state of the rail passengers. Thus, the music and the technological apparatus of the loudspeaker enter into a relationship with the train, creating an assemblage of estranging forces which converge in the railway station.

Christin Hoene, in an article about the sounds of postcolonial metropolises in the works of Amit Chaudhuri, describes six different ways in which novels can evoke sound,[8] and the literary sounds in the previous quote meet the criteria of three of these. First, there are 'descriptions of environments with predominantly auditory terms and a focus on auditory sensations' (Hoene 2016: 365) – in the above case, the station square is presented with a heavy emphasis on sound, and more specifically, the music which fills the square. Second, Hoene refers to cases in which 'objects and technologies of auditory perception are the subject matter' (2016: 365), and the public address system in the quote clearly represents such an acoustic apparatus. Third, Hoene cites 'characters' auditory perceptions' (2016: 365) – while Hoene most likely refers to instances where the sensation of sound is made explicit in the text (through verbs such as 'listen' or 'hear'), the use of free indirect speech at the end of the quoted paragraph ('[w]hat sort of music was this? What a programme!' Aitmatov [1980] 1988: 220) indicates that the sounds are conveyed to the reader through Yedigei's listening experience.

Shortly after, Yedigei and Zaripa find out why this music is broadcast all over the station square:

> The radio music played on all over the station, as if aware of Zaripa's bereavement, for it was mournful and exceedingly painful. . . . Lifting their heads, they were watching some men put up a ladder and set about hanging a large portrait of Stalin in military uniform, with a black mourning border around it, high above the door.
>
> Now he understood why the radio music had been so mournful. . . . He did not utter a word. Moreover Zaripa was not interested in anyone or anything else.
>
> The trains, however, were running as usual, as they had to, whatever else might be happening on earth. (Aitmatov [1980] 1988: 221–2)

Although at first it seems that the sorrowful music coincides with Zaripa's grief, the two characters are confronted with the real reason why the music plays – it is mourning music played to mark the occasion of Stalin's death in 1953. The internally focalized narration – which foregrounds the experiences of the two characters – adds to the effect of surprise, leaving the reader baffled, just as Yedigei and Zaripa appear to be. By presenting the events through internal focalization, the reader is also deceived by the sad solemnity of the music.

The sound dimension establishes a connection between Abutalip's death and Stalin's. However, as it turns out, the auditory environment serves entirely to commemorate Stalin's passing. The music announcing Stalin's death also seems to drown out Zaripa's and Yedigei's grief for Abutalip, assisted by the public address system at the train station. Barry Truax emphasizes the political effect of high-volume sounds that emanate from loudspeakers: 'The control of spatial communication . . . is essential to centralized power and domination. Therefore, acoustic power, amplified through the loudspeaker, . . . is linked to the domination of space. The loudest sounds have always been associated with the most powerful forces in the world, whether they represented physical or political power' (2001: 113). By incorporating the music broadcast by the public loudspeakers, the text marks the railway station as a site of sonic occupation. The music serves propagandistic purposes while announcing Stalin's death which, at this point in the novel, is contrasted with the death of a victim under Stalin's regime.

As Michael Denning argues, 'Empire . . . was a musical event: the conquest and colonization of territories was "accompanied" by the musical occupation of the space, and the projection of a new colonial order in sound' (Denning 2016: 35). In the case of Aitmatov's novel (which is situated in the Soviet Union), the occupation of space through sound is still in effect, and the music at the train station does, in fact, project a new colonial order – a colonial order in which the lost lives of the Indigenous population go unnoticed when they are juxtaposed with the passing of the leader of the political terror.[9] Furthermore, in the quote from the novel, there is a discrepancy in the intensity of sounds within the auditory environment. Yedigei and Zaripa are ascribed quiet behaviour, as opposed to the loudness of the music. By presenting this contrast in volume, the text also conveys the imbalance of power which becomes manifest at the train station. The reader becomes aware of this precarious power constellation solely based on the sound dimension of the narrated world and what effect it has on the characters.

Already during the Russian Empire, railway stations were imagined to be part of the *mission civilisatrice* because they represented a 'breeding ground for civilization' (Schenk 2014: 189; my own translation). As Aitmatov's text also shows, under the Soviet regime, the space of the railway station was renewed with acoustic technologies, which further enabled the sonic occupation of Central Asia. The next section will focus more closely on the train and how its sonic attributes are presented in the novel, and will also examine Abutalip's arrest before his death later on.

The literary sounds of the train and Soviet oppression

Another episode in the novel also heavily relies on a contrast of sounds, and the difference in the acoustic modes and behaviours is even more striking than in the example from the previous section. The following recollection of Yedigei is about the actual arrest of Abutalip, after being charged with 'hostile agitation' and 'counter-revolutionary tendencies' (Aitmatov [1980] 1988: 185) by the secret police. This time, sonic occupation becomes manifest in connection to the train on which the officers take Abutalip away. As will be shown, the scene in which the train arrives at the village and leaves with Abutalip is riddled with various sounds that establish a contrast of auditory phenomena and that further highlight the menacing presence of the train. It will also be noticeable that – similar to how train noises were perceived as a nuisance when they were newly introduced – the sounds of the train are a source of distress for the characters in the novel, and the text accentuates the adverse situation between the village inhabitants and the secret police through the train noise and the reactions to it.

Prior to a closer analysis of the text, however, it is important to note that Abutalip is arrested by the secret police because he writes down folk legends and his memories of the Second World War for his children; his writings and memories are deemed 'hostile to the State' (Aitmatov [1980] 1988: 187). While interrogating Yedigei, the officer presents his reasoning as to why Abutalip should not have written of his own accord: 'What matters is that when we describe the past . . ., we should do so in the way that is needed now, . . . for us. Things that are of no use to us at the present time must not be mentioned' (Aitmatov [1980] 1988: 189).[10] The dialogue between the officer and Yedigei is one of the most explicit historical references in the novel: the native population is denied their collective memory and, ultimately, their identity under the Soviet regime.[11]

Before the train arrives at the village, the acoustic behaviour of the inhabitants and the auditory environment is presented to set the scene. They are aware of Abutalip's arrest and they are portrayed to be mostly quiet. For example, 'Zaripa was weeping quietly' (Aitmatov [1980] 1988: 195),[12] and Daul, one of Abutalip's sons, 'was quiet' (Aitmatov [1980] 1988: 195). Likewise, the surroundings in the scene are described as equally quiet: 'The wind swept through the place. It chased the snowy air across the ground with a rustling sound and a scarcely audible whistle' (Aitmatov [1980] 1988: 195). In order to express utter silence in the text, some of the actions are relegated to the visual realm, even if they are commonly associated with specific sounds: 'The heavy sighs of Ukubala were revealed in the clouds of mist which came from her mouth' (Aitmatov [1980] 1988: 195). On the other hand, and in contrast to the acoustic behaviours of the village inhabitants and the quiet surroundings, there is the train which signals the imminent parting with Abutalip and which produces very loud noises. The image of the quiet, rural village is the direct opposite of how life in the city is presented in the novel. Those who move to the city to complete their education in the Soviet system become estranged and turn into modern-day *mankurts* (Aitmatov [1980] 1988: 347–8), whereas the rural village represents an environment where the traditions of the (pre-colonial) past can still be allowed to thrive and native identity is fostered. The rural village is strongly associated with nature, while the city stands for an affinity with technology. The sounds of the train thus evoke the processes of technologization and urbanization that run counter to the ideals of rurality in *The Day Lasts More Than a Hundred Years*. Consequently, the train is described as an intrusive element which disturbs the sorrowful quiet of the village in the chapter about Abutalip's arrest: 'With its headlight piercing through the thick, frosty, swirling mist, it came on, a dark, threatening, clattering mass. As it approached, the blazing headlight and the other lights seemed to rise above the ground; the snowy air above the rails became more visible in the beams, and the heavy noise of the cranks and pistons grew louder' (Aitmatov [1980] 1988: 195–6). The train is pictured as an obscure, menacing object by means of its acoustic characterization in the text. What follows next is a plethora of descriptions of the intimidating sounds produced by the train, making it out to be much more than simply a transport vehicle made out of steel. The train stops 'with a long, heavy screeching' (Aitmatov [1980] 1988: 196), its engine lets out 'a great hiss of steam' (Aitmatov [1980] 1988: 196), and later the train leaves with 'its wheels shrieking as they turned' (Aitmatov [1980] 1988: 198), to quote just a few examples. Remarkably, both in the Russian original and in the English translation, all of the words used for the sonic phenomena produced by the train have an onomatopoeic quality: 'screech' and 'скрежет' (*skrezhet*); 'hiss' and 'шипение' (*shipenie*); and 'shriek' and 'скрипучий' (*skripuchij*).[13] Furthermore, there are other noises connected to the train, such as the recurring sound of the whistle which is alternately described as 'piercing' (Aitmatov [1980] 1988: 196) and 'terrifying' (Aitmatov [1980] 1988: 197). The original uses a more figurative language in the last instance, presenting the effects of the whistle sound in an even more vivid way. It is described as 'свербящий душу' (Aitmatov [1980] 1981: 164), which can be loosely translated as 'soul-unsettling' or 'mind-troubling'.

In her readings of Western novels between 1875 and 1975, Karin Bijsterveld formulates a typology of mechanical sounds and sounds connected to technology. She suggests four different types of sound, one of which she calls 'intrusive sounds':

> *Intrusive* sounds are usually expressed as a multitude of different sounds or a series of recurrent sounds. These sounds threaten the existence of something or someone that is vulnerable or fragile, such as nature, harmony, or one's heart, mind, body or security . . .

> Intrusive sounds violently enter the protagonists' world, often all at once, and endanger something cared for. The simultaneousness of different sounds creates chaos or forms a deep rumble that affects a subject's body. (Bijsterveld 2008: 44–5)

The train in *The Day Lasts More Than a Hundred Years* produces such intrusive sounds, but the presentation of their intrusiveness and noisiness is rooted in the central themes of the text. While the sounds of the train may communicate the ideas of progress and modernity from the perspective of Soviet authority, the internally focalized narrator establishes the village and its tight-knit community as such a vulnerable and fragile sphere that Bijsterveld writes about and that is threatened by the train sounds. The suppression of Indigenous memory in the chapter is accentuated through the unpredictability and chaotic simultaneity of the different sounds produced by the train, which are important criteria for their intrusiveness (Bijsterveld 2008: 45). It is their disruptive nature that makes these sounds appear as noisy, whereas silence becomes synonymous with the calm of the countryside and the harmony of the rural setting. Bijsterveld herself discusses the noise of trains in conjunction with rurality as an example for intrusive sounds in her analysed texts: 'By positioning, in the auditory topos of the intrusive sound, the chaos of train sounds against the order of the countryside – the situation to be protected – mechanical noise is the symbol of social disruption' (2008: 51). Aitmatov's novel likewise presents 'sounds of technology . . . as powers ruthlessly invading a realm to be defended' (Bijsterveld 2008: 51), enabling a critical perspective on occupation through a textual focus on sonic phenomena. The disruptive force of the train also becomes evident when considering the reactions of the village inhabitants to its loud noise: 'The boy in Yedigei's arms had shivered with fright when it had come level with them, and had jumped as the train gave out steam with a sudden hiss' (Aitmatov [1980] 1988: 196). The boy's auditory perception illustrates once again the threatening nature of the train sounds.

The intrusion of the train is also illustrated through how the sounds are contrasted with the behaviour of the characters who witness the arrest of Abutalip and what kind of sounds are ascribed to them (as I have already shown in reference to their quiet demeanour). There are also occasional loud interjections by the village inhabitants which either fade away or are drowned out by the sounds of the train. For example, Abutalip's son Ermek falls silent when his father does not respond to his remark about the train: '"Papika! Papika! Look, the train's coming!" Ermek was shouting – then he too became silent, surprised that his father did not answer' (Aitmatov [1980] 1988: 196). Such transitions from loudness to quiet further highlight the villagers' silence in comparison to the train's overwhelming acoustic presence in the text. It is also of note that the loud sounds produced by the people in the village fundamentally differ from those of the train: with reference to a 'narrative sonography' (Vandevelde 2015: 61), the sound types can be classified as 'human/anthropomorphic' on the one hand and 'mechanical' on the other (63, 65). This differentiation is important because it reiterates the confrontation between the village community and Soviet authority. It is presented as a sonic conflict between 'organic' human voices and the 'cold' noise of machines, where the latter threatens to overpower the former.

The arrival and departure of the train are thus narrated with excessive reference to auditory phenomena, and the political conflict at the heart of this episode is transferred to the dimension of sound in the text. The interrogation by the secret police that takes place before the quoted passages and the arrest of Abutalip culminate in this very scene where they force Abutalip into the train to take him with them, as a provision to censor his writings and suppress the memory of the Indigenous population and their traditions.

As was the case in the example within the previous section in regard to the railway station, the train is strongly associated with the Soviet regime and its repressive measures, and Aitmatov presents the train as a menacing object mainly by depicting its sonic attributes.

Conclusion: Sonic occupation and sound culture

Aitmatov's novel highlights the imperial heritage of the Soviet Union by also focusing on the railway and its status as an imperial tool even a century after the Russian annexation of Central Asia, reaching beyond 1917 and the dissolution of the empire. In *The Day Lasts More Than a Hundred Years*, the railway also emblematizes the conflict between subjugated people and an oppressive political system. The text establishes the conjunction between the railway and occupation through references to the auditory environment. Whenever the political impact of the railway is foregrounded, the narrative heavily draws on phenomena which are of an acoustic nature. The two analysed examples from the text feature two different elements of the railway system – the railway station and the train – and in the context of the novel's opposition of the past and the present, both appear as objects and spaces that illustrate how the Indigenous population is oppressed by the political regime, forcing them to forget their traditions and values. When Abutalip is arrested for writing down folk legends and his memories of the Second World War, the train – with its screeching and shrieking wheels and hissing engine – provides, in a manner of speaking, the soundtrack to his imprisonment. Even after Abutalip dies, his death is overshadowed by the death of Stalin. The mournful music which is played in honour of Stalin over the loudspeakers at the railway station drowns out the grief of Abutalip's family and friends. The railway is thus closely connected to the occupation of Central Asia in the text, and Aitmatov uses references to the auditory dimension to highlight the political significance of this means of transportation. Literary sounds and the contrasts between them evoke the fundamental conflict between Soviet authority and the Indigenous people, as well as their traditions and culture. The sounds in the text point to the oppressive circumstances under which the Indigenous population lives, how they are not allowed to preserve their traditions and how the grief for the death of those who fall victim to the state's repressive measures cannot be adequately expressed.

In both discussed examples from the novel, the literary treatment of sounds conveys to the reader the political significance of the railway, and the various noises amplify the dramatic effect of each scene – but they also show that the Soviet regime relied not just on the occupation of the mind but also on the occupation of the ear. Carla J. Meier argues in regard to sound cultures that sound is 'part of complex cultural, social, and mediatized practices' and that sounds 'constantly re-constitute the world in which we live and how we perceive it and make sense of it' (Maier 2016: 179). Aitmatov's novel clearly demonstrates the impact sound can have on one's perception of the world and how one interacts with it. While Radano and Olaniyan rightly point out that there is no such thing as a 'sociopolitical "absolute sound"' and that sound cannot be 'observed separately from other territories of the imperial' (2016: 6), sonic occupation must be understood not just as an occupation's effect on a particular sound culture but also as how occupation works through sound culture itself, how it creates new auditory environments and new ways of hearing and listening which reinforce political, economic, social and cultural constellations of power.

Notes

1. The scholarly literature about Central Asia and its occupation by the Russian Empire in English alone is enormous. For recent scholarship about the Russian conquest of Central Asia, see Morrison (2021) and Keller (2020). A very comprehensive inquiry into the history of Central Asia since the mid-nineteenth century is presented in Adle, Palat and Tabyshalieva (2005). Allworth (1994) gives a critical overview of the developments in Central Asia under Russian and Soviet rule.

2. In the last twenty years, the Soviet Union and Central Asia have been increasingly studied from the perspective of postcolonial studies (Moore 2001; Ram 2003;

Etkind 2011; Adams 2008; Heathershaw 2010; Khalid 2007). For an analysis of Aitmatov's novel based on postcolonial theory, see Coombs (2011).

3 For an analysis of the *mankurt* within the novel, see Mozur (1995: 107–11). See also Mozur (1987: 13–24), Kolesnikoff (1999: 71–4) and Haber (2003: 137).

4 For a nuanced study of the linguistic and cultural hegemony within the Soviet Union in the first half of the twentieth century, see Martin (2001).

5 Mieszkowski describes 'literary sound studies' as a new research area which aims to 'build a bridge between the interdisciplinary field of Sound Studies and literary criticism' (2014: 9). Thus, literary sounds are understood here as 'silent' sounds, that is, as 'sounds and processes of hearing, which have been medialized by (written) words' (Mieszkowski 2014: 24). Philipp Schweighauser has also previously made a suggestion for a field called 'literary acoustics' (Schweighauser 2015: 483), which shares similar research interests with literary sound studies.

6 Ram (2006: 832) writes: 'The Soviet Union was expressly internationalist yet zealously territorial and expansionist, denying the autonomy of its constitutive peoples while retaining a federal structure that would nonetheless permit an elaborate discourse of local specificity.'

7 For a critical discussion of the term 'soundscape' and its problematic implications, see Kelman (2010).

8 Hoene derives her six modes of how sound enters the domain of literature from John M. Picker's groundbreaking monograph, *Victorian Soundscapes* (2003) (Hoene 2016: 365).

9 Yedigei's reaction to the monotonous music emanating from the loudspeakers is later contrasted with how deeply moved he is by Erlepes playing on his *dombra*; in this case, the long and old tradition of the music is highlighted multiple times in the text (Aitmatov [1980] 1988: 260–6).

10 In the Russian original, the statement by the officer is even more drastic because it does not just prohibit mentioning the things that are not useful to the Soviet regime but even remembering them, making the forceful process of forgetting even more explicit: 'Важно вспоминать, нарисовать прошлое ... так, как требуется сейчас, как нужно сейчас для нас. А все, что нам не на пользу, того и не следует вспоминать' (Aitmatov [1980] 1981: 157).

11 The events in the novel also appear to echo the cultural policies in the Soviet Union in the 1950s, when, for example, Kyrgyz epics were criticized during a 'general campaign against epics' (Grenoble 2003: 155; Haber 2003: 53–4).

12 The English translation does not exactly reflect the level of quietness which is present in the original: 'Зарипа неслышно плакала' (Aitmatov [1980] 1981: 162). A more literal translation of the quote would read 'Zaripa wept unhearably'.

13 'Поезд остановился с долгим, тяжким скрежетом' (Aitmatov [1980] 1981: 164); 'паровоз ... с шипением спустил пар' (Aitmatov [1980] 1981: 164); '[о]н пошел, скрипуче раскручивая колеса' (Aitmatov [1980] 1981: 165).

References

Abdurakhimova, N. A. (2005), 'Tsarist Russia and Central Asia', in C. Adle, M. K. Palat and A. Tabyshalieva (eds), *History of Civilizations of Central Asia*, vi: *Towards the Contemporary Period: From the Mid-Nineteenth to the End of the Twentieth Century*, 125–52, Paris: UNESCO.

Adams, L. L. (2008), 'Can We Apply Postcolonial Theory to Central Eurasia?', *Central Eurasian Studies Review*, 7 (1): 2–7.

Adle, C., M. K. Palat and A. Tabyshalieva, eds. (2005), *History of Civilizations of Central Asia*, vi: *Towards the Contemporary Period: From the Mid-Nineteenth to the End of the Twentieth Century*, Paris: UNESCO.

Aguiar, M. (2011), *Tracking Modernity: India's Railway and the Culture of Mobility*, Minneapolis: University of Minnesota Press.

Aitmatov, C. ([1980] 1988), *The Day Lasts More than a Hundred Years*, trans. J. French, Bloomington: Indiana University Press.

Aitmatov, C. ([1980] 1981), *Burannyj polustanok [I dol'she veka dlitsya den']*, Moscow: Molodaya gvardiya.

Allworth, E., ed. (1994), *Central Asia: 130 Years of Russian Dominance, A Historical Overview*, 3rd edn, Durham, NC: Duke University Press.

Applebaum, A. (2003), *Gulag: A History*, New York: Doubleday.

Ashcroft, B., G. Griffiths and H. Tiffin (2007), *Post-Colonial Studies: The Key Concepts*, 2nd edn, London: Routledge.

Baillargeon, D. (2020), '"On the Road to Mandalay": The Development of Railways in British Burma, 1870–1900', *Journal of Imperial and Commonwealth History*, 48 (4): 654–78.

Biermann, W. (1995), *Tanganyika Railways – Carrier of Colonialism: An Account of Economic Indicators and Social Fragments*, Münster: LIT.

Bijsterveld, K. (2008), *Mechanical Sound: Technology, Culture, and Public Problems of Noise in the Twentieth Century*, Cambridge, MA: MIT Press.

Birk, H. and B. Neumann (2002), '*Go-Between*: Postkoloniale Erzähltheorie', in A. Nünning and V. Nünning (eds), *Neue Ansätze in der Erzähltheorie*, 115–52, Trier: Wissenschaftlicher Verlag Trier.

Brower, D. R. (2003), *Turkestan and the Fate of the Russian Empire*, London: Routledge.

Bull, M. (2019), 'Introduction: Sound Studies and the Art of Listening', in M. Bull (ed), *The Routledge Companion to Sound Studies*, xvii–xxxii, London: Routledge.

Caffee, N. B. (2013), 'Russophonia: Towards a Transnational Conception of Russian-Language Literature', PhD diss., University of California, Los Angeles.

Carrère d'Encausse, H. (1994a), 'Civil War and New Governments', in E. Allworth (ed), *Central Asia: 130 Years of Russian Dominance, A Historical Overview*, 224–53, Durham, NC: Duke University Press.

Carrère d'Encausse, H. (1994b), 'The National Republics Lose Their Independence', in E. Allworth (ed), *Central Asia: 130 Years of Russian Dominance, A Historical Overview*, 254–65, Durham, NC: Duke University Press.

Chignell, H. (2009), *Key Concepts in Radio Studies*, London: SAGE.

Coombs, D. S. (2011), 'Entwining Tongues: Postcolonial Theory, Post-Soviet Literatures and Bilingualism in Chingiz Aitmatov's *I dol'she veka dlitsia den*', *Journal of Modern Literature*, 34 (3): 47–64.

Cuddy-Keane, M. (2000), 'Virginia Woolf, Sound Technologies, and the New Aurality', in P. L. Caughie (ed), *Virginia Woolf in the Age of Mechanical Reproduction*, 69–96, New York: Routledge.

Cuddy-Keane, M. (2005), 'Modernist Soundscapes and the Intelligent Ear: An Approach to Narrative Through Auditory Perception' in J. Phelan and P. J. Rabinowitz (eds), *A Companion to Narrative Theory*, 382–98, Malden, MA: Blackwell.

Denning, M. (2016), 'Decolonizing the Ear: The Transcolonial Reverberations of Vernacular Phonograph Music', in R. Radano and T. Olaniyan (eds), *Audible Empire: Music, Global Politics, Critique*, 25–44, Durham, NC: Duke University Press.

Das, P. V. (2015), *Colonialism, Development, and the Environment: Railways and Deforestation in British India, 1860-1884*, New York: Palgrave Macmillan.

Dave, B. (2007), *Kazakhstan: Ethnicity, Language and Power*, London: Routledge.

Dvořáček, J. and J. Záhořík (2018), 'Small but Strategic: Foreign Interests, Railway, and Colonialism in Djibouti', in J. Záhořík and L. Piknerová (eds), *Colonialism on the Margins of Africa*, 32–41, London: Routledge.

Etkind, A. (2011), *Internal Colonization: Russia's Imperial Experience*, Cambridge: Polity.

Gamst, F. C. (2006), 'The Eritrean Railway: Backbone of Colonialism: Phoenix of Transportation', in S. Uhlig (ed), *Proceedings of the XVth International Conference of Ethiopian Studies: Hamburg, July 20-25, 2003*, 1042–48, Wiesbaden: Harrassowitz.

Grenoble, L. A. (2003), *Language Policy in the Soviet Union*, Dordrecht: Kluwer.

Haber, E. (2003), *The Myth of the Non-Russian: Iskander and Aitmatov's Magical Universe*, Oxford: Lexington.

Hendy, D. (2013), *Noise: A Human History of Sound and Listening*, London: Profile Books.

Heathershaw, J. (2010), 'Central Asian Statehood in Postcolonial Perspective', in E. Kavalski (ed), *Stable Outside, Fragile Inside? Post-Soviet Statehood in Central Asia*, 87–102, Farnham: Ashgate.

Hoene, C. (2016), 'The Sounding City: Soundscapes and Urban Modernity in Amit Chaudhuri's Fiction', in C. Sandten and A. Bauer (eds), *Re-Inventing the Postcolonial (in the) Metropolis*, 363–78, Leiden: Brill.

Ishiguro, L. (2017), 'Northwestern North America (Canadian West) to 1900', in E. Cavanagh and L. Veracini (eds), *The Routledge Handbook of the History of Settler Colonialism*, 125–38, London: Routledge.

Keller, S. (2020), *Russia and Central Asia: Coexistence, Conquest, Convergence*, Toronto: University of Toronto Press.

Kelman, A. Y. (2010), 'Rethinking the Soundscape', *The Senses and Society*, 5 (2): 212–34.

Khalid, A. (2007), 'Introduction: Locating the (Post-) Colonial in Soviet History', *Central Asian Survey*, 26 (4): 465–73.

Kolesnikoff, N. (1999), *Myth in the Works of Chingiz Aitmatov*, Lanham, MD: University Press of America.

Maier, C. J. (2016), 'Sound Cultures', in K. Merten and L. Krämer (eds), *Postcolonial Studies Meets Media Studies: A Critical Encounter*, 179–96, Bielefeld: transcript.

Marcus, L. (2017), 'The Rhythm of the Rails: Sound and Locomotion', in J. Murphet, H. Groth and P. Hone (eds), *Sounding Modernism: Rhythm and Sonic Mediation in Modern Literature and Film*, 193–210, Edinburgh: Edinburgh University Press.

Martin, T. (2001), *The Affirmative Action Empire: Nations and Nationalism in the Soviet Union, 1923–1939*, Ithaca, NY: Cornell University Press.

Mieszkowski, S. (2014), *Resonant Alterities: Sound, Desire and Anxiety in Non-Realist Fiction*, Bielefeld: transcript.

Moore, D. C. (2001), 'Is the Post- in Postcolonial the Post- in Post-Soviet? Toward a Global Postcolonial Critique', *PMLA*, 116 (1): 111–28.

Morat, D., V. Tkaczyk and H. Ziemer (2017), 'Einleitung', in Netzwerk 'Hör-Wissen im Wandel' (ed), *Wissensgeschichte des Hörens in der Moderne*, 1–19, Berlin: De Gruyter.

Morrison, A. (2021), *The Russian Conquest of Central Asia: A Study in Imperial Expansion, 1814–1914*, Cambridge: Cambridge University Press.

Mozur, J. P. (1987), *Doffing 'Mankurt's Cap': Chingiz Aitmatov's 'The Day Lasts More than a Hundred Years' and the Turkic National Heritage*, Pittsburgh, PA: University of Pittsburgh Center for Russian and East European Studies.

Mozur, J. P. (1995), *Parables from the Past: The Prose Fiction of Chingiz Aitmatov*, Pittsburgh, PA: University of Pittsburgh Press.

Payne, M. J. (2001), *Stalin's Railroad: Turksib and the Building of Socialism*, Pittsburgh, PA: University of Pittsburgh Press.

Picker, J. M. (2003), *Victorian Soundscapes*, London: Routledge.

Poujol, C. and V. Fourniau (2005), 'Trade and the Economy (Second Half of Nineteenth Century to Early Twentieth Century)', in C. Adle, M. K. Palat and A. Tabyshalieva (eds), *History of Civilizations of Central Asia*, vi: *Towards the Contemporary Period: From the Mid-Nineteenth to the End of the Twentieth Century*, 51–77, Paris: UNESCO.

Radano, R. and T. Olaniyan (2016), 'Introduction: Hearing Empire – Imperial Listening', in R. Radano and T. Olaniyan (eds), *Audible Empire: Music, Global Politics, Critique*, 1–22, Durham, NC: Duke University Press.

Radjapova, R. Y. (2005), 'Establishment of Soviet Power in Central Asia (1917–24)', in C. Adle, M. K. Palat and A. Tabyshalieva (eds), *History of Civilizations of Central Asia*, vi: *Towards the Contemporary Period: From the Mid-Nineteenth to the End of the Twentieth Century*, 153–83, Paris: UNESCO.

Ram, H. (2003), *The Imperial Sublime: A Russian Poetics of Empire*, Madison: University of Wisconsin Press.

Ram, H. (2006), 'Between 1917 and 1947: Postcoloniality and Russia-Eurasia', *PMLA*, 121 (3): 831–3.

Rees, E. A. (1995), *Stalinism and Soviet Rail Transport, 1928–1941*, Houndmills:, Macmillan.

Revill, G. (2013), 'Points of Departure: Listening to Rhythm in the Sonoric Spaces of the Railway Station', *The Sociological Review*, 61 (1, supplement): 51–68.

Schenk, F. B. (2014), *Russlands Fahrt in die Moderne: Mobilität und sozialer Raum im Eisenbahnzeitalter*, Stuttgart: Franz Steiner.

Schrage, D. (2011), 'Erleben, Verstehen, Vergleichen: Eine soziologische Perspektive auf die auditive Wahrnehmung im 20. Jahrhundert', *Zeithistorische Forschungen*, 8 (2): 269–76.

Schweighauser, P. (2015), 'Literary Acoustics', in G. Rippl (ed), *Handbook of Intermediality: Literature – Image – Sound – Music*, 475–93, Berlin: De Gruyter.

Smith, M. M. (2001), *Listening to Nineteenth-Century America*, Chapel Hill: University of North Carolina Press.

Smith, M. M. (2007), *Sensing the Past: Seeing, Hearing, Smelling, Tasting, and Touching in History*, Berkeley: University of California Press.

Smith, M. M. (2012), 'The Garden in the Machine: Listening to Early American Industrialization', in T. Pinch and K. Bijsterveld (eds), *The Oxford Handbook of Sound Studies*, 39–57, Oxford: Oxford University Press.

Spalding, S. D. and B. Fraser, eds. (2012), *Trains, Literature, and Culture: Reading/ Writing the Rails*, Lanham, MD: Lexington.

Tabyshalieva, A. (2005), 'Social Structures in Central Asia', in C. Adle, M. K. Palat and A. Tabyshalieva (eds), *History of Civilizations of Central Asia*, vi: *Towards the Contemporary Period: From the Mid-Nineteenth to the End of the Twentieth Century*, 79–101, Paris: UNESCO.

Thompson, E. (2004), *The Soundscape of Modernity: Architectural Acoustics and the Culture of Listening in America, 1900–1933*, Cambridge, MA: MIT Press.

Truax, B. (2001), *Acoustic Communication*, 2nd edn, Westport, CT: Ablex.

Vandevelde, T. (2015), 'The Modernist Soundscape: Towards a Theory of the Representation and Perception of Sound in Narrative', PhD diss., KU Leuven, Belgium.

8

Auditory and spatial regimes of US colonial rule in Baguio, Philippines[1]

Russell P. Skelchy

Introduction

From its conception as a military hill station, the city of Baguio was intended to be a respite from the noise, oppressive heat and disease of the capital city Manila and the lowlands. Located around 240 kilometres north of Manila in the Benguet mountains, Baguio, by the 1920s, had become what the Filipino novelist Carlos Bulosan (1973: 66) describes as 'a small city in the heart of the [Benguet] mountains where the weather is always temperate. . . . Tall pine trees cover the mountains and at night one can hear the leaves singing in the slight wind'. A visitor in the 1930s describes Baguio as a place where 'the gardens sing and shout' as birds flutter (Cranston 1937: 300). Still others have described its natural environment poetically, sometimes using aural references such as the wind rustling, the 'talking' or 'whispering' of trees and the 'soundless' experience of quiet walks through pine forests (Subido 2009: 28–30). Hearing the vibrant natural sounds, in this context, sensorially complemented feeling the refreshing chill of the mountain air.

Although the auditory environment and landscape of Baguio today are quite different, and significantly less quiet, the city continues to proudly promote itself as the 'City of Pines' in the Philippines.[2]

The origins of the contemporary Philippine nation state are linked historically to the empires of Spain (1565–1898), the United States (1898–1946) and Japan (1942–5), making it, as Vicente Rafael (2018: 1) aptly observes, 'a kind of imperial artifact'. The name 'Philippines' itself derives from the Spanish '*las islas Filipinas*' named by Spanish explorers in 1565 to honour Felipe II, the heir apparent to the Hapsburg throne. Although the idea of instituting a summer capital at Baguio is often credited to the US administration, it was first proposed by the Spanish (Morley 2018: 87). Under American rule, officials modelled Baguio after Simla, the renowned British

Himalayan hill station known as the 'summer capital of India' (Woolley 1913). Colonial hill stations in Asia were a unique entity, neither a traditional Asian city nor a colonial/postcolonial metropolis (Kennedy 1996: 3). A preoccupation with health and climate drove the founding of various hill stations across Asia and Africa, and most were designed to enable colonials to supervise their subjects from isolated and commanding heights (Kennedy 1996; Crossette 1998). Hill stations were spaces of recreation and play, physically removed from contested lowland areas. In Simla, British officials enjoyed the climate and 'quiet remoteness' that enabled them to enjoy familiar outdoor activities such as riding, trekking and fishing (Owen 2004: 66). The sensory impact of India, according to Dane Kennedy (1996: 39), 'would have been difficult if not impossible [for colonials] to process without a shared aesthetic standard against which these unfamiliar landscapes could be measured and through which they could be given meaning'. The familiarizing of landscapes (and soundscapes) defined not only how colonials sensorially experienced being abroad but also how they re-engineered occupied space.

In Baguio, the United States constructed its own highland sanctuary in Southeast Asia. Nestled in the Cordillera Mountains of Luzon island at nearly 1,500 metres above sea level, Baguio was an ideal location due to its weather (considered enervating for white bodies), scenic mountain vistas and the opportunity for adventure. As Grace Subido (2009: xiv) observes, the US colonial narrative of Baguio as 'a romantic, exotic space and site for recreation and rejuvenation echoes in the contemporary narrative of the city as a tourist destination'. Baguio symbolized an urban, spatial and sonic order that the US colonial administration sought to replicate elsewhere in the Philippines. However, the Cordillera Mountains also represented a type of auditory wildness that required attention. Certain sounds that resonated nightly from surrounding native Igorot villages, such as loud chanting and the buzzing of bamboo musical instruments, were considered 'strange' and frightening for some Americans (Mock 1981). From a sensory standpoint, controlling Baguio's auditory environment paralleled the wider colonial project of controlling geographical space.

This chapter examines how the early colonization of Baguio was achieved sonically and spatially through the construction of its urban infrastructure in the early twentieth century. Focusing on the designs of US architect Daniel Burnham and his 1905 *Plan of Baguio*, I argue that US colonial reconfiguration of Baguio's auditory environment was foundational to how the highland military outpost would be transformed into a comfortable resort city.

Specifically, I focus on the sonic design of Baguio's urban core and its central meadow, which later became Burnham Park. My objective here is not to counter the ocularcentrism of others who have written on colonialism by over-representing the significance of sound. Instead, this chapter explores how sound was engineered and experienced through a wider sensory world shaped by US colonialism in the Philippines. Furthermore, this chapter contributes to a body of literature on Philippine colonialism that has been largely ocular and textual-centric. Although canonical historiographical works on colonialism in the Philippines have examined an array of topics, including language, racial hierarchy, hygiene and health, many have not adequately addressed the sensory features of the colonial experience (e.g. Rafael 1993, 2000; Ileto 1998, 2017; Anderson 2006). Some recent studies in sound and music, however, have begun to shift the discourse on Philippine colonialism towards listening practices, sensorial experience and musical performance (Rotter 2019; Tan 2018; Balance 2016; Buenconsejo 2017; Castro 2011; Irving 2010).

In this context, I am interested in how Baguio's urban spaces represented 'auditory contact zones', where subjects were constituted in and by their relations to each other through specific types of auditory encounters in a colonial context. Inspired by Lucy Burns's (2013: 16) conception of performing stages as 'contact zones', or complex terrains of interaction among US patrons and Filipino performers, I explore how sound in early Baguio configured and framed the interactive dimensions of imperial encounter. The semantic shift from terms such as 'colonial frontier' to 'contact zones', as Mary Louise Pratt (2008: 8) has suggested, extends readings of imperial encounters to emphasize how subjects get constituted in and by their relations to each other. Contact zones, according to Pratt, represent 'social spaces where disparate cultures meet, clash and grapple with each other, often in highly asymmetrical relations of domination and subordination such as colonialism, slavery or their aftermaths as they are lived out in many parts of the world today' (Pratt 2008: 8). In such settings, contact zones shift our focus away from expansionist expressions of the colonial frontier and diffusionist practices of domination and conquest. Auditory contact zones represent an analytic for better understanding how the colonial encounter was mediated by sound and the senses. In this context, the control of auditory environments in Baguio and elsewhere in the Philippines was integral not only to creating familiarized spaces but also in establishing sound as a material symbol of US imperial power.

Colonialism and the territorialization of sound

In a 2019 issue of *Sound Studies*, Leonardo Cardoso (2019) poses the question: 'How does the modern state hear?' Besides framing the journal issue, such a question, mostly absent from sound studies literature in the English-speaking world, forays into a wider relationship between sound, imperialism and Western modernity. As Veit Erlmann (2004: 4–5) writes, to assert the idea of Western modernity as essentially a visual age resting on technologies of surveillance, observation and seeing no longer holds much heuristic value. Although ideas about the 'colonial gaze' have inspired a questioning of Western monopolies of knowledge and representation, they have mostly resulted in more images and texts (Erlmann 2004: 405). While it makes little sense to map an alternative economy of the senses around a 'countermonopoly of the ear', understanding arguments about the hierarchy of the senses suggests how such arguments inevitably involve cultural and political agendas.

Sensory historians have argued that all human relationships, including imperial relationships, are shaped through the five senses (Rotter 2019; Smith 2007). Projects of imperialism are not effected by sight alone but instead require the wider human sensorium to make, accommodate and resist empire (Smith 2007: 18). Andrew Rotter (2019: 2–3) argues that empire was an embodied experience where people living in imperial spaces formed impressions and feelings about each other through the senses. Certain relationships, in this formulation, were as much determined by colonizer and colonized meeting face to face, hand to hand and body to body as they were by thinking about each other. As David Howes (2005: 4) observes, the senses are not merely another field of study but instead 'the media through which we experience and make sense of [fields such as] gender, colonialism and material culture'. Intersensoriality, defined as the 'multidirectional interaction of the senses or sensory ideologies considered in relation to a society, individual or a work', suggests ways to consider how sensations weave together in sequence and may be conveyed through sensory shifts (Howes 2005: 9). Howes describes how in Western cultures, the dominant group, whether conceptualized by race, class or gender, has been associated with the so-called higher senses of sight and hearing. Conversely, subaltern groups, including non-Westerners, women and workers, have been linked to the 'lower senses' of touch, taste and smell. Akin to sight, hearing has had strong associations with intellect in Western cultures – due to the importance of speech as a means of communication (Howes and Classen 2013: 2–4). For many centuries in Western law and society, the ability to hear and speak represented a prime indicator of an ability to reason, which is one reason why the deaf were considered mentally incompetent.

The hierarchy of senses, as constituted culturally through the relationship between the colonial and modern, was also expressed through the differentiation between the oral/aural bodily knowledge of the subaltern opposed to the ocularcentrism of the elite (Ochoa Gautier 2014: 14–17). The creation of the field of orality inspired theory and methodology for lettered elites to generate the idea of alterity as constitutive of the modern. In the audio-visual complex of modernity, sound appears as the interior, immersive and affective other of vision's exteriorization, privileging ocularcentric histories over orality and acousticity (Ochoa Gautier 2014: 14; Sterne 2011). The consolidation of modernity, in this respect, elicits not only an erasure of colonial history and the possibility for decolonial thought; it can also be read spatially through the 'silent ruins' of a landscape marked by the remnants of colonial architecture (Trouillot 1995). Marked by the sonic territories and terrains of empire, such remnants have been formulated through circuits of technology and sound that have undermined the neat boundaries of imperial geography (Bronfman 2014: 37; Douglas 2004). The ontological making of sonic space is implicated in the political agency of sound, defined according to sound's potential and capacity to be implicated in formal and informal cultural politics (Revill 2016: 240–1; Häkli and Kallio 2014). Sound is not merely an object but instead a set of processes and properties operating in and through materials as the agent creating space.

From the sixteenth century onwards, colonialism has produced an extensive and widely experienced rearrangement of physical space and people. The project of territorializing sound therefore must be contextualized within a wider transformation of space that gave effect to colonial claims on territory and the dispossession of Indigenous land. As Banivanua Mar and Edmonds (2010: 2) write, 'In geopolitical terms, the impact of colonialism on the land is starkly visible in the landscapes it produces: symmetrically surveyed divisions of land, fences, roads, power lines, dams, mines, expansive and gridded cities, and socially coded areas of human habitation and trespass that are bordered, policed and defended.' Land and the organized spaces on it echo the stories of colonization and Indigenous dispossession and resonate the ideological tools, language, policies and social infrastructure of colonialism. Projects of occupation and imperialism, in this context, have focused on controlling space over people (Hawkins 2012: 48).

This idea is no different for American occupation and control of land in Asia and the Pacific. As Vernadette Gonzalez (2013: 9) observes, occupied land in the form of colonial outposts and military bases along with the resources and markets of the Asia-Pacific region provide the stakes of past and continued US interest in the area. Forays into 'extracontinental empire' have defined sites of US occupation, such as the Philippines and Hawai'i, as 'feminized tropics' subject to masculinized modes of security (Gonzalez 2013: 9). Although not unique to the United States, the mutual deployment of tourism and militarism has enabled the United States to successfully navigate the complex global–local dialectics of mass tourism and exoticism projected onto the Pacific next to military occupation and interstate partnerships (Wilson 2000: xi; Gonzalez 2013: 16–18). In general, US imperial objectives in the Asia-Pacific region were no less territorial than previous colonial empires. Although the United States did not seek domination through colonial possessions per se, its ambitions were achieved using interconnected means through the domination of the global economy, fostered through capitalism as the basis for an integrated 'Free World', and militarization, which included short occupations, the maintenance of bases and the stationing of 'military advisory groups' (Man 2018: 6).

The Philippines under US rule was the site of 'a protracted social experiment' in using police as an instrument of state power (McCoy 2009: 16). The creation of a new internal security apparatus in the archipelago featuring the enhanced clandestine capabilities of the military police produced 'a virtual blueprint for the perfection of [US] state power' (McCoy 2009: 16). The occupation of the Philippines provided a favourable environment for the cultivation of covert techniques, institutional networks and systematic surveillance that were previously antithetical to US political institutions (McCoy 2009: 18–19, 38). Empire created a crucible for introducing new security procedures into Philippine and later US society. One such measure involved communications technology. For instance, in three years, the US Army laid over 16,000 kilometres of telegraph lines across the Philippine archipelago which expedited communication between its stations (May 1980: xv–xvii). Advancements in information technology, including the telephone and telegraph, also created an integrated information-based police panopticon that placed thousands of households and individuals under continuous surveillance (McCoy 2009: 34–5).

The organization of an occupied space, however, cannot simply be understood as the preserve of the colonial power alone but rather one diffused among a multiplicity of actors planning and implementing 'a structured chaos' (Weizman 2007: 5). In the Philippines, such actors included urban planners such as Daniel Burnham, the renowned American architect who, beginning in the late 1800s, designed distinctly modern urban spaces and auditory environments in the United States and fashioned templates for colonial policy in the Philippines. In the following sections, I examine how Burnham's philosophy of urban design, following the City Beautiful movement, guided the refiguring of colonial space and auditory environments in Baguio. Furthermore, I explore Baguio as an 'auditory contact zone' in which Indigenous subjectivities were constituted sonically in relation (and response) to environments created by the US colonial administration. Before addressing these topics, I turn my attention to Baguio as a symbolic space of US colonial authority.

The colonial project of Baguio

In the early twentieth century, Baguio became emblematic of 'new empire' acquisition; by definition a colonial enclave limited in its territory, it represented a process of transforming the pastoral from an aesthetic form into a colonial reality (McKenna 2017: 7, 154). What began as a US colonial 'reservation' of around 5 square miles (13 square kilometres) in 1905 eventually grew to cover 21 square miles (54 square kilometres) by 1907. Baguio was one of thirty-nine 'civil reservations' claimed by the colonial government from which the United States sought to exercise local authority while projecting a wider sphere of influence in Asia. The US colonization of the Philippines, according to Sarita Echavez See (2017: 51), plays a significant role in providing a historical and paradigmatic example of the interconnectedness between settler and military colonialisms at the turn of the twentieth century. As See suggests, the Philippines represents a 'pivotally ambiguous formation' that positioned the Filipino as proximate in time and space to Native Americans due to the ways that genocidal wars of conquest across the United States required the idea of the primitive for its legitimacy. Moreover, the conquest of the Philippines marked the transition between settler colonialism in the United States and a transoceanic imperialism that 'deployed the genocidal logic of the Indian Wars even if in the end it substituted military occupation for settlement' (See 2017: 51).

Baguio was representative of a space where acts of dispossession that underwrote its creation as a colonial capital would apply elsewhere. This was exemplified through US dispossession of Philippine Indigenous sovereignty and its enclosure of a political future (McKenna 2017: 7). Conversely, Baguio stood distinct from much of the Philippine archipelago in its geographical and climatic features. Located in the mountainous present-day province of Benguet, Baguio's topography, along with the region's large native population, suggests that US officials chose an upland retreat quite different from its lowland bases. An early report by the Philippine Commission, a group of five men appointed executive and legislative powers in the colony, describes the local Benguet native population (likely Nabaloi) as an 'awfully quiet' and 'harmless tribe' that was 'favorably disposed toward Americans' (Philippine Commission and Taft 1901: 66). Such words likely would not have been used to describe the Filipino revolutionaries of the lowlands.

It was in this context that Daniel Burnham journeyed to the Philippines in 1904, not long after the United States had acquired the archipelago from Spain. Burnham arrived with impressive credentials as an architect, city planner and businessman, having already received numerous awards for his White City designs at the 1893 Chicago World's Fair and work in US cities (McKenna 2017; Morley 2019; Hines 1972).[3] Despite only being in the Philippines for a few weeks, Burnham's impact was significant and remains so until today. Describing his role in reconfiguring Philippine urban spaces, Burnham wrote: 'No sooner had the United States come into possession of the Philippines than the War Department set about adapting the city of Manila to the changed conditions brought about by the influx of Americans, who are used to better conditions of living than had prevailed in those islands' (Burnham and Bennett 1909: 29). Burnham secured the commission to re-plan the Philippines through a series of social and personal circumstances that involved his growing reputation as an architect and his long friendship with W. Cameron Forbes, a wealthy banker who served as commissioner (1904–8) and governor-general (1909–13) of the Philippines. Burnham and Forbes shared similar pro-imperialist world views based on an ambivalence towards how US territories were acquired. Although both men agreed on the idea of eventual Filipino self-rule, they believed that Filipinos needed a period of tutelage in which US colonials could effect a 'progressive civilization' (Hines 1972: 40; Burns 2013).

Burnham focused on two projects in the Philippines: improvements to Manila and the plan for Baguio. Although the projects were distinct, his approach underscored the philosophical and aesthetic interconnections between them. Burnham did not explicitly discuss auditory aspects in his reports to US officials, yet his awareness of the relationship between sound and urban design was apparent. Burnham also was deeply inspired by design practices of the École de Beaux Arts in Paris which placed immense value on the creation of monumental, orderly public spaces and civic districts. As some writers have noted, Beaux Arts design did not function within a grid of any historical style but instead represented a way of thinking about form, and in this way, was open and 'liberal' (Van Zanten 2011: 26). Beaux Arts design, for instance, emphasized the idea that one should be able to sense the outside when inside of a building (Van Zanten 2011: 25). Likewise, Beaux Arts philosophy promoted the idea that cities represented spaces of moral, intellectual and governmental progress (Morley 2019: 49). The importation and propagation of the Beaux Arts-inspired City Beautiful planning in the Philippines, as Ian Morley (2018) suggests, stimulated advancements germane to the US regime's efforts to 'uplift' and 'civilize' the local population. More importantly, city planning was integral to revealing a new political and cultural era while distinguishing the US regime from the previous Spanish era.

The coupling of citizenship and urban design meant that urban planning represented the apogee of rational cultural development. The City Beautiful movement inspired the notion that planning was not only a tool to configure urban environments but also an instrument to enhance the social and cultural conditions of the nation state. Planners sought to resolve social and environmental flaws, such as poor housing and overcrowding apparent within urban communities while highlighting flaws with urban government (Morley 2019: 49–51). Burnham believed that urban design would lead to more effective city planning while promoting economy, efficiency and good citizenship (Morley 2019: 50). Aesthetically, City Beautiful borrowed generously from the Beaux Arts, privileging a neoclassical style 'signalled by the clustering of civic buildings, provision for open spaces around them, and the axial design of city streets' (McKenna 2017: 76). The aesthetic represented a reverence for public life and the aspiration that public spaces become an antidote to the noisy clamour of ethnic and class conflict. The US administration also trained Filipinos, such as Arcadio Arellano, a pioneer in Philippine architecture, in the aesthetics and values of City Beautiful planning, which were later utilized to promote ideas of social progress and national identity (Morley 2018: 434–5).

Urbanism, noise and the auditory

Sensorial aesthetics were embedded in the praxis of design in Burnham's plans. This was evident, for instance, in his incorporation of the European archetype of erecting water fountains in large parks. For instance, Burnham explains the value of having flowing water in parks as a source of refreshment to urban dwellers while using the city of Rome as a model. As Burnham writes, 'Wherever one goes in Rome, the gentle spray of water is ready to refresh the eye and the ear' (Moore 1921: 183). The refreshment of ear and eye, on one hand, suggests how Burnham emphasized visual and aural aesthetics working in tandem with nature. On the other, his assumptions about what constituted sensorial 'refreshment' or who exactly it refreshed also revealed elements of the modernist civilizational ideology driving City Beautiful. In Burnham's assessment, refreshment in the Philippine context involved the installation of 'playing fountains' that would 'help mitigate the trying effects of a tropical climate' (Moore 1921: 184). Implied in the statement above is an understanding that the transformation of Baguio into a modern city would entail adverse side effects. In other words, Burnham considered the aesthetic value of public parks, water and open spaces in urban environments because large-scale development, as he experienced it in an early-twentieth-century US context, had eradicated such sensorial experiences from the lives of residents of large cities. Considering the types of sounds, smells and sights associated with green spaces, swimming pools, running tracks and other outdoor facilities and venues for public entertainment (which included live musical concerts) was integral for healthy urban living, or as Burnham called it, 'breathing spaces for the people' (Moore 1921: 182). Burnham's resentment towards 'unpleasant sights and sounds' (as an issue of health and economy) was articulated in further detail in the 1909 *Plan for Chicago*. Pushing for the abolishment of excess noise of street and elevated railcars, Burnham argued that such noise deeply impacted residents and ultimately would have adverse effects on the local economy (Burnham and Bennett 1909: 74). Burnham's comments suggest how the experience of urban noise and the senses interweaved with wider issues of capitalist economic and social production, corporeal health and state citizenship. As Burnham writes,

> [T]he noises of surface and elevated road cars [are] often excruciating. . . . These conditions cause misery to a large majority of people who are subjected to constant strain . . . and undoubtedly cause a heavy loss of money to the business community. For the sake of the state, the citizen should be at his best and it is the business of the state to maintain conditions conducive to his bodily welfare. Noises, ugly sights, ill smells . . . tend to lower average efficiency. . . . Moreover, citizens have pride in and loyalty to a city that is quiet, clean and generally beautiful. (Burnham and Bennett 1909: 74–6)

Having designed public spaces for large American cities, Burnham understood that the economic benefits of modernizing would come with unpleasant sounds, smells and sights. Such concerns anticipated and paralleled other discussions about the effects of new technologies and noise on public health and urban acoustic settings beginning in the late nineteenth century (Bijsterveld 2008).

At this point, it is worth briefly explicating the differences between perceptions of sound and noise. The word 'sound' describes vibration that is perceived and becomes known through its materiality, often infused with diverse meanings and interpretations that reside in metaphor (Novak and Sakakeeny 2015: 1–2). The physical form of sound is the movement of particles of air that are the basis for hearing, listening and feeling that enable communication and social development. Sound represents the tangible basis for music, speech and spatial orientation – playing a significant role in determining how we locate ourselves in spaces through reverberation (Novak and Sakakeeny 2015: 1–2). Noise has widely been defined according to a subject-oriented framework that defines it as unwanted, undesirable, bad and unpleasant, anti-social or physiologically damaging or just excessively loud (Thompson 2020: 4; Novak 2015: 125; Voegelin 2013: 43). Noise is often juxtaposed with romanticized notions of 'natural silence', some of which have taken on moralistic tones reiterating the binarial position that noise is bad while silence is good.

Noise often is positioned as a material aspect of sound or a type of sound, constituted by particular sonic attributes (Thompson 2020: 4). Although difficult to define, noise is always 'coloured, filtered, limited, and changed by contexts of production and reception' (Novak 2015: 126). Moreover, noise has the 'imperial ability to distract and colonise . . . hearing' (Voegelin 2013: 44). In American, British and other colonial contexts, colonial agents used noise to further their own modernizing imperatives while simultaneously confronting and substituting the noise of the colony for a more 'civilized sound' (Rotter 2019: 147).

In nineteenth-century Britain and Europe, as James Mansell (2017: 1) writes, 'Noise was not just representative of the modern, it *was* modernity manifested in audible form.' The so-called age of noise equated Western modernity with the clash and clatter of urban and industrial life. This was representative of changing times where noise was thought to be 'clamorous, all-enveloping and unpredictable' in industrialized cities due to the introduction of technologies such as motor vehicles, airplanes, typewriters, gramophone loudspeakers, factories and telephones (Mansell 2017: 1–4). Discussions of noise constituted a conscious engagement with the politics of modernity in which the modern was not solely a set of ideas, institutions and practices but rather 'a sensed experience of an unnerving atmosphere' (Mansell 2017: 1–2, 11). The rise of industrial capitalism and increasingly dense concentrations of people in cities and towns meant that auditory respite was difficult to find. Vibrations of noisy urban life in the industrialized West resonated in a way where many people living in Western cities became accustomed to hearing such sounds. In the United States, the war on noise had important precedents in anti-noise activism throughout the 1900s and 1910s and later in New York City's Noise Abatement Commission (NAC), which from 1929 to 1932 undertook landmark studies of urban noise based on the premise that urban technological progress itself was the cause of the noise problem (Radovac 2011; Bijsterveld 2008; Thompson 2002; Smilor 1978). Other Depression-era anti-noise campaigns in New York City framed noise as not merely a behavioural or technological problem but a symptom of urban disorder, requiring that noise be conceived as a spatial problem necessitating a different set of strategies to control (Radovac 2011: 736). Ultimately, such strategies involved increased policing and surveillance and the reconfiguration of urban space as city officials and urban planners sought to protect the stability of the city's suddenly volatile social relations.

For colonial administrators across the world, one of the requirements for effective governance was the quieting of noise. Noise was culturally and racially defined so that it was not white colonizers who created noise but rather their subjects. As Andrew Rotter (2019: 135) observes in imperial India, 'Indians made noise, not sound, and Britons regarded it as something between a nuisance and a threat.' As the British Empire expanded across the globe, they removed noisy people in places such as Canada and New Zealand with 'more sonically dutiful white settlers' (Rotter 2019: 132). As noise abatement campaigns were undertaken across US and European cities in the late nineteenth century, changes in the dynamics of urban soundscapes 'transferred readily and deliberately to the sites of empire . . . where sonic environments were more noise than sound' (Rotter 2019: 134). As Rotter writes, 'In their presumed resemblance to Native Americans, immigrants, ethnic and racial minorities and the lower classes at home, Indians and Filipinos presided over undisciplined natural soundscapes abetted by their own primitive noise. Britons and Americans would try to impose their own auditory regimes. . . . If they could not get silence, they would at least demand quiet.' Imperial control of noise defined public space and, in some cases, even restricted certain noises as a matter of public safety. British colonial officials, for instance, created a series of Noise Ordinances that determined when and where Hindu musical processions could move in the British Empire (Sykes 2015: 384).

In the Philippines, noise was ominous and annoying to some American expatriates but did not prevent them from listening and trying to understand it. US governors took tours of the islands not merely as an exercise in reading the landscape but also to listen to acoustic environments and the people (Rotter 2019: 140–2). Although noise abatement was less of a concern, issues of noise were inherent to urban planning. In Burnham's Baguio Plan, the construction of buildings, roads and open spaces fused with its natural surroundings, and subsequently, the city acquired a reputation for being 'a place of park-like splendor' (Morley 2019: 91). Such spaces also promoted the acclimatization of US colonials, many of whom considered the tropical climate unsuitable for long-term and widespread settlement, due to the perception that tropical climates caused the deterioration of physical and mental health among white people (Anderson 1997). As a full-functioning city constructed out of the Philippine wilderness, Baguio's climate and beauty reminded both colonizers and the colonized that life under US rule was being transformed. In this sense, Baguio was conceived not as a place that would dominate the natural landscape but instead embrace it (Morley 2019: 17; see Figure 8.1).

Burnham's purposeful insistence on promoting beauty and functionality centred on the idea that the Baguio meadow would be the geographical centre (or central axis) of the city. The Baguio Plan intended for its natural environment to be more than just a backdrop for the city. Its rationale of blending urban and natural reinforced the character of US governance and its alleged benevolence by creating Baguio as a tool for the colonial regime to obtain influence and control over terrain previously belonging to the Indigenous Igorot people (Morley 2019: 92). As described earlier, such ideas extended settler-colonial practices of the US metropole to the Philippines.

Figure 8.1 Photograph of Burnham Park, Baguio, *c.* 1913. Courtesy of the Ammann-Irminger Collection, Filipinas Heritage Library, Ayala Museum, Philippines.

Prior to the arrival of American settlers, the grassland meadow, known as Kafagway to the local Igorot people, was mainly used to graze cows, carabao and horses, and bore the distinct soundmark of a horn that would be sounded at certain hours to summon livestock to feed (Tapang 1982: 82–3). The desertion of Kafagway by the Ibaloi, as one US expatriate noted, symbolized 'a silent protest against outside interference', and it was not unusual to hear Igorots state that if US colonialists were to leave 'we would quickly return to the happy life enjoyed by our ancestors' (Pérez 1904: 198). As Olivia Habana (2001: 10) observes, US colonials who laid claim to Baguio conveniently overlooked the fact that its streams, pastures and mines were already inhabited and owned by Igorots.

According to the Baguio Plan, the central meadow offered the largest area of level land and the most practical area for development, a site where 'all the more important activities, including business, municipal and government functions' would be located. This would leave the outlying areas on the surrounding hills to be a space for 'residence property' and 'detached institutions of public and semi-public nature'. Schools, universities, churches, hospitals, asylums and sanitariums were strategically placed on higher ground because, as Burnham explains, such institutions demanded 'a quiet location conveniently accessible to the city' (Burham and Bennett 1909). The distinction of higher ground as quiet and tranquil was indicative of how urban space was aurally differentiated according to the function of certain institutions.

Burnham's cultivation of separate auditory spheres along the gridded lines of noise and quiet also was reflected in the creation of street systems that laid down geometrical schemes that adapted to the contours of the Baguio valley (Moore 1921: 198). Different from the earlier Spanish colonials, the US administration considered road construction in the Philippines as key to economic development and nation-building, emphasizing specifically how roads productively linked regions, people and resources (McKenna 2017: 52–3). Besides providing ample sunlight, ventilation and strategic sight lines to government buildings, the street system concentrates traffic flow and the sounds of horse carts, carriages, motor vehicles and pedestrians to the far north-west quadrant of the valley, where businesses and government offices were located. Quiet spaces were preserved for schools, colleges and hospitals in outlying areas to the east and south, a significant distance from the municipal centre and its main roads. In this context, the hills surrounding the Baguio valley supplied visual grandeur and a physical sonic enclosure that would resonate colonial auditory power through the sounds emanating from the city's municipal centre.

As Blesser and Salter (2009: 4) observe, listening to a real environment, such as an urban street, concert hall or a dense jungle, is a sonically complex endeavour. This is due to the composite of numerous objects, surfaces and geometries in a complicated environment that creates an aural architecture. Sounds from multiple sources interact with various spatial elements that may displace familiar sounds in unfamiliar environments. Without delving too deeply into issues of aural architecture, it is worth emphasizing here the ways that visual and aural meanings often align and reinforce each other (Blesser and Salter 2009: 3). Hearing, and its active component listening, enables us to aurally visualize spatial geometry and propagate cultural symbols through aural architecture. In this sense, we may imagine that Burnham's aural visualization of Baguio's natural geometry followed a wider philosophy of embracing nature and more specifically, the sounds of nature. By differentiating spaces of noise and quiet, as I discuss in the following section, Burnham cultivated aural–spatial distinctions that both preserved and drastically re-engineered the auditory environment of the Baguio valley. The cultivation of separate auditory spheres would figure more prominently into Burnham's plans for Manila and Chicago, especially in the grouping of government buildings, courthouses, parks and green spaces versus areas of business and commerce (McKenna 2017: 104). From an ideological (and aural) standpoint, Burnham knowingly restricted what he called the 'clatter of commerce' from spaces that he considered 'majestic, venerable and sacred' (McKenna 2017: 104). The distinction between aural spaces would inform how and why park space would be central to Baguio's overall design.

Green spaces and urban aurality

The idea of preserving Baguio's natural environment, to a degree, was reflected in how it was originally idealized in its pastoral form. As I described earlier, building the hill station was not only about escaping the heat, overwork and exhaustion of the lowlands, which were arguably the realities of US occupation. Baguio also represented a retreat into nature, or more accurately, a re-engineered 'imperial pastoral' (William 1899; McKenna 2017: 11–12). Furthermore, the idea of a 'pastoral capitalism' was exemplified in the efforts of US corporations in the mid-twentieth century to refigure their suburban campuses to resemble a pastoral setting. Such efforts reflected a distaste for the sensorial realities of industrial production, namely the noise and congestion of dense urban cores (Mozingo 2011). As McKenna (2017: 14) aptly notes, the idea of the suburb as pastoral was not far off from how colonial administrators imagined Baguio. Like other 'progressive' imperialists of the time, Burnham had mixed feelings about the effects of the US invasion in the Philippines. For instance, he warned about the overdevelopment of its green spaces and protecting forests from exploitation by 'energetic lumbermen' (Moore 1921: 202).

The open space Burnham sought to preserve was the Baguio meadow, which bisected the valley to become a central *tapis vert* or 'greensward', a grassy mall between clusters of government buildings.[4] Setting Baguio's colonial offices amid grass and trees created a pastoral middle-ground landscape that associated the imposing structures and institutions of colonial power with the virtues of nature itself (McKenna 2017: 78). The preservation of green spaces was central to Burnham's plan and as such were intended to be aurally and visually appealing to American settlers. Burnham's 1909 *Plan of Chicago* more clearly articulated the ideal of parks as '*quiet* stretches of green' that would 'enhance its attractiveness' and 'develop its natural beauties' (Burham and Bennett 1909: 50). In Baguio, green spaces formed a continuous parkway meant for recreation, public events and performances in open-air theatres. Although such areas were created as 'quiet spaces', certain types of sound familiar to US colonials would become a dominant feature of the meadow and its surroundings. For instance, Western musical concerts, public speeches and sporting events featured sonic expression in the meadow that otherwise would be incommensurate with the soundscape of the Cordillera Mountains.

The *Plan for Baguio*, to an extent, became a blueprint for engineering urban space in the Philippines. It was not, however, conceived as an immutable model. After Burnham left the Philippines, he chose William E. Parsons, a fellow architect inspired by the French Beaux Arts, to implement the designs. Parsons altered the initial plan by establishing Burnham Park on the meadow, a redesign that included tree-lined open areas, walkways and a man-made lake for boating, all neatly arranged in a grand symmetrical layout. As Morley (2019: 100) observes, the creation of Burnham Park exploited urban space to aid the normalization of Filipinos living in what US expatriates considered 'culturally unacceptable ways' and represented the colonial imperative of drawing local people into the fold of modern US culture. Besides spatially fortifying the central axis of colonial administrative buildings and green spaces, Burnham Park symbolized a sonic order for which types of sounds would be deemed acceptable in a modern park, for instance light conversation, boating, Western music, sports activities and recreation. In other words, Burnham Park sonically represented how green spaces in the Philippines should sound (see Figure 8.1).

As Henri Lefebvre (1996) suggests, legitimized and authorized presence in a city centre structures membership in the urban public by determining who has ownership of a city and can represent it. Sounding the city in a present-day context, as Marina Peterson (2010: 18–19) observes, involves making urban space 'neutral' through projects such as concert programming and urban renewal which 'cleanse' public areas, such as corporate downtown plazas, by turning them into civic spaces. The idea of cleansing here assumes the wider ideological role of social reform wrapped in urban rationality: clean spaces create clean people, in both body and morals (Peterson 2010: 20). The function of sound in the cleansing of a colonized space reiterates an argument made by Michel de Certeau (1984: 94) that urban environments, in their design, can be employed for 'social betterment' when a rational organization of the environment takes place – a process that includes the production of new spaces to 'subjugate pollutants'.

Race was a significant factor in the process and the site of deep struggle in Philippine–US colonial history. As Paul Kramer notes (2006: 4–5), the result of such struggle was 'a novel racial formation' whose contours and texture emerged from a convergence of transnational forces implicating participants of the United States, the Philippines and Europe and its colonial outposts. The encounter between US and Filipino forces in the Philippine-American War (1899–1902) structured American racial ideas about Filipinos as tribally fragmented (therefore unfit for self-government) yet racially united in support of guerrilla warfare (Kramer 2006: 5). At the war's conclusion, the Philippine Commission and collaborating Filipino elites constructed a new racial state organized around the capacity of colonial power to shape 'a progressive, future oriented Filipino' under the tutelage and indefinite control of the United States (Kramer 2006: 5). Given that the binary of whites and non-whites in the United States did not exist in the Philippines, the racial landscape that existed in North America could not be transplanted to the colony without being altered (Molnar 2017: 5). American concepts of race were adapted to a Filipino racial hierarchy, creating a 'hybridized concept of race' that did not previously exist in that context. The new racial formation also reiterated a bifurcation of the population into Christian and non-Christian people, a binary categorization with deep roots in earlier Spanish colonialism. As Hispanized Filipino elites allied with US colonial rulers, both groups reinforced the widening gap between the 'civilized Christians' and 'non-Christians', especially those of Moro (Muslim) background on the southern islands of Mindanao, Palawan and the Sulu archipelago and the animist highlanders of Luzon island such as the Igorots.

In the context of colonial Baguio, the transformation of a rural mountain area inhabited by a significant native Igorot population into a summer resort town represented a form of class and racial segregation. The re-engineering of the Baguio valley created a distinctly colonized space to be used and enjoyed by colonials and members of the Filipino elite, a group that the US administration believed would eventually govern the Philippine state under US tutelage.

Re-engineering Baguio, in this respect, was not only about constructing modern concrete public edifices, such as city halls and government buildings, tree-lined boulevards and expansive green spaces. With the addition of colonial architecture came the simultaneous cleansing and erasure of acoustic characteristics previously distinctive to the Baguio valley and native communities. The colonial formula of adding and subtracting was symbolized by the creating and destroying of sensory worlds in Baguio. Furthermore, the engineering of a 'civilized' Baguio urban core addressed some of the unease felt by early US settlers who described 'strange' and 'frightening' sounds emanating from the surrounding forests and Igorot villages.

The role of colonial administrators and planners was to conceive and construct stable, isolatable and interconnected properties and organize the city's operations to eliminate identified pollutants. US officials such as E. J. Halsema, the Baguio mayor from 1920 to 1937, were best known for such a role. As a local newspaper of the period opined, 'A man forgets the burdens of democracy to quietly enjoy an atmosphere of cleanliness, of orderliness, and paradisiacal tranquility [in Baguio] . . . the roads are always kept in good order [and] no deafening noises are heard' (Halsema 1991: 205–6). The cleansing (or neutralization) of auditory space in colonial Baguio had different implications. For Burnham's protégé William Parsons, the establishment of Burnham Park in the city centre kept with the original intention of the urban park as a cleansing space of sensorial refreshment. The park, however, also marked a space of white colonial domination that, to an extent, cleansed Baguio of the sounds that frightened and caused unease among some US expatriates, especially in terms of the sounds emanating from the nearby Igorot villages and forests.

Conclusion

If the project of Western imperialism is to be understood widely as a complex phenomenon implicating multiple purposes of cultural and religious power, militarism, capitalism, tourism and other imperatives of progress, it is also about how Westerners have tried to control parts of the world with which they were (and are) largely unfamiliar. Unfamiliarity, as Uday Singh Mehta (1999) writes in *Liberalism and Empire*, is not merely ignorance but rather quite the opposite. As Mehta observes, many British liberal thinkers of the 1800s met fastidious standards of knowledge about the parts of the British Empire they wrote about. What Mehta (1999: 2) means by 'unfamiliarity' is the idea that Western colonizers did not share the 'various ways of being and feeling' that shape experience and give meaning to the communities and the individuals that constitute them, or in other words, not being familiar with what was experientially familiar to others in the empire. Unfamiliarity fuelled a liberal preoccupation with empire as a legitimate form of political and commercial governance. As was the case with many liberal and progressive thinkers of the time, what was understood as knowledge about colonized people easily became justification for the empire, especially as liberal European thought and Eurocentrism gained confidence in its universality and cosmopolitanism (Mehta 1999: 9; Quijano 2008: 197). Unfamiliarity, in this context, also inspires the desire to familiarize. This feature of Western colonial projects was evident from its earliest days and is ongoing – for instance, in the desire to make familiar spaces of US military outposts across the world as symbols of power and consumer consumption (Gillem 2007). Colonial contexts of intense contact, as Anna Maria Ochoa Gautier (2014: 34–5) observes, mobilize an 'acoustic regime of truths' where certain modes of perception, description and inscription of sound are considered more valid than others in the context of unequal power relations. Acoustic knowledge is formed at the nexus of what we can make sense of and what we cannot yet still affects us.

In the colonial Philippines, liberal-thinking planners such as Daniel Burnham designed modern urban spaces that would aurally and visually appeal to the increasing population of US expatriates. Such ideas ostensibly differentiated 'benevolent' US rule from the previous period of Spanish rule. Urban spaces like Baguio were constructed as material symbols of imperial power, and Burnham's designs transformed the secluded military outpost into a bustling highland summer retreat and tourist destination in the early twentieth century. This process included the introduction of new communication technologies and the construction of urban infrastructure (roads, railway), green spaces and other facilities (e.g. amphitheatre, country club, golf course) that would dramatically transform Baguio's natural landscape and auditory environment. Burnham's plans for Baguio were implemented and replicated across the Philippines by William E. Parsons and Filipino planners such as Juan Arellano and Antonio Toledo from 1905 to 1914. In addition to the Manila capital, cities such as Cebu, Zamboanga and provincial capitals including Tarlac, San Fernando, Lucena City, Legazpi City and others were redesigned to fit US standards (Morley 2018: 252).

Features of the redesigns included the classically built concrete edifices, such as city halls and capital buildings, wide boulevards lined with trees and the creation of spacious parks and green spaces. Baguio's auditory contact zones were sonic spaces of interaction where disparate cultures met under the asymmetrical power relations of colonialism. Such complex and rugged terrains framed the interactive dimensions of the imperial encounter sensorially. The 'smoothing out' of Baguio's rough and rocky terrain, in this respect, involved complex layers of re-engineering of sonic and spatial architecture that prefigured a wider infrastructural strategy that would replicate across the Philippine archipelago under US colonial rule.

Notes

1   An earlier version of this chapter was first published as Russell P. Skelchy (2021), 'Auditory and Spatial Regimes of United States Colonial Rule in Baguio, Philippines', *Sound Studies*, 7 (2): 187–205. It is reproduced here with the permission of Taylor and Francis. Research for this chapter was funded by the European Research Council under the European Union's Horizon 2020 research and innovation programme (Grant Number 682081).

2   For instance, see 'Top 19 Tourist Sites in Baguio, Philippines: The City of Pines': https://guidetothephilippines.ph/articles/things-to-do/baguio-city-tourist-spots (accessed 15 May 2020) as well as Reed (1976).

3   White City's neoclassical buildings evoked the architecture of imperial Rome or Athens. Burnham's design demonstrated that he was well acquainted with European precedents (McKenna 2017: 76).

4   The word 'greensward' gained popular currency in Olmstead and Vaux's 1858 winning scheme for the design of Central Park in New York City. These park designers and their clients believed that spatial practices, such as promenading, riding and boating, engendered a sense of 'communicativeness' and 'commonplace civilization' that fostered a 'democratic community' through the enactment of everyday recreational spatial practices (Meyer 2007: 61).

References

Anderson, W. (1997), 'The Trespass Speaks: White Masculinity and Colonial Breakdown', *American Historical Review*, 102 (5): 1343–70.

Anderson, W. (2006), *Colonial Pathologies: American Tropical Medicine, Race and Hygiene in the Philippines*, Durham, NC: Duke University Press.

Balance, C. B. (2016), *Tropical Renditions: Making Musical Scenes in Filipino America*, Durham, NC: Duke University.

Banivanua Mar, T. and P. Edmonds, eds. (2010), *Making Settler Colonial Space: Perspectives on Race, Place and Identity*, Houndmills: Palgrave Macmillan.

Bijsterveld, K. (2008), *Mechanical Sound: Technology, Culture and Public Problems of Noise in the Twentieth Century*, Boston, MA: MIT Press.

Blesser, B. and L. Salter. (2009), *Spaces Speak, Are You Listening? Experiencing Aural Architecture*, Cambridge, MA: MIT Press.

Bronfman, A. (2014), 'Birth of a Station: Broadcasting, Governance and the Waning Colonial State', *Small Axe*, 18 (2): 36–52.

Buenconsejo, J. S., ed. (2017), *Philippine Modernities: Music, Performing Arts and Language, 1880–1941*, Quezon City: University of the Philippines Press.

Bulosan, C. (1973), *America is in the Heart: A Personal History*, Seattle: University of Washington Press.

Burnham, D. H. and E. H. Bennett (1909), *Plan of Chicago*, Chicago: Commercial Club.

Burns, L. M. (2013), *Puro Arte: Filipinos on the Stages of Empire*, New York: New York University Press.

Cardoso, L. (2019), 'Introduction: Hearing like a State', *Sound Studies*, 5 (1): 1–3.

Castro, C. A. (2011), *Musical Renderings of the Philippine Nation*, Oxford: Oxford University Press.

Cranston, C. (1937), *I've Been Around: Seen and Heard Circling the Globe in Six Months from New York to New York*, Philadelphia, PA: J. B. Lippincott Company.

Crossette, B. (1998), *The Great Hill Stations of Asia*, Boulder, CO: Westview Press.

Czerniak, J. (2007), 'Introduction/Speculating on Size' and 'Legibility and Resilience', in J. Czerniak and G. Hargreaves (eds), *Large Parks*, 19–34, New York: Princeton Architectural Press.

de Certeau, M. (1984), *The Practice of Everyday Life*, Los Angeles: University of California Press.

de Gracia Concepcion, M. (1931), 'Silent Trails', *Philippine Magazine* (September): 173.

Douglas, S. (2004), *Listening In: Radio and the American Imagination*, Minneapolis: University of Minnesota Press.

Erlmann, V. (2004), 'But What of the Ethnographic Ear? Anthropology, Sound, and the Senses', in V. Erlmann (ed), *Hearing Cultures: Essays on Sound, Listening, and Modernity*, 1–20, Oxford: Berg.

Gillem, M. L. (2007), *America Town: Building the Outposts of Empire*, Minneapolis: University of Minnesota Press.

Gonzalez, V. V. (2013), *Securing Paradise: Tourism and Militarism in Hawai'i and the Philippines*, Durham, NC: Duke University Press.

Habana, O. M. (2001), 'Gold Mining in Benguet: 1900–1941', *Philippine Studies*, 49 (1): 3–41.

Häkli, J. and K. P. Kallio (2014), 'Subject, Action and Polis: Theorizing Political Agency', *Progress in Human Geography*, 38 (2): 181–200.

Halsema, J. (1991), *E.J. Halsema, Colonial Engineer: A Biography*, Quezon City: New Day Press.

Hawkins, A. (2012), 'Appropriating Space: Antarctic Imperialism and the Mentality of Settler Colonialism', in T. Banivanua Mar and P. Edmonds (eds), *Making Settler Colonial Space: Perspectives on Race, Place and Identity*, 29–52, New York: Palgrave Macmillan.

Hines, T. S. (1972), 'The Imperial Façade: Daniel Burnham and American Architectural Planning in the Philippines', *Pacific Historical Review*, 41 (1): 33–53.

Howes, D. (2005), 'Introduction: Empires of the Senses', in D. Howes (ed), *Empire of the Senses: The Sensual Culture Reader*, 1–20, New York: Berg.

Howes, D. and C. Classen. (2013), *Ways of Sensing: Understanding the Senses in Society*, New York: Routledge.

Ileto, R. C. (1998), *Filipinos and Their Revolution: Event, Discourse, and Historiography*, Quezon City: Ateneo de Manila University Press.

Ileto, R. C. (2017), *Knowledge and Pacification: On the US Conquest and the Writing of Philippine History*, Quezon City: Ateneo de Manila University Press.

Irving, D. R. M. (2010), *Colonial Counterpoint: Music in Early Modern Manila*, Oxford: Oxford University Press.

Kennedy, D. (1996), *The Magic Mountains: Hill Stations and the British Raj*, Berkeley: University of California Press.

Kramer, P. A. (2006), *The Blood of Government: Race, Empire, the United States, and the Philippines*, Chapel Hill: University of North Carolina Press.

Lefebvre, H. (1996), *Writings on Cities*, trans. and ed. E. Kofman and E. Lebas, Cambridge, MA: Blackwell.

Man, S. (2018), *Soldiering Through Empire: Race and the Making of the Decolonizing Pacific*, Berkeley: University of California Press.

Mansell, J. G. (2017), *The Age of Noise in Britain: Hearing Modernity*, Urbana: University of Illinois Press.

Manuel, A. E. (1978), *Towards an Inventory of Philippine Musical Instruments: A Checklist of the Heritage from Twenty-three Ethnolinguistic Groups*, Quezon City: Asian Studies.

May, G. A. (1980), *Social Engineering in the Philippines: The Aims, Execution, and Impact of American Colonial Policy, 1900–1913*, Westport, CT: Greenwood Press.

McCoy, A. (2009), *Policing America's Empire: The United States, the Philippines, and the Rise of the Surveillance State*, Madison: University of Wisconsin Press.

McKenna, R. T. (2017), *American Imperial Pastoral: The Architecture of US Colonialism in the Philippines*, Chicago: University of Chicago Press.

Mehta, U. S. (1999), *Liberalism and Empire: A Study of Nineteenth Century British Liberal Thought*, Chicago: University of Chicago Press.

Meyer, E. K. (2007), 'Uncertain Parks: Disturbed Sites, Citizens and Risk Society', in J. Czerniak and G. Hargreaves (eds), *Large Parks*, 59–86, New York: Princeton Architectural Press.

Mock, C. B. (1981), 'Childhood, Love and War in Manila: A Memoir', *Bulletin of the American Historical Collection*, 30 (1): 7–30.

Molnar, N. T. (2017), *American Mestizos, the Philippines and the Malleability of Race, 1898–1961*, Columbia: University of Missouri Press.

Moore, C. (1921), *Daniel H. Burnham: Architect, Planner of Cities, Volume Two*, Boston: Houghton Mifflin Company.

Morley, I. (2018), 'The First Filipino City Beautiful Plans', *Planning Perspectives*, 33 (3): 433–47.

Morley, I. (2019), *Cities and Nationhood: American Imperialism and Urban Design in the Philippines, 1898–1916*, Honolulu: University of Hawai'i Press.

Mozingo, L. A. (2011), *Pastoral Capitalism: A History of Suburban Corporate Landscapes*, Cambridge, MA: MIT Press.

Novak, D. and M. Sakakeeny, eds. (2015), *Keywords in Sound*, Durham, NC: Duke University Press.

Novak, D. (2015), 'Noise', in D. Novak and M. Sakakeeny (eds), *Keywords in Sound*, 125–38, Durham, NC: Duke University Press.

Ochoa Gautier, A. M. (2014), *Aurality: Listening and Knowledge in Nineteenth-Century Colombia*, Durham, NC: Duke University Press.

Owen, R. (2004), *Lord Cromer: Victorian Imperialist, Edwardian Proconsul*, Oxford: Oxford University Press.

Pérez, A. (1904), *Relaciones Agustinianas de Las Razas del Norte de Luzon*, Department of the Interior, Ethnological Survey Publications, Vol. 3, Manila: Bureau of Public Printing.

Peterson, M. (2010), *Sound, Space and the City: Civic Performance in Downtown Los Angeles*, Philadelphia: University of Pennsylvania Press.

Philippine Commission and William H. Taft (1901), 'F. H. Donaldson-Sim, Interview by the Philippine Commission, 26 July 1899', *Reports of the Taft Philippine Commission*. General Records of the Department of State, Records of the US Commission to the Philippine Islands, 1898–1909, RG 59, Entry 1027, 250: 48/28/01–02, Box 2, National Archives and Records Administration, Washington, DC.

Pratt, M. L. (2008), *Imperial Eyes: Travel Writing and Transculturation*, 2nd edn, Abingdon: Routledge.

Quijano, A. (2008), 'Colonialism and It's Replicants', in M. Moraña, E. Dussel and C. A. Jáuregui (eds), *Coloniality at Large: Latin America and the Postcolonial Debate*, 181–224, Durham, NC: Duke University Press.

Radovac, L. (2011), 'The "War on Noise": Sound and Space in LaGuardia's New York', *American Quarterly*, 63 (3): 733–60.

Rafael, V. L. (1993), *Contracting Colonialism: Translation and Christian Conversion in Tagalog Society under Early Spanish Rule*, Durham, NC: Duke University Press.

Rafael, V. L. (2000), *White Love and Other Events in Filipino History*, Durham, NC: Duke University Press.

Rafael, V. L. (2018), 'Colonial Contractions: The Making of the Modern Philippines, 1565-1946', in D. Ludden (ed), *Oxford Research Encyclopedias: Asian History*, 1–32, Oxford: Oxford University Press.

Reed, R. R. (1976), *City of Pines: The Origins of Baguio as a Colonial Hill Station and Regional Capital*, Berkeley: University of California Press.

Revill, G. (2016), 'How Is Space Made in Sound? Spatial Mediation, Critical Phenomenology, and the Political Agency of Sound', *Progress in Human Geography*, 40 (2): 240–56.

Rotter, A. J. (2019), *Empires of the Senses: Bodily Encounters in Imperial India and the Philippines*, Oxford: Oxford University Press.

See, S. E. (2017), *The Filipino Primitive: Accumulation and Resistance in the American Museum*, New York: New York University Press.

Skelchy, R. (2021), 'Auditory and Spatial Regimes of United States Colonial Rule in Baguio, Philippines', *Sound Studies*, 7 (2): 187–205.

Smilor, R. W. (1978), *Confronting the Industrial Environment: The Noise Problem in America, 1893–1932*, Austin: University of Texas Press.

Smith, M. M. (2007), *Sensing the Past: Seeing, Hearing, Smelling, Tasting, and Touching in History*, Berkeley: University of California Press.

Sterne, J. (2011), 'The Theology of Sound: A Critique of Orality', *Canadian Journal of Communication*, 36 (2): 207–25.

Subido, G. C., ed. (2009), *The Baguio We Know*, Manila: Anvil Publishing.

Sykes, J. (2015), 'Sound Studies, Religion and Urban Space: Tamil Music and the Ethical Life in Singapore', *Ethnomusicology Forum*, 24 (3): 380–413.

Tan, A. Q. (2018), *Saysay Himig: A Sourcebook on Philippine Music History, 1880–1941*, Quezon City: University of the Philippines Press.

Tapang, B. P. (1982), 'Innovation and Economic Change: A Case History of the Ibaloy Cattle Enterprise in Benguet', MA diss., Centre for Research and Communication, Manila.

Thompson, E. (2002), *The Soundscape of Modernity: Architectural Acoustics and the Culture of Listening in America, 1900–1933*, Cambridge, MA: MIT Press.

Thompson, M. (2020), *Beyond Unwanted Sound: Noise, Affect and Aesthetic Moralism*, London: Bloomsbury.

Trouillot, M. (1995), *Silencing the Past: Power and the Production of History*, Boston, MA: Beacon Press.

Van Zanten, D. (2011), 'Just What Was Beaux Arts Architectural Composition?' in J. W. Cody, N. S. Steinhardt and T. Atkin (eds), *Chinese Architecture and the Beaux Arts*, 23–37, Honolulu: University of Hawai'i Press.

Voegelin, S. (2013), *Listening to Noise and Silence: Towards a Philosophy of Sound Art*, London: Bloomsbury.

Weizman, E. (2007), *Hollow Land: Israel's Architecture of Occupation*, London: Verso.

William, J. (1899), 'The Philippine Tangle', *Boston Evening Transcript*, 1 March.

Wilson, R. (2000), *Reimagining the American Pacific: From South Pacific to Bamboo Ridge and Beyond*, Durham, NC: Duke University Press.

Woolley, M. (1913), 'Baguio, Simla of the Philippines', *Overland Monthly*: 292–3.

9

Soundscapes of diversity in the port cities of British Malaya

Cultural convergences and contestations in the early twentieth century

Tan Sooi Beng

Introduction

British colonization brought rapid political, economic and cultural transformations to Malaya in the nineteenth and early twentieth centuries. Port cities such as Singapore, Malacca (now Melaka) and Penang were established as administrative centres for the import and export of products. These cities attracted multiracial and multilingual communities of Europeans, Chinese, Arabs and Indians who sojourned to trade or to work in the tin mines or rubber estates, or to work on the construction of roads and railways. Even Malay-speaking Muslim merchants, religious teachers, journalists, artisans and entertainers who came from the surrounding islands to such port cities represented diverse communities. With the advent of the steamship and the opening of the Suez Canal in the nineteenth century, these port cities became regional hubs for the circulation of cargo, people, print, technology and ideas, as well as popular entertainment. Commercial theatre and dance troupes from Europe, India and China stopped in such cities to entertain a growing and diverse urban population. New media technologies such as the gramophone, cinema and radio broadcasting introduced Anglo-American music and European lifestyles to a variety of audiences.

To sanction their control of Malaya, the British attempted to create the notion of the 'Anglicized Malayan' in the consciousness of the diverse populations of port cities via English education, literature, culture and propaganda, all of which was disseminated through newspapers and radio, as well as film censorship policies, particularly in the late colonial era (Harper 2001: 275). However, the colonial construct of the 'Anglicized Malayan' was not entirely successful. Educational opportunities, printed materials, travel and transnational trade networks contributed to the emergence of a new middle class that was exposed to a wide variety of political ideas and which contested colonialism in the first half of the twentieth century (Lewis 2016). A multiethnic population debated their own ideas about Malayan identities, nationalisms and decolonization through their respective newspapers, theatrical performances, creative arts and social organizations.

This chapter looks at how the local Malay opera entertainers and musicians negotiated colonial cultural hegemony in British Malaya by fusing Anglo-American theatre and music with local Malay, Chinese, Arabic and Indian elements. Despite living under British colonial rule, they created their own hybrid theatre and music that was disseminated via live performances, gramophone recordings and later radio in British Malaya and in the islands of the Malay Archipelago. The soundscapes of colonial Malayan port cities articulated the merging of diverse cultures and the creation of new mixed identities. Yet, the hybrid sonic cultures that developed in such places were not mere replications of Anglo-American culture. The notion of difference is not simply a set of dichotomies such as colonizer–colonized, European–local or hegemony–resistance. As Homi K. Bhabha (1992) notes, 'hybridity' provides an avenue for local people to challenge imperial cultures and aesthetics. Indeed, local musicians reworked European theatrical and musical genres into a counter-discourse to the dominant colonial culture.

Through hybrid music and Malay song lyrics about progress and self-advancement, as well as multilingual songs about the anxieties of the working classes who lived in these colonial port cities, *bangsawan* performers promoted a vision of local modernity that was cosmopolitan and inclusive. This type of cosmopolitan modernity was built on cultural difference, interculturalism, self-advancement and a sense of connection with others through values (Appiah 2007). It was based on the tenets of European liberal humanism as well as reformist Islam, a modernity that emphasized human agency, autonomy, progress and moral values (Hooker 2000). Not only was this kind of modernity different from the British vision of the 'Anglicized Malayan', it also differed from the narratives promoted by mainstream nationalists who began to essentialize the meaning of *Melayu* (Malayness), linking it to a rigid terrain and 'race' (*bangsa*).

By looking beyond empire-centric and state-dominated auditory histories and suppositions about national borders and identities, this chapter (like this volume as a whole) contributes to the decolonization of sound studies as a field. Malay music and language have always been mixed and have changed in time and space. The popular imagination of the Malays of the 'Nusantara' in the early twentieth century was hybrid and not bound by the national boundaries that exist today; it articulated performers' experiences of performing, travelling and networking in the region. The Malays of the region referred to this organic type of cultural mixing, particularly in language, as *kacukan* (translated here as 'hybridity') (cf. Andaya 2019; Weintraub 2014). Drawing on alternative sources such as gramophone recordings, oral histories and newspaper reports from the early twentieth century, this chapter shows that external developments such as empire-building, migration, travel, trade networks, communication technologies and the spread of Anglo-American popular music all had a significant impact on the changes and types of hybridity that developed in the music and soundscapes of Malaya's colonial port cities.

Cultural convergences in the Malay opera

In the late nineteenth and early twentieth centuries, travelling theatre groups from Europe and other parts of Asia visited Malayan port cities via maritime trade routes. Besides Chinese operas that were performed for temple festivities, vaudeville shows from Europe and Parsee theatre troupes from Bombay (now Mumbai) stopped in Malaya following their tours of China, India and Burma. The foreign groups included the Anglo-American Troubadors,[1] the Stanley Opera and Dramatic Co.[2] and the Parsi Curzon Theatrical Co. of Calcutta (now Kolkata).[3] Additionally, travelling American, British and Japanese cinematograph companies screened silent movies in the cities.

It was at this time that the local *bangsawan* (Malay opera) theatre that toured the islands of the Malay Archipelago emerged. *Bangsawan* (literally meaning 'nobility' in Malay and referring to the main characters) was the first Malay commercial musical theatre in British Malaya that used the proscenium stage and a Western orchestra. *Bangsawan* performers adapted stories and stage conventions from Parsee theatre troupes (Tan 1993). In its heyday prior to the Second World War, well-known *bangsawan* troupes traversed the Straits of Malacca and the South China Sea to perform for diverse populations living in the islands of the Malay Archipelago. In his essay 'The Malay Opera, A Study', published in the *Straits Chinese Magazine*, Shaik Othman bin Sallim (1898) observed that the Malay opera catered to all those who spoke Malay, including the Jawi Peranakan (locally born Indian Muslims) and Straits Chinese or Baba communities (i.e. local-born Chinese communities who had acculturated to Malay language and culture):

> The Malay opera is, as far as I know, the only kind of dramatic performance for the large section of the community speaking the Malay tongue. It is as popular among the Straits Chinese as among the Malay people; and it is no uncommon thing to see the ladies' galleries filled en masse by the Straits Chinese women.

The diverse Malays in the port cities who performed and watched the Malay opera included people from Riau, Sumatra, Borneo, the Malay Peninsula, the southern Philippines and southern Thailand. These Malay-speaking Muslims travelled throughout the region and recognized themselves as part of a greater Malay world, which they referred to as 'Malaya Raya', 'Indonesia', 'Malaya' or 'Nusantara' (literally 'archipelago'). They interacted with other Malays and non-Muslim immigrants using the Malay language as a lingua franca and formed an emerging cosmopolitan urban middle class in the Straits Settlements (Kahn 2006: 174–5).

The owners, managers and performers of the Malay opera came from diverse ethnic backgrounds. The earliest *bangsawan* group, known as the Pushi Indera Bangsawan, was formed by a Jawi Peranakan named Mamat Pushi in Penang; this company performed in the Straits Settlements, Sumatra and Java.[4] In the early days, this troupe used the Malay lingua franca to stage fairy-tale stories that had been adapted from the repertoire of touring Parsee theatre groups. As the names of the *bangsawan* troupes indicate, these stories were based on the characters and activities of the celestial court of Indra (or, in Malay, 'Indera'). In between scenes, while sets were being changed, extra turns of singing, dancing or comic sketches were performed to the accompaniment of Western instruments. Since its inception, the Malay opera fused cross-cultural elements in the music, costumes, stage settings and props.[5]

Some of the travelling troupes that emerged in the early twentieth century included the Wayang Kassim of Singapore that was started by Shaik Kassim of Bombay; the Wayang Yup Chow Thong of Selangor, which was founded by a Chinese proprietor; and Wayang Tuan Ali, which was founded by a Malay-Muslim from Medan in Sumatra. In the 1900s, these troupes added new stories and styles from Europe and various parts of the world to attract Europeans, Straits Chinese and the other ethnic groups living in port cities under British rule. Wayang Kassim, the Indra Zanzibar Royal Theatrical Co of Singapore, one of the most admired groups to tour the Straits Settlements and the islands of the Malay Archipelago in the 1900s, was said to have combined the styles of the Dutch East Indies with those of the Pushi Indera Bangsawan of Penang (van der Putten 2014; Cohen 2002). In 1903, the *Straits Echo* newspaper, printed in Penang, reported that Wayang Kassim staged new stories such as 'East Lynne' (2 August), 'Prince Hamlet' (5 August), 'Cinderella' (8 August), 'Edward William' (12 August), 'Romeo and Juliet' (17 August) and 'Ali Baba and the Forty Thieves' (21 September) in 1903.

Furthermore, Wayang Kassim added English language and comic music hall songs from Europe as well as Dutch and Eurasian performers from Batavia in order to attract English-speaking and European audiences.[6] The newspaper reported that the extra turns, which included three European clowns from Harmston's Circus ('Guillarme, Baby and August') and a Spanish dancer called Lolita, drew Chinese and Malays to the shows.[7] This type of performance, which incorporated a variety of stories, music and dances from different parts of the world, was fashionable in the popular theatre of the Malay Archipelago in the early twentieth century.

In an article entitled 'Malayan Wayang', Ann Nacter gives an interesting account of how 'Grimm's fairy tales' and 'classic productions such as Hamlet, The Merchant of Venice, Othello, Carmen, Comedy of Errors, A Midsummer Night's Dream, etc, as well as Genevieve of Brabant, Griselda, or East Lynne' were put together through a process of improvisation by *bangsawan* performers, most of whom were not formally educated:

> If the piece chosen is an adaptation of one of Grimm's fairy tales, the stage manager calls all the artistes together and reads the story to them, exploring any point that may not be understood in the meantime. When he has finished, and everyone understands the piece in question, the performers are given their respective parts, and told to play the story that same night, which they do by 'gagging', but at the same time keeping to the plot of the play.
>
> Then, as regards the singing – and everybody has to sing – the musicians notice who steps on to the boards and the leader of the band strikes up an air that he knows the particular person can sing, the actor putting in his own impromptu words as he goes along.
>
> When witnessing a Malay play one requires a great deal of imagination, and has to take the actor's word for it when he comes out in front of a street scene, and explains that he has now arrived in a certain country and then perhaps five minutes later comes on the same scene again and sings that he is now 1,000 miles away, and so on. (Nacter 1910)

In order to attract diverse Malay-speaking audiences to their performances, such troupes emphasized novelty and comic interludes. For instance, Wayang Yap

Chow Thong, the Indra Permata Theatrical Co of Selangor, owned by a Chinese proprietor Yap Chow Thong and managed by Abu Bakar, called on audiences to see their new costumes and backdrops, watch Dutch and Malay performers and see their 'comical clowns'.[8]

In an earlier newspaper report in the *Straits Echo* on 19 May 1904, an anonymous reviewer of Wayang Yap Chow Thong praised the 'acting and singing' of the Dutch actresses and the Malay clown who kept the audience amused:

> The acting and singing of Miss Dora van Smith, the Queen of King Khoda Dosh, were all that could be desired and elicited loud applause from the audience. . . . During the performance Miss van Cantarfischer, at one time the belle of the Zanibars, sang a song from 'The Geisha' in a most pleasing manner. Mention must also be made of the Clown Abu Bakar who took the part of 'Saudagar Bada Meah' and kept the audience in roars of laughter from start to finish. The play was a decided success and we are glad to notice that several Europeans were present. We hear that another six lady artistes will arrive here in the course of next week, when the public of Penang will be sure of an even better performance. The play tonight will be 'Ali Baba and the 40 Thieves' and another bumper house is expected. (*Straits Echo* 1904)

Another reputable group that toured the region at the turn of the twentieth century was the Wayang Tuan Ali, Wayang Comedy India Ratoe of Medan. This company also boasted of its European actresses who performed tricks during the extra turns:

> Interspersed through the performance were some cleverly Japanese conjuring tricks by Miss Sorset and Miss Jahara, who made torn up paper turn into flames, and produced silk handkerchiefs from their empty fingers. . . . A really clever cakewalk was given and I hope will be repeated at our next visit.[9]

The *bangsawan* was popular among diverse Malay speakers not only because of its hybridity but also because it was flexible and could be adapted to the preferences of target audiences in specific locations. To attract Chinese Peranakan audiences in Penang, for instance, it was reported in the local paper, *Straits Echo*, that new stories from Batavia that included Peranakan characters would be introduced. As reported in the *Straits Echo*, Wayang Kassim featured a Chinese Baba character called Kee Ah Sam, as well as his wife Kun Neo in the play 'Radent Adjeng Rohaja' (*Straits Echo* 1906). Chinese legends were also staged. The Alfred Theatrical Company of Selangor staged the Chinese legend 'Aw Chua Pek Chua' (Black and White Snake) in 1928. An advertisement for the show in the *Straits*

Echo on 26 March 1928 called on audiences to 'See the Thunder Pagoda', 'The Broken Bridge', 'The Flying Mountain' and 'The Temple of Golden Mount'.

By the 1920s, *bangsawan* star directors, such as Khairuddin or Dean of the Union Star Opera and Nani of the Gnani Star Opera, began to introduce 'moral and educational stories' to their performances, as well as Malay historical plays in tandem with the rise of Malay nationalism.[10] On 13 December 1926, the Union Star Opera of Singapore advertised, 'An extra special Malay historical play in 4 parts Siti Zubaidah (Produced by Inche Zainol, Directed by K Dean. . . . The greatest of Malay plays).' As a heterogeneous and flexible form, *bangsawan* remained popular in British Malaya until the post-Second World War period.

Hybridity as counter-discourse

Besides incorporating new stories from Europe and other parts of Asia, the Malay opera stimulated the blending of European music with the music of the multiethnic populations of cosmopolitan port cities in British Malaya. Shaik Othman (1898) commented that he heard European songs such as 'Ta-ra-ra-boom-de-ay', 'Daisy-Bell', 'After the Ball' and 'Two Little Girls in Blue' at the Jawi-Peranakan Theatrical Company from Penang's performance in North Bridge Road, Singapore. He added that the singing was, however, often soft and drowned out by a 'strong orchestra consisting of a trumpet, drum and two fiddles'.

Ann Nacter recalled hearing European tunes such as 'Annie Laurie' or Gounod's 'Serenade' and 'Her Golden Hair Was Hanging Down Her Back' being sung at Malay opera shows. Nacter (1910) added that 'the latest idea' in 1910 was 'to introduce English Music Hall numbers into the night's performance, such as songs, cake-walks, national dances, sketches and the like'. Nevertheless, by the 1920s, vaudeville shows featuring multiethnic actors and actresses performing songs and dances from all parts of the world had become the trend. The Malay orchestra (*orkes Melayu*) comprising instruments such as the violin, trumpet, trombone, clarinet, saxophone and piano was created to accompany *bangsawan* performers. Sometimes the Malay frame drum and Indian *tabla* would also be added if the stories being performed were associated with Malaya or India, respectively (Tan 1993).

The gramophone has left an auditory record of the *bangsawan* songs of the early twentieth century that would otherwise have disappeared. The main companies that recorded Malay music in British Malaya were from Europe and included the Gramophone Company or His Masters Voice (HMV; this went by the names of 'Chap Anjing' or 'Dog Brand' in Malaya), Beka, Odeon, Columbia Gramophone Company, Pathé (known locally as 'Chap Ayam' or 'Rooster Brand') and Pagoda. HMV was the largest producer of Malay recordings in British Malaya with its own local subsidiaries or sister companies such as Chap Kuching ('Cat Brand') and Chap Singa ('Lion Brand') in the 1930s. Recording engineers from these gramophone companies carried out recording sessions in Singapore, the main port of call for entertainers travelling in the region. As I have shown in earlier work, local agents who selected artists, repertoire and venues assisted recording engineers in their work. The recordings were made on hard wax, and the wax matrices were shipped to factories of various companies to be pressed (Tan 1996/97; Murray et al., 2013). As these records were played in public spaces such as amusement parks, theatres and outside record shops, they were accessible to all types of Malay-speaking audiences in colonial port cities.

Malay folk social and dance music (*ronggeng*) formed a large part of the repertoire that was recorded by these gramophone companies in Malaya in the first half of the twentieth century. These 'song-dance genres' were performed live at Malay and Peranakan social occasions such as weddings and other festivities in various parts of Malaya. They were also staged in the *bangsawan* stories and interludes known as extra turns.[11] An analysis of some recordings of Malay songs from the 1920s to the 1950s gives us an idea of the intercultural mixing and cultural convergences that occurred. For instance, 'Chek Siti I'[12] is a *bangsawan* song in which a male singer (H. Dolmat) and a female singer (Miss Saianah) exchange Malay verses (*pantun*). The *ronggeng* ensemble comprising the European violin (*biola*), Malay frame drum (*rebana*) and Malay gong accompanies the singers. The two singers perform the *joget*, a fast and lively dance song that uses a four-beat rhythmic pattern, which juxtaposes units of two notes and three notes played in succession (H. Dolmat and Miss Saianah 1935). It is believed that the Portuguese brought this type of ensemble and music to Southeast Asia when they first arrived in the sixteenth century (Matusky and Tan 2017).

Gramophone companies such as HMV and Pagoda also recorded prominent Malay and Peranakan Chinese *dondang sayang* (love song) singers in the early twentieth century. Stylistically, the *dondang sayang* combines the Western and Malay instruments of the *ronggeng* ensemble, the Malay *asli* social dance rhythmic cycle, Malay *pantun* singing as well as Western triads and the diatonic scale. Singers try to outwit each other in a repartee style using the *pantun* to debate topics of interest such as love, good deeds, business, fruit or the sea in the

Baba (Peranakan) Malay patois. As in 'Dondang Sayang Tanaman 1' (Dondang Sayang about Plants 1), (Miss Piah, Mr Poh Tiang Swee and Mr Koh Hoon Teck, *c*.1930s), a typical five-bar melody begins all singing that can last for several hours depending on the abilities of the vocalists. The rhythm played by the frame drum (*rebana*) and placements of the gong beats resemble the Malay *asli* rhythmic pattern from the *ronggeng* dance repertoire. As in traditional Malay music, the vocalist sings in heterophony with the violin or *biola* in Malay.

Through *bangsawan* theatre and gramophone recordings, the *ronggeng* social folk music evolved into modern popular genres in the interwar period. In order to appeal to multiethnic urban audiences, new musical arrangements and melodies were composed. The piano often played the parts of the violin and gong while the Western drum set was used in place of the frame drum. Sometimes the ensemble was supplemented with a plucked bass and extra violins. The Tin Pan Alley musical arrangements disseminated by gramophone records and Hollywood talkies influenced the new *ronggeng* music.

In addition to the Malay and Anglo-American elements, other foreign elements were often added to the recorded *bangsawan* and folk songs of the 1920s to 1950s. 'Tandi Tandi' portrayed Indian influence and was accompanied by a harmonium, *tabla* and piano (Che Tijah *c*. 1930s). The addition of a short, unmetered introduction (*alap*) by the harmonium, as well as vocal ornamentations, articulated Indian folk and light classical singing styles. 'Gambos Betjerai Kasih' (Gambos Separation of Lovers) (Ahmad CB 1939) had a Middle Eastern flavour that highlighted the use of the Middle Eastern *ud* (called a *gambus* locally) together with small *marwas* hand drums and a cone-shaped drum (*dok*) that played the characteristic four-beat *zapin* rhythm.[13] The *gambus*, and other instruments such as the accordion, violin and double bass, played an Arabic-type of mode. Another older recording, *Gambos Ya Omar* by Salih, featured the Arabic *zapin* in the village setting in which the vocalist, *gambus*, violin and harmonium performed the melody while the *marwas* executed the *zapin* rhythm (Salih 1911).

Hybridity was a way to contest the dominant colonial culture that was being fostered under British rule. Nevertheless, the idea of variance in the Malay opera was ambivalent as local performers mixed European music with Malay texts, folk tunes and rhythms and added other elements from Chinese, Indian, Javanese and Arabic cultures. In so doing, the *bangsawan* theatre could attract multiracial audiences in port cities. The music also mirrored a Malay entertainment community that was open to and tolerant of other races and cultures. The performers themselves came from and networked in different parts of the Malay Archipelago.

Education, progress and independence

Gramophone recordings also indicate that Malay popular music based on Anglo-American and Latin American social dance rhythms, such as the waltz, tango, foxtrot and rumba, was widespread in British Malaya. Marches, comic songs (*lagu klakar*) and Hawaiian songs were also recorded. These new songs were originally performed by dance bands at British clubs but were later adopted by local bands in the *bangsawan* extra turns and at cabaret dance halls in Malaya's amusement parks; they were also disseminated through gramophone records, radio broadcasts and films. The new dance music and rhythms appealed to consumers as they were up-to-date and resembled the novel and popular music showcased in films from Europe, Hollywood, Shanghai and India.

Local musicians in British Malaya appropriated Anglo-American music to create their own musical idiom that was 'modern' (*moden*). Even though the new popular music used Tin Pan Alley instrumentation, strophic structure, dance rhythms and the open-throated crooning style of singing, nevertheless, the songs retained specific Malay folk elements and texts. The fusion of Malay social dance rhythms, musical textures, singing styles, drums and other foreign elements led to a local form of modernity – one that was current yet different from the European version.

In fact, the modern songs advocated change; they helped to educate and raise the consciousness of Malay audiences to prepare them for eventual independence. Through Anglo-American-style popular songs, *bangsawan* performers and recording artists contributed to contemporary discourses about reform and the creation of a more progressive or advanced society. These issues were being debated in Malay newspapers and other public texts by modernist reformist Muslims and Malay nationalists in the 1930s and 1940s in British Malaya and throughout the greater Malay world (Kahn 2006).[14] Although the two main nationalist groups advocated different ways forward, both focused on concerns about Malay poverty and backwardness, decolonization, fears that immigrants were taking over the Malay land (*Tanah Melayu*) and the need for the Malay race (*bangsa*) to protect its political sovereignty. Debates in vernacular newspapers, journals and new fiction centred on solutions to such problems, the necessity of change and strategies for progress (*maju*) (Hooker 2000; Muliyadi 2004).

Newspapers such as the *Jawi Peranakan* (first published in 1876) and *Warta Malaya* (1936) stressed the importance of education as a vehicle for progress. *Al-Imam* (1906) urged Malays to 'wake from their slumber', to work hard, change their behaviour and be active in education, trade, agriculture and the development of the community. In tandem with such discourses, *bangsawan* performers and singers such as the late Ahmad CB called on audiences to 'wake up from sleep' and to 'study' from his songs. Ahmad CB hailed from Sumatra and was known for his nationalist songs. He used lively (*rancak*) rhythms such as the march, rumba and foxtrot to bring vitality to these songs. In an interview with the author, Ahmad CB stressed that as he 'travelled from island to island . . . while earning a living, he was educating the young . . . [and] . . . educating the community so that they could move forward' (Ahmad CB 1986).[15] He declared that his performance group staged many songs and stories that called on children to 'wake up' (*bangun anak-anak*). When I interviewed him in 1986, he sang the song 'Bangun Anakku' (Wake Up My Child) to me, which he had also recorded with Chap Singa in 1938 (Ahmad CB 1938). The song's lyrics are as follows:

Bangun anakku dari tidurmu	(Wake up my child from your sleep)
Semua kawan-kawanmu sudah menunggu	(All your friends are waiting)
Jikalaunya sudah, segera berpakaian	(If you have woken up, quickly get dressed)
Menuntut ilmu, jangan-jangan dilupakan	(Pursue knowledge, do not forget)
Ini semua demi masa depan.	(All this is for the future).

Ahmad CB's 'Bangun Pagi' (Wake Up in the Morning) – a *kerconcong* foxtrot – was based on the English nursery rhyme 'Early to bed, early to rise, makes a man healthy, wealthy and wise' (Ahmad CB 1947a). In 'Menuntut Ilmu' (Claim Knowledge) (Ahmad CB 1947b) – a rumba – Ahmad CB asks 'children to go to school so that they will be safe, meritorious and become useful to society and can help the old in time to come'.[16]

Furthermore, singers advised women to pursue an education so that they could be respected as mothers and leaders of the nation. A vibrant swing, foxtrot rhythm was used in 'Gadis Malaya' (Women of Malaya) (A. Rahman *c.* 1950s), which included the lyrics:

Gadis Malaya, oh	(Women of Malaya, oh)
Belajarlah kamu seakan setia	(Be devoted to your studies)
Majukanlah kamu punyalah cita-cita	(Develop yourselves and have ambitions)
Menjadi pemimpin ibu yang berharga	(To become leaders and mothers of esteem)

Recording artists also sang about the way forward proposed by modernist Islamic reformists. In her analysis of Malay prose fiction, Virginia Hooker (2000: 5, 85) shows that for the new generation of modernist reformists, the 'way forward' was through 'individual initiative' and humanitarian values such as concern for the poor and the marginalized.[17] There was a longing for moral guidance and advice about how to progress. In line with this trend, *bangsawan* troupes staged moral stories, but there was also a considerable increase in songs about virtuous behaviour through the 1930s to the 1950s. Keywords pertaining to values were often printed in the HMV advertisements, catalogues and song lyrics. Showing sympathy (*belas kasihan*) to the less fortunate and to women, and generosity to the needy, was often presented in recorded songs. Singers advised (*nasihat*) audiences to take care of the poor, orphans and their aged parents. Song titles published in recording catalogues in the 1930s and 1940s include 'Kesian' (Pity) (Che Aminah *c.* 1930s); 'Yatim Piatu' (Orphans) (Mohd. Yatim *c.* 1930s); 'Yatim yang Miskin' (The Orphan Who Is Poor) (Miss Rambat *c.* 1930s); and 'Ibu' (Mother) (Mr Jani *c.* 1930s). Songs about children who were ill-treated by their stepmothers, such as 'Anak Tiri' (Stepchild) performed by the child star Miss Emmy, were also common (Miss Emmy *c.* 1930s).

Through their songs, the *bangsawan* stars helped to raise the awareness of their audiences concerning progress, change and a Malayness that was not fixed to any one place or ethnic group. Some musicians even encouraged the building of a Malaya which included other (i.e. non-Malay) ethnic groups. For example, Ahmad CB wrote the lyrics and melody of the song 'Malaya' (Malaya) (Ahmad CB 1935), which praised the beauty of the country and the different races living in it. The song 'contained an ensemble of many sounds and voices including members from the Malay, Chinese, Indian, Eurasian, Filipino, Portuguese and English ethnic groups'[18] (*Filem Melayu*, 1941):

Malaya, tanah pesaka	(Malaya, inherited land)
Malaya, Malaya, maju dan jaya	(Malaya, Malaya, developed and successful)
Malaya, Malaya, indah dan permai	(Malaya, Malaya, precious and beautiful)
Berbagai bangsa hidup aman damai	(Different races living peacefully)

In the 1950s, musicians composed and recorded the first patriotic songs that referred specifically to the formation of a new independent nation. Of the many patriotic songs by Zubir Said, 'Majulah Singapura' (Onward Singapore, 1958) is the most well known of these, as it became the national anthem of Singapore. During this era, Zahara Agus (*c.* 1930s) was acknowledged for her 'Malaya

Merdeka' (Independence of Malaya) while Ahmad CB encouraged youths to unite and work towards independence in his song 'Pemuda Melayu' (Malay Youths) (Ahmad CB and Osman Ahmad Orchestra *c.* 1950s):

Pemuda mesti berbakti	(The youths must be devoted)
Membela ibu pertiwi	(Defend the motherland)
Marilah bersama bertegak bersatu	(Let us together stand united)
Merdeka tetaplah Merdeka	(To be free is to attain independence)

Malay recording artists articulated their ideas about modernity, progress and decolonization by composing lyrics that emphasized universal values such as humanity and responsibility towards the disadvantaged, including the working-class poor, orphans and women. They advocated change and ways to achieve independence through education, hard work and unity, as well as moral guidance. By combining pivotal terms employed by nationalists and modernist Islamic reformists in hybrid popular music, such musicians promoted a form of cosmopolitanism that was inclusive of the diverse Malays and immigrants living in the islands of the Malay world. The performers advocated a broader type of Malayness and debated the relationship between Malay nationalism and their regional identity through their songs.

Multilingual songs chiding colonial authorities

Beginning in the 1930s, multilingual comic songs performed in the *bangsawan* extra turns provided an avenue for raising frustrations with the colonial authorities. These songs incorporated topical issues such as the plight of taxi drivers, trishaw men and street hawkers. Such songs were often invigorated by humour in the tone of voice and musical accompaniment. These songs did not use the Malay verse form (as in other *bangsawan* and Malay social dance songs) but were sung in 'bazaar Malay'; they incorporated English, Chinese and Tamil words to speak to multiethnic audiences. As in the modern tracks about change and progress described earlier, these comic songs were also accompanied by upbeat rhythms such as the rumba, foxtrot or tango that were played by dance orchestras.

'Taxi Rumba' (Rumba Taxi) is a lively comic song about the problems faced by taxi drivers (Che Tarminah and Piet S 1939). It is sung as a duet between a female passenger and a male taxi driver in conversational Malay with a sprinkling of English words included. The song informs the audience about a policeman who often took away the driver's license if his lights were not working or if his number plates disappeared:

Sabarlah nona, lampu tidak nyala	(Be patient lady, [my] lamp is not lighting)
Number belakang tidak ada	(There is no number [plate] at the back)
Gohed *lah saja, hari sudah gelap*	(*Go ahead*, the day is getting dark)
Jangan takut kena tangkap.	(Don't wait till the rain comes).
Kena saman saya takut	(I am scared of getting a summon)
Saya khuatir lesen kena chabut.	(I am afraid [my] licence will be confiscated).[19]

After the Second World War, comic topical songs that concerned ordinary working people of all races remained popular and were also sung in Malay films. 'Saudagar Minyak Urat' (The Nerve Oil Merchant) (Aman Ballon King Clown, Nooran Opera and HMV Orchestra *c.* 1950s); 'Che' Mah Dengan Tukang Becha' (Che Mah with the Trishaw Man) (Aman Ballon *c.* 1950s); and 'Uncle Murtabak' describe the hardships faced by ordinary peddlers and small businessmen who are inevitably harassed by the police.[20] The lyrics for 'Uncle Murtabak' (Mohd. Yatim *c.* 1950sa), for example, are as follows:

Uncle Murtabak tersalah cakap	(Uncle Murtabak said something wrong)
Mata gelap datang tangkap	(the secret police came to catch him)
Kena masuk dalam lokap	(he had to go to jail)
Central polis tiga tingkat.	([At the] Third Floor of the Central Police Station).

Such comic songs can also be seen as tongue-in-cheek comments on decolonization and the challenges of living in a modern city. The singers mix Malay, English and other languages to mock those who imitate the British by drinking excessively, playing the violin or dancing at cabarets. One song advising the audience about the woes and consequences of excessive drinking, 'Yam Choi Chow', mixes Malay, English and Cantonese (Mohd. Yatim *c.* 1950sb):

My darling broke my heart	(My darling broke my heart)
Yi kar ngo mo sweetheart	(Now I do not have a sweetheart)
Ngo yo lok soon badan ku tak sehat	(I am ugly, my body is not fit)
Ngo pangkau sama nyamok and moksat.	(I sleep together with mosquitoes and lice).

It is interesting to note that the melody for 'Yam Choi Chow' was adapted from a song featured in the French movie *Sous Les Toits De Paris* (Under the Roofs of Paris) (1930), directed by René Clair. This film had voice and sound in some parts and was about dance halls in Paris in the late 1920s. The melody must have been a hit in the 1930s as it was appropriated and rendered with different lyrics in various parts of the world. In Germany, the melody was sung during men's drinking sessions.[21] Mohd. Yatim may have adapted the German version and changed the text to express his thoughts about the consequences of excessive drinking. His version also had comic effects played by brass instruments at the end of each phrase.

Another song which lampoons the common Malay man's attempt to imitate the European is 'Wak Kasban Belajar' (Wak Kasban Learns) (Mohd. Yatim *c.* 1950sc). In this song, the singer ridicules Wak Kasban who tries to learn Anglo-American dances such as the tango and foxtrot and European instruments such as the violin and saxophone as was the fashion at the time. According to the song, Wak Kasban created such a din at the cabaret that the manager threw him out. He also made so much noise playing his musical instruments until late at night that the neighbours reported him to the police. This song resembled some of the cartoons that were featured in the Malay newspapers and which criticized locals such as Wak Ketok who tried to mimic British ways (Muliyadi 2004).

P. Ramlee, who dominated the Malay-language cinema field and recorded more than 350 songs in the 1950s and 1960s, was also known for his multilingual comic songs. In both his films and songs, P. Ramlee combined humour and conversational Malay to portray the contradictions faced by ordinary Malays in a modernizing society.

Multilingualism in such songs exemplified everyday realities and social relations among the working class in colonial society. By using several languages – colloquial Malay (the common language in the urban and rural areas), Hokkien, Cantonese, Hindi and English – such comic songs became relevant to diverse communities. The use of Western popular tunes, dance rhythms and musical instruments gave the songs a feeling of modernity and progressiveness. Through humour in the lyrics, singers were able to expose the problems of the common man regardless of race, be they taxi drivers, *murtabak* sellers or youths adjusting to life and the authorities in the city. The comic songs engaged audiences in social transition; audiences could laugh at their own faults and outdated customs. Humour also helped to ease anxieties about modernity and change in an urban colonial environment. By focusing on the similarities rather than the differences of the ethnically diverse urban population, the comic songs mediated inter-ethnic interaction in a plural society.

Conclusion

In this chapter, I have shown that the soundscapes of diversity in the port cities of British Malaya prior to Malaya's independence were derived from cultural convergences as well as contestations in the first half of the twentieth century. The vitality of these soundscapes stemmed from the creativity of musicians who lived in a period of change and their openness to the variety of cultures around them. Such musicians created modern popular music by combining European musical instruments, Anglo-American dance rhythms, and Malay and other folk music with song texts about Malay progress and the problems of the common man. Hybridity became a means of challenging the colonial culture that was being disseminated via radio and film as well as the British construction of an 'Anglicized Malayan' identity. However, the notion of difference was ambiguous and portrayed a multiethnic intertexuality that was localized. Unlike the exclusive music-making of the British colonizers, this new hybrid music was performed live at amusement parks and was accessible to people of all classes and backgrounds, Malay and non-Malay, throughout the Malay world.

Furthermore, artists communicated a form of vernacular modernity that was cosmopolitan, open to the transnational exchange of culture, and crossed boundaries of class and ethnicity. They performed a type of 'colonial cosmopolitanism' that was 'rooted', which they experienced as they travelled and created networks in the Malay Archipelago where there was no rigid interpretation of the Malay *bangsa* (race), identity or language (Anderson 2012). Such performers interacted with and married into the many and varied ethnic groups living in this archipelago; they spoke and performed in a variety of languages and dialects. Many were of mixed ancestry. They spent long periods of time outside Malaya, exchanging knowledge with and learning from one another as well as from performers from China, India, the Middle East, Europe and the Philippines who visited these port cities. Mobile *bangsawan* performers absorbed new ideas about education, morality and progress that circulated widely in the region. They mixed European and Malay music with those of the diverse ethnic groups with whom they interacted to disseminate these cosmopolitan ideals. They used Malay, the local lingua franca that had no fixed form at this time, and merged it with other languages to voice their opinions about the problems of the common man of different races in the port cities. This type of modernity differs from the present-day mainstream Malay ethno-nationalist narrative that essentializes the notion of Malayness (*Melayu*).

Notes

1 As per an advertisement in the *Straits Echo*, 23 March 1904.

2 As per an advertisement in the *Straits Echo*, 30 June 1904.

3 As per an advertisement in the *Straits Echo*, 15 June 1904.

4 Details can be found in *Bintang Timor*, 29 November 1894.

5 See Tan (1993) for an in-depth analysis of the historical development, dramatic elements, backdrops, extra turns, dance and music of *bangsawan* theatre or the Malay opera in early-twentieth-century Malaya.

6 As per reports in the *Straits Echo*, 15 October 1903.

7 As per reports in the *Straits Echo*, 15 June 1907.

8 As per advertisements in the *Straits Echo*, 1 February 1907.

9 As per advertisements in the *Straits Echo*, 8 October 1906.

10 Advertisements in the *Straits Echo*, 12 November 1926 and 26 October 1929.

11 For analyses of *bangsawan* songs and Malay social dance music, see Tan (1993) and Matusky and Tan (2017). In *bangsawan*, slow-paced *asli* songs were often sung as *lagu nasib* (songs of fate) or *lagu sedih* (sad songs) to accompany characters who were in extreme sorrow. Fast-paced *asli* accompanied dances and happier songs. *Inang* became associated with lighter dramatic situations such as lovers and dancers in the garden. *Joget* songs accompanied fighting scenes. *Zapin* (sometimes called *gambus*) songs were performed during sad scenes or to accompany dance. All four genres were popular in the extra turns.

12 The recordings and annotations of 'Chek Siti 1', 'Wak Daing' and 'Gambos Ya Omar' are available in Murray et al. (2013). This box set has a collection of four CDs and ninety tracks of 78 rpm recordings from Burma, Vietnam, Thailand, Malaysia and Indonesia. Other recordings analysed are from the collections of Naina Merican and Jaap Erkelens.

13 The Malay *zapin* is an adaptation of the Arabic *zapin* that was brought to the state of Johore (now Johor) by Arab immigrants. The dance was performed by men only in the early days. The *zapin* was modernized and adapted by *bangsawan* performers for Middle Eastern stories. New *zapin* dance motifs and choreography were created for both men and women dancers in *bangsawan*. Western instruments like the piano, violin and double bass were added (Matusky and Tan 2017).

14 Milner (1995) discusses the various intellectual debates in Malay public texts in the late nineteenth and early twentieth centuries. While the Malay mainstream nationalists led by vernacular-educated Malays upheld essentialized notions of the Malay *bangsa* (race), another group of reformist Muslims educated in modern Islamic schools provided an alternative discourse. According to the latter, the inhabitants of the Malay Archipelago constituted a community and formed the Malay *bangsa* or nation. The mainstream nationalists gained mass support in the post-war period and led Malaya to independence in 1957 (Kahn 2006: 68, 96).

15 '*pulau ke pulau jalan sambil cari makan sambil kita bimbingan anak-anak, bimbing masyarakat supaya boleh maju sikit*' (Ahmad CB 1986).

16 '*anak-anak yang mesti bersekolah supaya selamat berjasa kemudian menjadi berguna kepada masyarakat dan dapat membantu tua kemudian hari*' (Ahmad CB 1986).

17 For example, Syed Syekh al-Hadi, a teacher, journalist and writer who was inspired by reformist Islam from Egypt, wrote a series of stories called *The Moral Trainer* that was published by the Jelutong Press. He advocated morals and values (which included concern for people, responsibility, fidelity, initiative and education for women) in stories such as *Faridah Hanum* (Hooker 2000: 85).

18 '*Mengandongi pasokkan bunyi-bunyian dan nyanyi suara ramai ia-itu termasok-lah ahli-ahli daripada bangsa Melayu, China, India, Eurasia, Manila, Portuguese dan Inggeris*'.

19 '*Gohed*' was sung in English.

20 A *murtabak* is a stuffed pancake that is sold throughout Malaysia, as well as in other countries in Southeast Asia, South Asia and the Middle East.

21 I thank Uwe Patzold who alerted me to this and pointed out that the melody of the French song was probably adapted by the Germans in the song 'Lech Misch Am Arsche, Marie!' (Lick Me on the Arse, Marie!), a type of 'vernacular men's party song' often sung during drinking sessions where vulgar words were used (Uwe Patzold, personal communication, 28–29 September 2012). A version of 'Lech Misch Am Arsche, Marie'/'Sous Les Toi[t]s De Paris' was recorded on vinyl record by the German singers 'Klaus und Ferdie' (http://www.discogs.com/Klaus-Und-Fe rdl-Das-Berglandecho-Ein-Abend-Auf-Der-Heidi/master/257358). According to Patzold, the texts of this recording include some words which refer to the Second World War.

References

Ahmad CB (1935), *Malaya*, Chap Singa QF 87, 78 rpm.

Ahmad CB (1938), *Bangun Anakku*, Chap Singa, 78 rpm.

Ahmad CB (1939), *Gambos Betjerai Kasih*, Chap Singa QF 105, 78 rpm.

Ahmad CB (1947a), *Bangun Pagi*, HMV P 22924, May, 78 rpm.

Ahmad CB (1947b), *Menuntut Ilmu*, HMV P 22934, October, 78 rpm.

Ahmad CB (1986), Interview with the author.

Ahmad CB and Osman Ahmad Orchestra (*c.* 1950s), *Pemuda Melayu*, HMV, Nam 238, 78 rpm.

Aman Ballon (*c.* 1950s), *Che' Mah Dengan Tukang Becha*, HMV P 13179, 78 rpm.

Aman Ballon King Clown Nooran Opera and HMV Orchestra (*c.* 1950s), *Saudagar Minyak Urat*, HMV P 13078, 78 rpm.

Andaya, L. Y. (2019), 'The World of the Southern Malays', in M. Kartomi (ed), *Performing the Arts of Indonesia, Malay Identity and Politics in the Music, Dance and Theatre of the Riau Islands*, 40–57, Copenhagen: NIAS Press.

Anderson, B. (2012), 'Colonial Cosmopolitanism', in Zawawi I. (ed), *Social Science and Knowledge in a Globalising World*, 371–88, Petaling Jaya, Malaysia: Malaysian Social Science Association and Strategic Information and Research Development Centre.

Appiah, K. A. (2007), *Cosmopolitanism: Ethics in a World of Strangers*, London: Penguin Books.

Bhabha, H. K. (1992). 'Of Mimicry and Man: The Ambivalence of Colonial Discourse', in P. Waugh and P. Rice (eds), *Modern Literary Theory: A Reader*, London and New York: E. Arnold, 1992.

Che Aminah (*c.* 1930s), *Kesian*, HMV P. 13186, 78 rpm.

Che Tarminah and Piet S. (1939), *Taxi Rumba*, HMV P 13172, July, 78 rpm.

Che Tijah (*c.* 1930s), *Tandi Tandi*, HMV P. 16489, 78 rpm.

Cohen, M. I. (2002), 'Border Crossings: Bangsawan in the Netherlands Indies in the Nineteenth and Early Twentieth Centuries', *Indonesia and the Malay World*, 30 (87):101–5.

Filem Melayu (1940), 'Hanchur Hati: Ahmad C. B. masok dunia film', 1 May: 7.

H. Dolmat and Miss Saianah (1935), *Che siti*, Pagoda V 3666, 78 rpm.

Harper, T. N. (2001), *The End of Empire and the Making of Malaya*, Cambridge: Cambridge University Press.

Hooker, V. M. (2000), *Writing a New Society: Social Change Through the Novel in Malay*, Sydney: Asian Studies Association of Australia in association with Allen and Unwin and University of Hawai'i Press.

Kahn, J. S. (2006), *Other Malays: Nationalism and Cosmopolitanism in the Modern Malay World*, Singapore: Asian Studies Association of Australia in association with Singapore University Press and NIAS Press.

Lewis, S. L. (2016), *Cities in Motion. Urban Life and Cosmopolitanism in Southeast Asia, 1920–1940*, Cambridge: Cambridge University Press.

Matusky, P. and S. B. Tan (2017), *The Music of Malaysia: The Classical, Folk and Syncretic Traditions*, London and New York: Routledge.

Milner, A. (1995), *The Invention of Politics in Colonial Malaya: Contesting Nationalism and the Expansion of the Public Sphere*, Cambridge: Cambridge University Press.

Miss Emmy (*c.* 1930s), *Anak Tiri*, Pathé No. 61073, 78 rpm.

Miss Piah, Mr Poh Tiang Swee and Mr Koh Hoon Teck (*c.* 1930s), *Dondang Sayang Tanaman 1*, Pagoda V3770, 78 rpm.

Miss Rambat (*c.* 1930s), *Yatim yang Miskin*, HMV P. 2296, 78 rpm.

Mohd. Yatim (*c.* 1930s), *Yatim Piatu*, HMV P. 13187; P. 22936, 78 rpm.

Mohd. Yatim (*c.* 1950sa), *Uncle Murtabak*, HMV P 22945, 78 rpm.

Mohd. Yatim (*c.* 1950sb), *Yam Choi Chow*, HMV NAM 13, 78 rpm.

Mohd. Yatim (*c.* 1950sc), *Wak Kasban Belajar*, HMV NAM 13, 78 rpm.

Mr. Jani (*c.* 1930s), *Ibu*, Chap Ayam # 61085, 78 rpm.

Muliyadi, M. (2004), *The History of Malay Editorial Cartoons (1930s–1993)*, Cheras: Utusan Publications.

Murray, D., J. Gibbs, D. Harnish, T. Miller, S. B. Tan and K. Young (eds), *Longing for the Past: The 78-Rpm Era in Southeast Asia*, Atlanta, GA: Dust-to-Digital.

Nacter, A. (1910), 'Malayan Wayang', *Straits Echo*, 2 July.

Rahman, A. (*c.* 1950s), *Gadis Malaya*, Columbia GEM 502, 78 rpm.

Salih (1911), *Gambos Ya Omar*, HMV P 2784, 78 rpm.

Shaik Othman, S. (1898), 'The Malay Opera, A Study', *Straits Chinese Magazine*, 12 (8): 129–32.

Straits Echo (1904), 'Wayang Yap Chow Thong', 19 May.

Straits Echo (1906), 'Radent Adjeng Rohaja', 22 September.

Tan, S. B. (1993), *Bangsawan: A Social and Stylistic History of Popular Malay Opera*, Singapore: Oxford University Press.

Tan, S. B. (1996/7), 'The 78 Rpm Record Industry in Malaya Prior to World War II', *Asian Music*, 28 (1): 1–42.

van der Putten, J. (2014), 'Bangsawan, the Coming of a Popular Malay Theatrical Form', *Indonesia and the Malay World*, 42 (123): 268–86.

Weintraub, A. N. (2014), 'Pop Goes Melayu: Melayu Popular Music in Indonesia, 1968–1975', in B. Barendregt (ed), *Sonic Modernities in the Malay World: A History of Popular Music, Social Distinction and Novel Lifestyles (1930s–2005)*, 165–86, Leiden: Brill.

Zahara Agus (*c.* 1950s), *Malaya Merdeka*, Pathé PTH 189, 78 rpm.

Index